Praise for *Malcolm*

'In Apter's hands it _____
Young's guitar riffs.'

—Helen Pitt, author

'Love, love, love this book. [It's] a must for any true AC/DC
fan.'

—Reader's review (five stars) Amazon.com.au

Praise for *The Book of Daniel: From Silverchair to Dreams*

'A great story, well told.'

—Rod Quinn, ABC Overnights

'A cracking read.'

—Nick Rheinberger, ABC Illawarra

'I could now, like never before, relate to Daniel and apply
some of his own struggles (and successes) to my own.
Brilliant read.'

—Reader's review (five stars) Booktopia.com.au

Praise for *High Voltage: The Life of Angus Young*

'*High Voltage* is a great read, easy to whip through and take
in.'

—Shane Murphy, *Daily Review*

Jeff Apter is the author of more than 20 music biographies, many of them bestsellers. His subjects include Johnny O'Keefe, Keith Urban, John Farnham, the Bee Gees, the Finn brothers and Malcolm and Angus Young of AC/DC. As a ghostwriter, he has worked with Kasey Chambers, Mark Evans (of AC/DC) and Richard Clapton. Jeff was on staff at *Rolling Stone* for several years and has written about legends such as Aretha Franklin, Patti Smith, Robbie Robertson, Bob Dylan, Chrissie Hynde and Lucinda Williams. In 2015, he worked on the Helpmann award–nominated live show *A State of Grace: The Music of Jeff and Tim Buckley*. Away from music, Jeff has also worked on books with soldiers and diplomats and sports greats such as Michael Slater and Tim Cahill. Jeff, who speaks about music regularly on ABC Radio, lives in Wollongong, New South Wales, with his wife, two children, a cat that's so damned cool it needs no name, and a very blue dog named Neela.

www.jeffapter.com.au

FRIDAY ON MY MIND

the life of
GEORGE YOUNG

JEFF APTER

ALLEN&UNWIN
SYDNEY • MELBOURNE • AUCKLAND • LONDON

First published in 2020

Copyright © 2020 Jeff Apter

All chart placings for Australia are taken from *The Book: Top 40 Research 1956–2010*, by Stephen Scanes and Jim Barnes. Gorokan: Scanes Music Research, 2011.

Allen & Unwin
83 Alexander Street
Crows Nest NSW 2065
Australia
Phone: (61 2) 8425 0100
Email: info@allenandunwin.com
Web: www.allenandunwin.com

A catalogue record for this book is available from the National Library of Australia

ISBN 978 1 76087 510 7

Internal design by Post Pre-press Group
Set in 13/17 pt Adobe Garamond by Post Pre-press Group, Australia
Printed and bound in Australia by Griffin Press, part of Ovato

10 9 8 7 6 5 4 3 2 1

The paper in this book is FSC® certified. FSC® promotes environmentally responsible, socially beneficial and economically viable management of the world's forests.

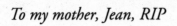

To my mother, Jean, RIP

Contents

Prologue

Late 2008, somewhere in Portugal

George Young had no time for bullshit. No time whatsoever. Nor did he have any time for celebrity; the dazzle of celebrity faded pretty damned quickly when his band, The Easybeats, exploded in the mid-1960s. In fact, he described that frantic period of screaming fans and fawning press and chart hits as the moment 'when the bullshit started'. It was simply too much, and it was the turning point in his evolution from pop star—albeit a very reluctant one, at best—to respected musician.

He just wasn't interested in playing the game. Not 40 years ago, and not now.

George Young was much more comfortable letting his music do the talking. After all, at almost 60 years old, he was the man who'd helped create the Great Australian Songbook: as a writer/performer with The Easybeats and Flash and the Pan, as a producer/mentor for AC/DC, and as the man who, along with long-time musical partner and friend, Harry Vanda, presided as in-house producer for Alberts, the fabled 'house of hits'. 'Friday on My Mind', 'Evie (Parts 1, 2, 3)',

'Love is in the Air', 'Hey, St. Peter', 'Bad Boy for Love', 'It's a Long Way to the Top (If You Wanna Rock 'n' Roll)', 'Dirty Deeds Done Dirt Cheap', 'Am I Ever Gonna See Your Face Again'—all these and so many other Oz classics bore the mark of George Young.

This was also a man whose maxims were legendary. 'Don't polish a turd' was one of George's favourites, as was 'Never bastardise your sound'. 'That's your thing,' he once told his brothers, AC/DC's Malcolm and Angus, 'stick with it.' 'Keep it simple, stupid,' he'd tell the bands he worked with. 'Don't fuck around.' George's advice was always on the money, and it was rarely rejected. The man was respected.

In November 2008, when Australian *Rolling Stone* was preparing a special Easybeats edition, it was understood that the reclusive George, now living the quiet life in Portugal, wasn't expected to contribute. After all, he hadn't taken part in *Easyfever*, the tribute album that led to the magazine's celebration of the band, or shown up when The Easybeats were inducted into the ARIA Hall of Fame in 2005. What would he have to say to some pesky journo? Wasn't his life's work—and the wisdom—enough?

So it came as a huge shock for *Rolling Stone*'s Michael Dwyer to receive an email response from George. Okay, it was long after the issue's deadline had passed, but a message from George Young was as rare as a sighting of the Loch Ness monster—and, with all dues to Nessy, far more real.

Young had quit 'the game' several years earlier—fittingly, his last major project had been producing an AC/DC album, *Stiff Upper Lip*, in 2000, and even then he'd had to be coaxed out of retirement—but he hadn't softened one bit. He still held fast to certain principles about the industry, hard lessons he'd learned and then adopted for all of his five decades in the business of making music. That was clear when he was asked about the 'biz' since the heyday of Alberts.

Was there anything that remained unchanged between then and now?

'The clash between the creative types and the number crunchers,' replied Young. 'But that'll always exist.'

And it was best not to get the man started on hype—the dreaded 'bullshit'. That, too, would never go away; neither would his resistance to the dark art of spin.

'Avoid over-hype,' he said when asked if he had any advice for young hopefuls starting out. 'Too many very talented Australian acts have been ruined by being on the receiving end of it.'

Young knew this well. At their peak, the mere presence of The Easybeats whipped up what became known as 'Easyfever', the Australian pop world's answer to Beatlemania. And George, the straight-shooting, Scot-slash-Aussie that he was, saw right through it. 'We weren't really playing anymore,' he once said. 'We were satisfying demand, trying to please the record company, promoters, record stores, radio stations, fan magazines, here, there and everywhere.' Rather than continue to play the game, he chose to play his guitar and help write the songs that made him a legend.

Did he have any other advice?

'Focus on what you do best,' he wrote. 'Stick to your guns and don't compromise your music to get airplay. Compromising is usually the kiss of death. If you do your own thing and bomb, then at least you go down on your own terms, not someone else's . . . Give it your best shot.'

These were all the beliefs that helped build Young's stellar career. His message was crystal clear. Do your own thing. Don't sell yourself short. Believe in your talent. And if you go down in flames, well, at least it was you who lit the fire, not some suit.

Even in retirement, George Young still had no time for bullshit.

It was the last interview he ever gave.

1

The Hostel Hillbillies

When George Young arrived in Sydney with his family in June 1963, he was greeted by a miserable scene. And it had nothing to do with the grim weather or the rough living conditions at the Villawood Migrant Hostel, the Youngs' first port of call.

No, the misery the sixteen-year-old was faced with was the sad state of the local pop charts. It was the blandest of times. It was as though the airwaves were coated in vanilla. Up top of the 2UE 'Official Top 40', which was the chart of choice for Sydneysiders—'the original and authentic survey of hit tunes', boasted the station—were cardigan-clad crooners Perry Como and Mel Tormé. Novelty songs were big, such as 'Tamoure (The Dance of Love)' by Bill Justis, the end result of someone suggesting to Bill that he mix sugary pop with faux-island rhythms. There was also Johnny Cymbal's 'Mr Bass Man', known chiefly for a lyric that offered seemingly endless variations on the word 'boom'. Even Elvis Presley had traded his gyrating pelvis for the rocking chair with the eminently forgettable 'One Broken Heart for Sale'.

Eydie Gormé was prepared to 'Blame it on the Bossa Nova', while Lesley Gore was reminding the good people of Sydney that 'it's my party and I'll cry if I want to'.

As leading Sydney DJ Bob Rogers has written, this was a time when 'all recorded foreign music had to first go through a public service cleansing bath in case it might contain anything that would contaminate us'.

And yet when the Youngs—ten of them, if you included extended family—left Glasgow for a new life in Oz, the UK charts were ablaze with a musical revolution: Merseybeat. By mid-1963, Liverpudlians The Beatles had twice topped their home charts, with 'Please Please Me' and 'From Me to You' ('She Loves You' and 'I Want to Hold Your Hand' were waiting in the wings), with Gerry and the Pacemakers, Brian Poole and the Tremeloes, and Billy J. Kramer with The Dakotas all soon to follow them directly to the top of the charts. The music was exciting and fresh and new—unlike the hits on the 2UE charts.

These 'Beat' groups were fast overrunning the British establishment acts, the old guard, represented by middle-of-the-road warblers such as expat Aussie Frank 'I Remember You' Ifield and Cliff Richard, still on his endless 'Summer Holiday', which seemed even more saccharine when stacked up against The Beatles' hits. 'Please Please Me' was possibly the raunchiest record ever made by four pale-faced Scousers; it was two minutes of raw sexual energy.

But in Australia this cultural revolution was still some way off. Recently re-elected prime minister Robert Menzies was an archconservative; *Coronation Street* was on the telly (for those who owned a set), and the one show that did cater for 'the youngsters', Channel 9's *Bandstand*, was hosted by the very square Brian Henderson, who could have passed for a staid suburban librarian. The biggest locally produced 'film' of the year was *The Queen Returns*, a documentary about Her Maj's recent visit to the colony. In fact, an oil rendering of Queen Elizabeth II looked down upon the Youngs, and their 1500-odd fellow residents at Villawood Migrant Hostel, whenever they gathered in the communal dining room.

Soon after, when George's star began to blaze brightly with The Easybeats, he summed up the local situation with his trademark precision: 'Australia,' he said, 'wasn't very fashion conscious.'

★

The Youngs were from Cranhill, a rough, hardscrabble slice of working-class Glasgow. They lived on the eastern end of the Cranhill housing estate. The only defining feature of the Young family home at 6 Skerryvore Road was the water tower that sat directly behind their house, a weird, spindly beast that rested on a series of pylons rooting it to the ground. It could have been mistaken for something out of a sci-fi movie depicting the end of the world. The same could be said for parts of Cranhill; this was no boomtown.

Established in the 1950s and bordered to the north by the M8 and to the south by the River Clyde, Cranhill was, by the early 1960s, hit hard by unemployment and poverty, with many local businesses shutting down. As a writer from *The Guardian* noted, 'When . . . the yards went quiet and the furnaces turned cold, no redundancy payments would ever be big enough to heal the gaping wounds in the psyche of generations of Glasgow men and, latterly, women. There were no enterprise zones, no tax inducements for inward investment, and no re-training.'

George was born in Glasgow on 6 November 1946, the fifth son to William and Margaret (whose maiden name was also Young). The sibling pecking order ran like this: Stephen, the eldest, was born in 1933; Margaret, the only girl among them, in 1935; then John in 1937, Alex in 1938 and William Jr in 1940. Two other boys followed George: first Malcolm, born in 1953, then 'wee' Angus two years later. It was quite the clan, and a very full house.

Cranhill would leave its mark on George. He came to understand that working-class people need an outlet, an escape from the grind. His most famous song, the classic 'Friday on My Mind', was, to George, 'really working-class rock and roll . . . That's what you dream about: Fridays.'

Cranhill also toughened him up. George was no push-over; he didn't mind a scrap. Fights were simply part of everyday life on the estate and at Cranhill Secondary. He was a regular kid, a bit dour, with a fondness for Irn-Bru (a caffeinated Scottish soft drink), steak pie and the music of Little Richard. George also had an eye for Hollywood actress Natalie Wood. Paul Newman impressed him, too—a classic tough guy, someone who could hold his own in a conflict.

George's father, William—a lively character known as 'Pop'—was born in 1911, and had bounced between jobs since finishing service as a flight mechanic with the RAF at the end of World War II. He'd worked as a spray painter, a 'wheel boy'—a stretch for a man well into his forties— and a machine operator. He'd also been a postman. George's mother, Margaret, suffered from arthritis and was often bedridden. She was a heavy-set woman, described as 'stoutish' on a medical examination card from 1963, which also noted that she was probably suffering from 'pleural thickening' of the lungs, affecting her breathing. Her poor health meant that George's only sister ran the household. She was quietly referred to as The Thunder; Margaret Jr took no crap. George lived in fear of crossing his sister.

William's work life may have been unsteady, but there was one constant at the house in Cranhill: music. Everyone played an instrument of some sort—Alex played the accordion, and Alex and John played guitar—the instrument was eventually handed along to George (and later on, to Malcolm and then Angus). Stephen, who had a ken for country music—so much so that he sometimes dressed in rhinestones and cowboy boots—played the accordion and the banjo. ('He was a rhinestone cowboy,' said a family acquaintance.) Sister Margaret was a big music fan, with an impressive collection of records that she'd tracked down at the Glasgow markets. She'd bring home music from the classic rockers of the time, such as Chuck Berry, Little Richard and Fats Domino, which seeped into the musical DNA of her siblings.

'She turned the rest of the family onto it,' recalled George when he spoke with Australian *Rolling Stone* in 1976. 'Their influence spread among young fellows like myself.'

George's interest in playing rock and roll, however, didn't really develop until the family emigrated, as he explained in a 1978 interview: 'Glasgow was one of the centres for blues music in Britain, and it wasn't till I came to Australia that I started playing rock music.'

George was right: acts such as The Poets, a Glaswegian blues outfit, were big local stars, dubbed Scotland's very own Rolling Stones. They scored a UK hit in 1964 with a song called 'Now We're Thru''. Lonnie Donegan, who'd taken the rootsy handmade genre known as skiffle to the top of the UK charts—he had an astonishing run of seventeen Top 10 hits between 1956 and 1962—was also a Glaswegian.

Still, the new Merseybeat groups had made a big impact on Scotland: The Beatles toured Glasgow as early as 1963, promoting their debut single 'Love Me Do'. It would take another year before they sank their claws into George Young. But when they did, the impression they left was as indelible as a tattoo.

★

Moving to Australia was the idea of George and his brother, John. They'd heard about the Assisted Passage Migration Scheme, which allowed UK citizens and their families to immigrate to Australia for the princely sum of £10 (hence the nickname 'Ten Pound Poms'). The original plan was for just John and George to migrate, but their parents, and eventually much of the rest of the family, also decided to leave Scotland. In early 1963, the UK was in the grip of the 'Big Freeze'. It was never especially warm in Scotland, but in that winter they were dealing with some of the worst weather the entire island nation had experienced for 200 years. It was a good time to leave.

And Pop was unemployed, again, so the opportunity to start afresh in another country—one with actual sunshine— must have seemed too good to pass up. The ad for the Assisted Passage Migration Scheme actually promised good weather: 'Come over to the sunny side now! Australia: a great place for families.' The family was given the green light to immigrate by the Office of the High Commissioner for Australia on 22 February 1963.

Twenty-five-year-old Alex Young, however, had no intention of going to Australia. He'd started working as a musician and believed, with some justification, that there were more opportunities right where he was. He told his family that he was staying put in the UK (though soon enough he'd be in Germany, with a band named the Bobby Patrick Big Six, playing the same clubs The Beatles had played during their Hamburg apprenticeship). George recalled that his mother's reaction to Alex's news was a simple: 'Oh no!' She didn't see any future in life as a musician.

It would be another four years before George saw his brother again. Even then he wouldn't dare tell his mother, who was still angry at Alex for staying behind.

The Youngs were a well-known family in Cranhill, so much so that when they left for Australia they were fare-welled at the train station by a brass band. But there was one family member missing: John. He'd gone AWOL, and no one knew where he was. John was hot-tempered and a big drinker; according to a family acquaintance, he was 'red faced, excited all the time, even in a normal conversation'.

So it was the Youngs, minus Alex and John, but with the addition of Sam Horsburgh, who was married to George's sister, Margaret, and their son, Samuel Jr—known as 'Wee Sammy'—who flew to Australia on Qantas flight QF738064. On the paperwork required by the Department of Immigration, sixteen-year-old George listed his occupation as 'apprentice draftsman', which was a bit of a stretch. He was using some documentation supplied by brother Alex, who had trained as a draftsman. George easily passed his medical but, like all the Youngs, he was small, standing just 5 feet 2 inches (157 centimetres) and weighing a slight 104 pounds (47 kilograms).

The family reached Sydney on 22 June 1963 and boarded a bus for Villawood. On their first night at the hostel, George walked in on his parents, who were both crying. They feared they'd made a huge mistake.

John did eventually make the trip to Australia, but some time after the rest of his family. He'd been arrested in London for a crime that allegedly involved violence, but when he was released on bail the judge didn't confiscate his passport. He contacted his family in Australia who arranged an air ticket for him. He skipped bail and flew to Sydney on the next flight, with nothing more than the clothes on his back. It became the Young family's closely guarded secret.

*

Some of the less friendly Villawood locals referred to kids like George as 'the hostel hillbillies' and would regularly wander over to the centre and thump anyone who got in their way. In the words of one soon-to-be-famous Villawood resident, Harry Vanda, aka Johannes van den Berg, 'When you're raised in a place like the Villawood Hostel, there's always a bit of a ghetto mentality . . . So we really didn't know many Australian guys—except when we used to meet them in fist fights.' George would meet Johannes soon enough, on friendly terms.

However, it was due to a fight that George first met Stephen Wright. He had been worked over by a local; it was neither the first nor last time for Wright, who, even then, had an eye for the ladies but usually fancied the girl with the angry boyfriend. And Wright was no pugilist; a strong wind would have blown him halfway to New Zealand.

After one of his fights, Stephen—soon to be Stevie—approached George. He was actually sixteen but looked much younger; George thought he was twelve, maybe thirteen tops.

'Gooday,' Wright said. 'Your brother sure knows how to throw a punch.'

'What?' George replied, a bit confused. 'They know how to throw a punch but none of them has thrown one at you.'

Wright had mistaken George for someone else.

Born in Leeds, England, Wright had immigrated to Australia with his family in 1956; they moved to Sydney in 1960, after a spell in Melbourne. He no longer lived in the hostel, but he knew Villawood well enough—he and his family lived across the street. His father was a sergeant, a military man and an Anglophile, who wore his uniform around the house and sported a handlebar moustache. Interestingly, the first thing Wright did when he arrived in Fremantle with his family, en route to Melbourne, was buy a 'Boomerang Songster'—a songbook produced by Sydney-based company J. Albert & Son.

And George? The first thing he did when he reached Australia was step lively to avoid the spray of young Angus, who was throwing up. His eight-year-old kid brother hadn't enjoyed the plane ride.

Wright described the Nissen huts that families such as the Youngs occupied as 'beehives'. He spent a lot of time at the hostel, hanging out, causing mischief, chasing girls. There was a lively social scene there, especially among the younger immigrants.

George learned that Wright had a musical background, having spent some time on the circuit of suburban Sydney clubs and talent shows. Wright had recently met a gangly kid with teeth that were a dentist's worst nightmare, a fellow expat Pom, also a singer. His name was Robin Gibb. Robin had played The Beatles' 'She Loves You' for Stevie—and turned Stevie's world upside down. Surf music was out and The Beatles were definitely in for Stevie Wright, who held down a day job selling menswear.

George wondered whether he might be able to form a group with Wright, especially after seeing him in action with his band at a Sydney venue named Suzie Wong's. The kid certainly looked the part, with his cheeky grin and boundless energy, on stage and off. And the girls in the crowd loved him.

*

'To pass the time,' George said of his relatively short stay at Villawood, 'we'd go to the recreation hall, play table tennis, strum guitars and so on. That's basically where The Easybeats started.'

George was rarely seen without his guitar. He didn't know many people in this strange new place, and music was the perfect escape. One Australian friend he did make was Brian Lee, who lived at Chester Hill and attended high school with a Villawood kid named Dingeman 'Dick' van der Sluijs. (George briefly attended Chester Hill High, too.) Lee would hang about the hostel's rec room; one day, George had wandered in and found Lee trying his best to play 'Pop Goes the Weasel' on the guitar.

'Did you pay money to learn that?' George asked, stifling laughter.

George taught Lee the basics: twelve-bar blues, some simple rock songs, a few moves he'd cribbed from John Lennon when he'd watched The Beatles on TV.

'I was strongly attracted to George; he was a Scorpio and I was a Taurus,' said Lee. 'He had all the traits of a Scorpio, a small person [in stature] who did really big things.'

'He was really friendly and warm, a pleasure to be with. We were great friends,' Lee recalled. 'I got into regular jamming with him.' Charlie, a Polish friend of George and Brian's, sometimes jammed with them.

They'd play a handful of songs over and over again, mostly covers that The Rolling Stones had recently made their own: 'Around and Around', 'It's All Over Now' and 'Under the Boardwalk'. When George played music with his family, the songs they favoured were more sentimental, such as 'I Belong to Glasgow' and Hank Williams' 'The Wild Side of Life'.

It was clear to Lee that George's horizons were very narrow. 'These lads [in the hostel] were so isolated,' said Lee. 'They didn't have cars, a peer group, friends.' So he began driving George to different places, introducing him to his mates at Parramatta and sometimes driving as far as the Northern Beaches, which was most likely the first time George had set foot on an Aussie beach. (There wasn't much sand and surf at Villawood, only blazing sun and hungry insects.) Lee took George to a dance at Hurstville to see a band called The Denvermen, whose guitarist had taught Lee—and George wasn't impressed.

'They're out of tune,' he told his new buddy.

One night, the three Gibb brothers—lanky Barry and twins Robin and Maurice—paid a visit to the hostel. The Gibbs were, like the Youngs, Ten Pound Poms, and had been 'in country' since 1958. They were living in the Sydney suburb of Lakemba and had recently signed a recording contract with Leedon Records; pop star Col Joye was their mentor. There was a PA and microphone set up in the rec room, and Barry tried to encourage his brothers to have a sing. But the twins were so short that they couldn't reach the microphone, and they were distracted by the sports equipment and the other kids in the rec room, so Barry sang a few songs by himself on acoustic guitar. George introduced himself to Barry and, as the evening set in, they sat on the grass outside the hostel general store singing and strumming together. Neither could have imagined what lay ahead for them both.

By early 1964, George had left school and had worked as an apprentice panelbeater, a short-lived job arranged by his friend Brian Lee. George's parents were keen on him getting a trade. His father knew what it was like to be unemployed, and 'he didn't want any of us to have trouble getting a job', George would tell a reporter from Sydney's *Daily Mirror*. But the call of music was strong.

George was killing time at the hostel when he met Harry Vanda. He was a lanky, fair-haired seventeen-year-old whose family had arrived at Villawood around the same time as the Youngs, having emigrated from The Hague. He was an only child and, like George, had few, if any, friends. (Unlike the Youngs, who would settle permanently in Australia, Harry's people moved back to the Netherlands after a couple of years.)

Harry was strumming a guitar, which was all the encouragement George needed to start talking with him. Or to try to talk with him, because Harry's English was still very much a work in progress—most of his English came from the lyrics of British bands that he admired.

'I think I'm getting sunstrike,' Harry would exclaim.

'You mean sunstroke,' George would correct him.

'It's too hot for that,' Harry would insist. 'I think it's sunstrike.'

George made a mental note to work on Harry's English.

There were two things that stood out about Villawood, Harry later recalled: 'the mud in the winter and the dust in the summer'. He especially hated rainy nights, when the dash to the communal bathrooms would leave him drenched. The flies bothered him, too.

But his musical CV impressed George. Back in the Netherlands, he'd played guitar in a band known as The Starfighters and had been playing since he was seven. Harry loved the guitar; as he'd admit, 'it was my whole reason for existence'. Just as The Starfighters began to build a following, Harry's parents told him they were moving to Australia. So here he was in Villawood, dreaming about forming another group.

Harry had already befriended Dick van der Sluijs, a fellow Dutchman. He was a few inches shorter than Harry, with slightly darker features. They, too, had met in the rec-room-cum-laundry and bonded over Harry's struggles with English. Dick lived nearby with his family, who were devout Jehovah's Witnesses, which instilled in him an interest in such arcana as numerology and astrology. Dick's sister, Henja, was a missionary, as was her husband, Roger.

As Dick's former classmate Brian Lee observed about Dick, 'He was the only one among [The Easybeats] that was cosmic, who believed in intuition, saw things, made predictions.'

Dick's mother, in particular, didn't share her son's enthusiasm for rock and roll—she must have been appalled when he adopted the stage name Dick Diamonde. 'She says the people most affected by pop music are followers of the creative, rather than the Creator,' Dick admitted in 1967. 'And it's something she doesn't care for.'

The van der Sluijs family had been in Australia since 1951; Dick's father was a cook at the hostel. Dick was working on the railways and, like Harry, he was a budding musician. But what interested Harry even more was the fact that Dick's family owned a car. That was a big deal—Harry had only been in a car a few times in his life. 'I thought he must be rich,' Harry remembered.

As for George and Harry, despite the differences in their characters (George was forthright, often blunt, whereas Harry was quiet) and physical disparities (George was short and dark, Harry tall and fair), there was a connection between the two teenagers, in part because of their shared dilemma: they were strangers in a strange land, with few friends. George had his own problems with English, too, or at least the English spoken by the locals. It took him some time to understand what Aussies were actually saying. His Scottish accent remained thick enough, meanwhile, to carve with a knife. That didn't help.

George and Harry had differing musical tastes: Harry loved the instrumentals of The Shadows, which he'd play with The Starfighters, while George was soaking up the new British bands that were gaining exposure on local radio— 'She Loves You', the Beatles song that had converted Stevie

Wright, reached number 3 in late 1963, and 'I Want to Hold Your Hand' did even better, topping the local chart in early 1964—and also in concert venues. In April 1964, Sydney promoter Harry M. Miller toured a troupe of British bands under the banner 'The Liverpool Sound'. Gerry and the Pacemakers, and Brian Poole and the Tremeloes were the two big groups, along with solo acts Dusty Springfield and Gene Pitney (whom George would befriend a few years down the line).

An even bigger tour from a certain Liverpool outfit was just around the corner. And its impact on George would be huge.

★

The songbook that Stevie Wright had bought in Fremantle, the 'Boomerang Songster', was a cash cow for J. Albert & Son, a successful Sydney family empire that had been thriving for 80 years. Alberts also did a lively trade in a harmonica range named the Boomerang, which was also the name of the building in Sydney's CBD that housed the Alberts company. The family yacht was named—you guessed it—*Boomerang*. Prince Philip, Queen Elizabeth's husband, was a family friend who'd enjoyed a few pleasant afternoons on Sydney Harbour on board *Boomerang*, with Alexis Albert and his wife, Elsa. The Alberts were Sydney royalty.

But Alberts' core products were on the wane by the early 1960s. They'd discontinued production of the harmonica, while changes in publishing were becoming problematic for the company's main line of business, which was importing and republishing sheet music. In 1963, 26-year-old Ted

Albert—the second of Alexis and Elsa's three sons, and the one most involved with the family business—was hoping to push the company into hitherto uncharted waters: producing their own musical artists. He'd identified the changes in the musical landscape led by groups such as The Beatles. New acts were now writing and recording their own music instead of relying on their record labels to source songs from songwriters-for-hire.

Ted told his fellow board members that Alberts was missing the boat. He wanted to enter into recording contracts with local artists and produce their records. Among the Albert family's sizeable real estate portfolio was the 2UW Theatre in Sydney, which Ted planned to convert into a recording studio.

A new division of the company was created and named Albert Productions. Ted hired Tony Geary, who'd be the company's 'A&R guy'—a talent-spotter, essentially. A deal was struck with record label EMI, who would lease recordings from Alberts and then manufacture and distribute them on the Parlophone label. Albert Productions was Australia's first independent pop music production company—and it was Ted's baby.

Ted signed a few artists, including Tony Barber (not the famous whistler and game show host). Then, in June 1964, Ted signed Billy Thorpe and the Aztecs, at the time the country's most popular 'Merseybeat' group—Tony Barber was their rhythm guitarist. The Aztecs were holding down a successful residency at Sydney hotspot Surf City and had just reached number 1 on the Oz charts with their cover of 'Poison Ivy' (a big hit for US group The Coasters in 1959). Within months of the creation of Albert Productions, the company had its first Top 10 hit with Billy Thorpe and the Aztecs' cover of novelty dance hit 'Mashed Potato'. The group's next recording, the double-sided 'Sick and Tired'/'About Love', reached number 2. Billy Thorpe and the Aztecs went one better with their sincere if schmaltzy take on the Judy Garland ballad 'Over the Rainbow', a national number 1 for the band—and for Alberts—in January 1965.

These hits were covers of existing songs; Thorpe and the band's original compositions were used strictly as B-sides. This was good for Alberts, which owned publishing rights on both the covers Thorpe and the band recorded and their originals, which generated some healthy royalties for the company.

But what Ted Albert really needed was an act that could write its own songs. *Ideally hit songs.*

★

At the same time that Thorpe and his band signed to Alberts, George Young witnessed a musical phenomenon at close range. It was an event that would rock his world. For most Aussies under 25, the June 1964 tour by the Beatles was far more significant than any royal tour; these four mop tops were superstars.

Bob Rogers, at the time a top-rating DJ for Sydney's 2SM, was with the group throughout the tour, which stretched from 11 to 30 June (broken up by a quick trip across the ditch for shows in New Zealand). It was chaos, both on stage and off.

'To be on tour with the Beatles meant living every minute upside-down and inside-out,' Rogers told *The Sydney*

Morning Herald. 'It was mentally and physically exhausting. And everything The Beatles said or did was of momentous importance, even if they'd said or done it many times before. That was part of Beatlemania.'

In Adelaide, upwards of 250,000 people, roughly a third of the city's population, packed the streets as they followed the Fab Four's motorcade from the airport to the city centre. In Sydney, the band traversed the airport on the back of a truck, a gale almost blowing them backwards, acknowledging the thousands of fans who'd braved a fierce storm. All up, more than 70,000 punters attended the six shows they gave at the Sydney Stadium, where the band played on an unreliable revolving stage—sometimes Ringo Starr had to manually relocate his kit between songs.

Madness aside, it was the band's playing and performing that most interested George, who attended one of the Sydney concerts with his sister, Margaret, brother Malcolm and his friend, Brian Lee. Even though he could barely hear the group over the incessant shrieking of their lovestruck female fans, George could tell that they had the chops. And, crucially, a lot of the material they were playing was their own, including hits such as 'I Want to Hold Your Hand', 'She Loves You' and 'Can't Buy Me Love'. That was interesting—it definitely wasn't the norm with local stars such as Billy Thorpe and Johnny O'Keefe, whose hits were songs that had already charted overseas for other acts.

Those even closer to the action could see the impact that The Beatles had on budding local musicians. Noel Tresider, who played keyboards with The Phantoms—one of the support bands on The Beatles' 1964 roadshow—noted the shift. 'The Beatles tour changed Australian pop music completely,' he said. 'Previously, the popular style had been a lead singer with his backing band or instrumental bands in the style of The Shadows. Now, the fashion was for bands . . . where everyone sang.'

The Beatles' impact went beyond music. Hairstyles rapidly changed; the brushed-back rocker look was on its way out, updated by a brushed-forward style known as the 'jazzer'. The gaudy lamé outfits that a lot of Australian acts had favoured were ditched for much sharper suits and leather 'Beatles' boots. The Beatles actually laughed at the outfits of some of the Oz bands on their tour; the locals were, as George Young had already observed, not very 'fashion conscious'.

George was inspired. He now set to work building his own band. He already had Harry and Dick; then Stevie wandered into the rec room one day and announced his availability as a singer. This meant that Villawood resident John Bell, who'd been singing with George's band-under-development, was out. Bell was gutted, later admitting, 'I had to carry my heart home—it was broken. I'd already seen what was in George Young; I'd seen the brilliance and where it was gonna go.'

But George knew that Stevie was the right singer for the band. Now all he needed was a drummer.

★

Some workmates had told Dick about a fellow named Gordon Fleet, another Ten Pound Pom. He was told that Fleet was an 'inmate' at the East Hills Migrant Hostel, living with his wife and baby daughter. Diamonde tracked the drummer down—East Hills was about 12 kilometres south of Villawood—and slipped a note under his door, asking if he'd be interested in trying out with a new band.

What no one yet knew was that Fleet didn't just thump the tubs—he had a notable musical past. Back in his native Liverpool, the twenty-something Fleet had drummed for a band called The Mojos—he even knew Beatle Paul McCartney. He'd only been in Australia for a few weeks when Dick sought him out; he had found a job as a tool-maker, which paid a handy £40 a week, but Fleet was feeling the same sense of dislocation as George and Harry.

'It's the weirdest feeling to land in a country and you don't know anybody. It's weird. I'd never seen the bush before,' he recalled later for an Easybeats documentary.

Fleet missed the camaraderie of a band and, with wife Maureen's encouragement, he met with George and the others, who'd now moved their rehearsal base to the shed at the rear of the van der Sluijs family home. Their rehearsals were occasionally interrupted by Dick's devout parents, reminding their son that rock and roll was 'the devil's work', before serving tea.

George was immediately impressed by Fleet's playing and his love of the 'British Invasion' bands—having met Paul McCartney gave Fleet real credibility as far as George was concerned. The name Gordon, however, wasn't going to cut it: soon enough, he was renamed Snowy. He'd also trim a few years off his age to fit in with the others.

One day, discussion turned to the band's name. They were currently using The Starfighters, the name of Harry's band back in the Netherlands, as they did the rounds of local gigs and talent quests—'We went down like a lead balloon,' George recalled—while working on original songs in the van der Sluijs shed.

'What about The Easybeats?' Snowy suggested.

George thought it through for a minute. 'Yeah, I like it,' he said.

It was settled. They were now The Easybeats.

2

'Waar Kom Je Vandaan?'

George knew that the band needed to get known beyond the wild west(ern) suburbs if they were to stand a chance of making it big. Sydney, fortunately, had a strong live scene, built on the back of the heady nightclub circuit of the 1950s, when large-living expat American promoter Lee Gordon—who hosted Sydney's wildest parties and liked to sleep in a coffin—had been the toast of the town. Meanwhile, Abe Saffron, the notorious 'Boss of the Cross', controlled much of the red-light action, opening the city's first strip clubs and gay venues, his friends and clients including high-ranking politicians and fellow crims.

In early 1963, local promoter John Harrigan had converted the 5000-seat Kings Cross Theatre into a live room that he named Surf City, a venue ruled in 1964 by Billy Thorpe and the Aztecs—but only when their arch rivals, Ray Brown & the Whispers, weren't in town. (Harrigan managed both acts and also ran his own booking agency.) Harrigan was also in charge of Sydney venues The Beach House, Star Club and Sunset Disco. Another key room was Beatle

Village, located at 124 Oxford Street, next door to the Oxford Hotel. The club was the owner's attempt to replicate Liverpool's legendary Cavern Club, The Beatles' old stomping ground. Beatle Village was a favourite hangout of the local sharpies—gangs with short hair, shorter fuses and a taste for ultra-violence, usually administered in packs. And, of course, there was Suzie Wong's, a Chinese restaurant in the CBD, which hosted afternoon and evening gigs. This was where Stevie Wright had performed.

It was a vibrant scene for both punters and players. Musos and 'colourful local identities' would gather after gigs at the Mandarin Club in Goulburn Street, a relatively new hotspot run by brothers Denis and Keith Wong, which stayed open until dawn. Denis ran another venue named Hawaiian Eye and owned the Chequers nightclub, which would soon become a rock-and-roll venue, having long been the upscale room of choice for visiting superstars such as Sammy Davis Jr and Liza Minnelli. Wong would soon open the Whisky a Go Go in Kings Cross, where sleaze and sounds collided every night of the week.

Band elder Snowy Fleet took on the role of manager, along with a friend of the band named Allan Kissick, and tried to hustle bookings. George's brother-in-law, Sam Horsburgh, helped lug their gear, as did George's mate, Brian Lee. Towards the end of 1964, they managed to secure an inner-city pub gig, but it didn't last long. According to George, they were turfed out for being 'too loud and filthy—you know, the long hair thing in a pub full of sailors'.

One night, Fleet tried to talk the bouncer at Beatle Village into letting the band audition for the owner, but he was sharply shut down. No chance. As they walked away,

Dick and Harry started speaking Dutch. The bouncer called them back.

'*Waar kom je vandaan?*' he asked the pair. He wanted to know where they were from.

When Harry replied that he was from Den Haag—The Hague—the bouncer became his new best friend, welcoming Harry and the others into the venue. He, too, was from The Hague; the owner was also Dutch.

'We could use a Dutch band here,' the bouncer told them. 'Why don't you go down[stairs] and have a blow?' (A 'blow' meant a jam.)

'They liked what they heard,' George said simply when interviewed by Australian *Rolling Stone* in 1976.

The audition went so well, in fact, that The Easybeats played Beatle Village several times in early October 1964, to mainly female crowds that slowly built in numbers. Soon enough they were playing late every Thursday, Friday and Saturday, for £15 a night. The venue—pretty much a dusty cellar with no fire escape—was entered via a narrow stairway that led down to the band room. At night it was dimly lit and moody, but when George and the band loaded their gear in during the day, they could see that the air was thick with dust. There was no stage at Beatle Village: the band set up and played on ground level.

Fifty people would fill the room to the brim. Among the crowd most nights was Sandra Ramsey, George's future wife. Not only did she own a cool black Mini Minor, but she also had two girlfriends, Eve and Livia, both teenagers, who also became staunch Easybeats fans. 'Livia' was a fair-haired ingenue named Olivia Newton-John, the granddaughter of Nobel Prize–winning physicist Max Born, who would begin her own musical journey before too long.

But The Easybeats soon accepted a better-paid offer at a rival venue named The Bowl, which alienated the owner of Beatle Village and resulted in fights between the two venues' crowds. According to George, this 'rolled along every Saturday night for a month, with big brawls'.

These early gigs were the making of Stevie Wright, whose onstage persona—a whirling, spinning, grinning ball of mad energy, constantly in motion—rapidly emerged. His MO seemed to be 'anything to get the audience involved', and George was hugely impressed. At the time, the most a frontman like Billy Thorpe would do was try a few dance steps, but Stevie and the band ripped it up. It was mad.

'Stevie as a frontman was phenomenal,' George said. 'At the time he was quite extraordinary . . . He influenced many singers in their approach to how they performed and their need to entertain.'

'Stephen wasn't a very good singer,' remembered Brian Lee, 'but his performance was magical, really attractive. He was a real performer and had an enormous ego. You'd speak with him and he wasn't there; he'd be thinking and wouldn't hear anything around him.'

George and Harry, too, were developing their own stagecraft, harmonising closely as they leaned in towards a shared mic, standing shoulder to shoulder, their physical contrasts on full display. Yet while Stevie was a man of the people and Harry a blithe spirit, George was all business on stage, his rhythm guitar resting high up on his chest like a shield as he chugged away, hitting the strings hard, leaving Harry to handle the solos on his Gretsch Jet Firebird. Sometimes George cracked a smile, but typically he was too focused on getting the job done.

While George wasn't as 'cute' as Stevie, he had presence; like John Lennon, he took a slightly pigeon-toed stance as he played, his feet firmly planted in place, knees bent, accentuating the sharp crease in the lower half of his trousers. Bassist Diamonde, meanwhile, stood as still and mysterious as an Easter Island statue, coolly plucking at his bass, seemingly in a dream. Snowy sat high on his drum stool, hitting the skins with confidence and precision—sometimes he rose out of his seat as he played, as if he'd just hit a speed bump.

'We were scruffy long hairs then,' George told *Bomp* magazine. 'But in England, where we had come from, fashions were taking off, so we got into it, wearing matching suits and other gear like that.' Thanks to Stevie's connections in the rag trade, they were soon sporting some fab gear. Their natty dress sense—favouring suits, either pinstriped or plain, sometimes worn with ruffled sleeves or turtlenecks—became an Easybeats trademark. Most bands were 'suiting up' by then, but with mixed results: some looked ridiculously stiff in suit and tie. But The Easybeats radiated cool. Occasionally, Stevie would fasten all the buttons on his jacket and flip up his collar, but that usually didn't last long—it was hotter than hell in the band room at The Bowl. He would have played naked if they'd let him.

The band's set list was starting to develop, too. They'd usually open with a few instrumentals; George and Harry would follow with a duet on 'She Said Alright'—one of George's earliest songwriting efforts—then 'Little Stevie' would hit the stage and the temperature in the already sweaty room would increase significantly.

★

Mike Vaughan was a clean-cut Sydney real estate agent who'd caught the rock-and-roll bug. He saw one of those early Easybeats gigs at The Bowl and was blown away by the band's energy, exuberance and musicality.

In his estimation, 'They were vital.'

Vaughan introduced himself and offered his services as manager. As George would recall, Vaughan told him that 'he had good connections with Ted Albert'. Vaughan mentioned that Albert was a big wheel in the music biz, and that he was working with Billy Thorpe. Vaughan said that he could get the band a meeting with Ted.

'He's one of the finest human beings I've ever met,' Vaughan told them.

None of this meant a thing to George. 'We didn't have a clue what Alberts was . . . I knew very little about the music business . . . The notion of signing a record contract, it just didn't register.'

George had been a migrant hostel kid; he felt a bit wary of outsiders, but agreed to at least consider Vaughan's offer to manage the band. Their current manager, Allan Kissick, wasn't working out. Encouraged by Vaughan's enthusiasm, George chucked in his traineeship and set his sights fully on a life in rock and roll. His parents were less than impressed, although they never failed to encourage George when it came to his music.

When Stevie Wright decided to quit his job, too, and sing full-time with the fledgling band, it also didn't sit well with his parents, especially his stern father. 'My father was a sergeant in the army,' Stevie told a reporter from the *Daily Mirror*, 'and you know what sergeants think about long hair.'

In order to escape the domestic tension, he took up an offer from George's mother to move in with the Youngs at Burwood, the family having left the hostel after a relatively short stay. They now lived at 4 Burleigh Street in a 60-year-old semi-detached suburban house. George and Stevie would sit at the family piano, trying to write their own songs—when they weren't being distracted by Margaret's son, 'Wee Sammy', who was a chess fanatic and would run around the house challenging everyone to a game, or by Malcolm and Angus, who liked to play 'Chopsticks' on the piano. As for Harry, he was still struggling with the local language—George said 'he could barely spell English'—so he was content to offer the occasional musical idea. Lyrics weren't Harry's forte, but he did start coming up with melodies and riffs.

Soon enough, all the band—even Snowy, a husband and father—would follow Stevie's lead and chuck in their day jobs.

There were even bigger developments behind the scenes: eighteen-year-old Harry married his teenaged girlfriend, Pamela, on 11 December 1964. The newlyweds moved into Albert Crescent in Burwood, not far from George and Stevie.

Just before Christmas 1964, the band set out on some regional dates, which included a series of shows at Mildura in Victoria, playing the Teen City Cabaret at the Murray Moon ballroom. It was the band's first rock-and-roll road trip, an exciting time. Diamonde drove the van while the others were squeezed together like sardines in the back, along with all their gear, but their spirits were high. And so what if the entire band would be forced to sleep in a single room above the local dance hall? They were a rock band on the road.

Yet when Christmas Day rolled around, homesickness hit them hard. As Stevie Wright told *Go-Set* magazine, a local took pity on them and invited the band to dinner. 'All went well,' said Wright, 'until one of her sons had too much to drink and started belting his father up, and then [the mother] got into her other son. This all went on as we sat quietly eating our plum pudding.'

The next day, George and the others learned that the owner of the venue was broke. They'd been ripped off. 'The last anybody heard of him,' said Wright, 'he had joined an outlaw band in the woods north of Mildura.'

It was a disaster—a rude awakening to the realities of life in a band.

'The van broke down three times,' George reported from the road, 'we were hungry and by the time we got back to Sydney we hadn't a penny left.'

That's when George agreed that it was time to hire Mike Vaughan.

★

Back on safer ground in Sydney, The Easybeats played a show at a girls' high school—'our usual twenty minutes with the bum shaking', as George described it. Mike Vaughan brought Ted Albert along to the gig, as well as Tony Geary, the Alberts A&R man. George didn't quite know what to make of Albert: with his bespoke suit and 'proper' manners, he was, in George's words, 'a bit square'. How could he understand rock and roll? But George and the others were more than happy to accept Ted Albert's offer of an audition at the 2UW Theatre. It was a start—a great start.

In person, George referred to him as 'Mr Albert', a clear sign of his respect for the man, even though Ted was only 27. Harry called him 'Mr Ted', also with due reverence, as did Mike Vaughan.

When George and the band convened in the 2UW Theatre in January 1965, Albert, who was producing the session, had a simple request: 'Play everything you know—even things that aren't complete.' He'd tape the lot, then take the results back to Alberts so he could further scrutinise the songs. 'We felt quite excited about the first session,' George told his niece, author Jane Albert, even though it was an intimidating experience.

But there was one thing George understood as this first session rolled along: 'We'd locked in on Ted's passion for sound.' Albert was mad for technology; he loved gadgets. Producing and recording music were his obsessions. As the band worked their way through their entire repertoire, Albert would leave the booth and walk among them, adjusting microphones and tweaking amplifiers, standing and listening, ears tuned to capture the perfect sound.

Albert was hugely influenced by the pop recordings coming out of the UK. It was a golden age: producer George Martin was making great records with The Beatles, Shel Talmy was doing likewise with The Kinks and The Who, and Albert hoped to re-create a bit of that magic. 'He looked at England as being the place,' George told Jane Albert. '[He'd say] "gotta try to match what they do sound wise".' But Albert also sought something more: 'He was looking for the hooks,' George remembered.

The band did exactly what Albert requested and played everything they knew. As many as 40 songs were recorded, including a cover of Chuck Berry's 'Little Queenie', and a version of the big ballad 'I Who Have Nothing', which was an English-language version of the Italian song 'Uno Dei Tanti' with lyrics by American hitmakers Jerry Leiber and Mike Stoller. 'I Who Have Nothing' struck Albert as a potential single. They also cut 'For My Woman', a sinuous, bluesy rocker that George had written with Stevie.

But it was another original, 'Say That You're Mine', that convinced Albert to sign The Easybeats. Upon hearing it, 'I almost broke my neck getting a contract drawn up', Albert told rock historian Glenn A. Baker.

While the song wasn't destined to become an Easybeats classic, it had all the necessary pop trappings of the moment: strong vocal harmonies, neat guitar picking by Harry, and rock-solid rhythm guitar from George. It also proved that the band could pen a decent tune. 'Ted liked it and we were on our way,' said George.

Over the years, these first recordings, which came to be known collectively as the 2UW Theatre Session, have gone down in Easybeats folklore as marking the beginning of their mad journey to the top and back. Just as crucially, this was also the start of George's long and fruitful relationship with 'Mr Albert'.

The 2UW Theatre became a handy refuge for the band, too; even when they were moving in fancier circles, they'd often return to the theatre to write and practise. Sometimes George's mate, Brian Lee, would drop in and listen to the band rehearse. 'I lost a few jobs,' Lee said, 'because I'd rather hang with George than go to work.'

★

Within a few months of the 2UW Theatre Session, in March 1965, Albert had a deal in place with George and the band. He'd produce their recordings, which would then be leased to EMI; they would then manufacture and promote the music and release it on their Parlophone label. This was The Beatles' label—surely a good omen. Albert's company would control the publishing of the band's songs, which meant that they collected the band's royalties—and also took their percentage.

Ted Albert still had his eyes on 'I Who Have Nothing', which had been a hit for Ben E. King in 1963 and which Albert thought might work as the group's first single. But the band was unintentionally gazumped by local pop-star-on-the-rise Normie Rowe, who cut his own version. As an alternative, Albert chose 'For My Woman' as The Easybeats' debut. It was released in March 1965, with 'Say That You're Mine' on the B-side. It wasn't a bad time, chart-wise, for a new 'Beat' band, with acts such as The Animals ('Don't Let Me Be Misunderstood'), Gerry and the Pacemakers, and the ubiquitous Beatles all riding high in the Australian charts.

But 'For My Woman' didn't connect.

George had a theory as to the problem. 'They had trouble getting radio stations to play it, that old reluctance to get in deep with an Australian band,' he later said. 'At the time there seemed to be a feeling amongst the radio stations . . . that Aussie artists couldn't write their own songs.'

He had a point: the majority of new entries in the charts originated in the UK. Local radio didn't seem quite ready for an Oz group that dared to write its own songs. Normie Rowe, who shared what George described as 'a friendly rivalry' with

The Easybeats, had the two biggest hits of the year, and both songs—'Que Sera Sera' and 'Shakin' All Over'—were covers. Rowe's third smash of 1965, 'It Ain't Necessarily So', was his rocked-up version of the Ira and George Gershwin standard from the opera *Porgy and Bess*. Rowe sang the socks off all these songs and his performances were great, but there wasn't an original track among them.

'For My Woman' mightn't have set the charts on fire— George conceded that it was a 'minor hit in Sydney and probably skidded in and out of the charts in other states'— but the band's live following was growing. In March, they were asked to open for Billy Thorpe and the Aztecs at Surf City. This was Thorpe's 'home turf', his patch. Thorpe was upstairs when The Easybeats came on stage, and he heard such a commotion—screaming and wailing, mainly—that he feared the place might be on fire. Many, many years later, in 2005, when Thorpe inducted The Easybeats into the ARIA Hall of Fame, he explained exactly what he had witnessed that night when he wandered downstairs.

'I heard what was then and remains to this day one of the greatest, tightest, bawdiest, kick-arse rock-and-roll sounds ever created,' Thorpe said. 'Within a year they had the country by the balls.'

★

Ted Albert maintained his faith in the band, especially in the songs of George and Stevie, and encouraged them to keep writing, so they stuck at it in the front room of the family home at Burwood. George had an incessant riff stuck in his head and finally managed to translate it to his guitar. It was simple, catchy and hugely effective—and 'She's So Fine' quickly took shape.

'I thought we needed something really in your face, really up and at 'em,' George said, 'so I came up with that riff. That and the chorus—and it seemed to do the job.'

That was an understatement; within a couple of weeks of its release in May, The Easybeats had their first number 1 single in Sydney. It was a smash. A stone-cold classic.

The band was ready and willing to help push 'She's So Fine' any way they could. They hand-delivered copies of the record to local DJs, and one night they all crammed into a phone booth, repeatedly calling 2UE's phone-in line to request the song. George could hardly believe it when he was told that calls were coming in from all over the city requesting 'She's So Fine'. They needn't have bothered.

An immediate upside of the success of 'She's So Fine' was that 'For My Woman' got a second run at the charts. Yet The Easybeats were still a Sydney phenomenon, this being long before the era of national radio networks, and years before programs such as *Countdown* could transform an act from local heroes to national stars in three minutes of airtime and with a 'Do yourself a favour' from Molly Meldrum.

Before the release of 'She's So Fine', the ever-eager Mike Vaughan had managed to swing a deal to get the band to Melbourne. The concert scene there was every bit as lively as Sydney; there were literally hundreds of groups in action every Saturday night, mainly playing local halls, as well as band-friendly clubs such as Sebastian's and the Thumpin' Tum. Vaughan had spotted Ron Blackmore outside the 2UW studios; Blackmore was a Melburnian, the manager of pop duo Bobby & Laurie. Vaughan encouraged Blackmore to check out 'my band', and Blackmore was taken with The Easybeats to such an extent that he floated Vaughan £150 to get the band to Melbourne.

Vaughan traded in his Jaguar for a station wagon; the band packed their gear in the back and drove south. Stevie, who'd lived in Melbourne for a couple of years before shifting to Sydney, took the time to point out the sights to his bandmates: 'Over there is my old school.' Then, when he spotted a VFL field: 'Look, George, two big ones and two little ones.' (George hadn't seen an Aussie Rules ground before.)

Blackmore had put in some solid legwork, securing them more than £1000 worth of work. But their overheads were such that the band hunkered down at night in a sordid St Kilda boarding house and had to scrounge for food. A starving Stevie collapsed on the set of TV's *The Go!! Show* and was whisked away to hospital.

This had changed by the time of their second Melbourne visit in May 1965. With their hot single 'She's So Fine' to plug, Vaughan organised a meet-and-greet for the band with influential local DJs at the Windsor Hotel, known locally as The Duchess of Spring Street, which was often frequented by politicians (Parliament House was nearby). Melbourne radio was dominated by characters such as 3KZ's Stan 'the Man' Rofe, who'd been playing rock and roll since 1956, long before other DJs dared to stray from easy listening. He also booked bands for weekly dances at Preston Town Hall, so befriending a figure like Rofe would be a huge leg-up for the band. 'We were supposed to be nice and generally get them to play our records,' George said of the get-together at the Windsor.

All was going swimmingly until a group of nearby drinkers started throwing a few verbal darts in the direction of George and the band—'Look at the poofters!' and 'What's with the hair, girls?'

The smart move for George and the others would have been to turn away, but they were still kids—George was all of eighteen—and the barbs stung. It was never revealed who threw the first punch, but George admitted that a taunt of 'English bastards' was what had set him off. He was Scottish and proud of it.

Fuck it, George thought. 'We tore into these guys,' he later recalled.

A rolling brawl between band and agitators quickly spilled out into Spring Street, as the congregation of DJs gathered on the footpath to check out the action. 'I don't know how well they can play,' one DJ said to an incredulous Ted Albert, 'but they sure can fight.'

However, George and the band were outnumbered and outmuscled; as he later admitted, 'we got a hiding in the end'. But a surprising upside came about the next day: 'We got word back later from the DJs that it was the most enjoyable lunch they'd ever had, and they put the record on the air the same day.'

'She's So Fine', and The Easybeats, were soon a national sensation. Alberts were chuffed, too. 'The record company was pleased,' George told *Bomp* magazine, 'because it was the first time . . . that they had managed to get a local act off the ground with original material.'

He thought it best not to mention the punch-up.

★

'She's So Fine' was a huge turning point for George and the band. They'd proved that it was no longer necessary to cover an existing hit to make the Australian charts. Another local act who would make inroads with their own music was the Bee Gees, but their breakthrough hit, 'Spicks and Specks', was still a year away; likewise The Loved Ones and their signature song, 'The Loved One'. The Easybeats were going it alone. Tellingly, while 'She's So Fine' was on top of the charts, Aussies Billy Thorpe, Ray Brown and Normie Rowe all had Top 10 hits: 'I Told the Brook', 'Fool, Fool, Fool' and 'It Ain't Necessarily So', respectively. Not one of them was self-penned.

But there was a downside to success, especially for George. Up until then, he'd been more than ready to 'play the game', to call phone-in lines and press the flesh with DJs and other people of influence. He had a good memory, too: during an interview with *Bandstand*'s Brian Henderson, he and Stevie rattled off the names of all the DJs who mattered: 'Mike Walsh and Tony Murphy, Stan Rofe and Ken Sparks, Bill Gates . . .'

Yet the band's live shows were becoming little more than an opportunity for their many female fans to scream their lungs raw or pass out in excitement. It was a kind of hysteria rarely witnessed this side of The Beatles. Stevie Wright would further ramp up the madness when he turned away from the crowd during his soggy ballad 'In My Book', and rub onion peel in his eyes. The tears that rolled down his cheeks induced even louder screams. (If he didn't have an onion handy, Wright would simply poke himself in the eye—anything to get the waterworks flowing.)

The press swiftly dubbed this phenomenon 'Easyfever', and it was on full and fervent display during a gig at Festival

Hall in Melbourne during September 1965. Local journalist Maggie Makeig covered the show. 'A high-pitched roar hit the ceiling,' she wrote. 'Little Stevie, hair flying, hips gyrating, hands stabbing the air, threw himself into the spotlight.' According to Makeig, it was 'She's So Fine' that inspired the chaos that abruptly ended the concert. 'They stopped the show before The Easybeats had finished their bracket.'

George and the band were now confronted with the problem of leaving the venue. That wasn't easy because the streets around Festival Hall were clogged with fans, some angry at the show being cut short, others simply in thrall to their new heroes and determined to get one more look at them, maybe even grab a souvenir. A tuft of hair would do the job.

The band jumped into a taxi and the driver slowly made his way through the crowd. However, when he stopped for a red light, kids clambered like insects all over the car.

'Get out!' the cabbie roared at the band.

'Mate,' George told him, 'we'll be killed if we get out. And our manager is seven foot four and he'll kill you!'

The cabbie reluctantly drove on and finally got the band back to their hotel unscathed.

However, the drama didn't end there. The next day the driver returned, demanding restitution. 'He was Italian and was shouting mightily at the outrage on his taxi,' said George, who knew exactly what to do.

'We served him many bottles of beer,' George reported. He also slipped him some cash.

A similar situation eventuated post-gig when the band played in Brisbane. Wright recalled 'about five to seven hundred kids . . . pulling aerials off the taxi and jumping all over it, trying to let the tyres down and rocking the taxi to reach us inside'.

Talking with *Go-Set* magazine, Stevie described the madness that occurred at a Sydney Stadium show called Gala Night of Stars, in July 1965: 'As we walked down the aisle towards the stage, the kids stood on the seats of stadium and screamed like I'd never heard screaming before.'

When the band shared a Sydney Stadium bill with Normie Rowe, it was the first time that George's friend, Brian Lee, caught a whiff of Easyfever. 'I'd seen The Beatles at the Stadium, but when they introduced The Easybeats—and the Stadium was absolutely packed—and Stephen came out, his hair was really long, and the sound reached that peak where you can't hear your voice, then I realised, *My god, they're really famous.* Ten thousand people were screaming like mad. They couldn't quieten the crowd. And the band just flayed them.'

Things went from mad to manic when George and Stevie returned to Burwood for what they hoped would be a brief respite from the chaos. In a gesture that must have irked George hugely, local magazine *Everybody's* printed his address, and, as *The Sydney Morning Herald* reported in mid-July, that's when the Burleigh Street riot began.

'Crowds of young fans several hundred strong started to gather around the house,' the *Herald* reported, 'breaking windows, obstructing the street and even breaking into the house. Several times the police have been called to restore order.'

George's ten-year-old brother Angus returned home from school just as the riot broke out. He slowly made his way to the front gate but was challenged by a policeman who was trying to hold back the crowd.

'I live here,' Angus insisted. 'Let me in!'

'They're all saying that,' the copper told Angus. 'Get lost.'

Angus was forced to jump the back fence to get into his own home.

George once let slip that he thought meeting girls was a great by-product of being in The Easybeats, but finding them in his wardrobe was a step too far. 'We've found them under our bed and everything,' he told the *Herald*. 'My parents are furious.' George's mother chased overzealous fans out of the house with a broom. George and Stevie were forced to move out. It wasn't fair on George's family.

This type of chaos was taxing enough, but more crucially it was the sonic roar generated by fans at their shows that didn't sit well with George. The Beatles were facing a similar situation; they, too, were fast growing tired of not being heard when they played live. George wanted to grow as a musician, and that wasn't going to happen when he could just as easily mime their songs on stage.

Brian Lee remembered George talking to him about how the shows were losing their appeal for him. 'We're now playing concerts, not gigs,' George said. 'With a gig you can finish, go to the bar, have a drink, mingle with the audience, but concerts, with rows of cops and security, well, it's just not the same.'

George said something similar years later when asked about Easyfever. 'We went out and did one half-hour, nobody could hear, we could have gone out and picked our noses, it wouldn't have made any difference.'

George was just eighteen years old, and the transition from migrant hostel to top of the pops had come about at break-neck speed. His family, especially his younger brothers, were enormously proud of him. Malcolm and Angus had taken to introducing themselves as 'the brother of George Young from The Easybeats' at every opportunity, which was quite the badge of honour in working-class Burwood. But George was discovering that there were more interesting things to pursue in music than fame. From then on, George would concentrate on writing great songs. He'd leave the 'bullshit' to everyone else.

3

Easyfever

As a songwriter, George was about to hit a purple patch—almost everything The Easybeats recorded between mid-1965 and late 1966 turned to gold, at the very least. Yet apart from making him more wary about the 'bullshit', success hadn't changed George a great deal, and it didn't take much to bring out the 'hostel boy' in him.

When the band toured northern Queensland in November 1965 with Melbourne's The Purple Hearts, that group's guitarist, Lobby Loyde, got into a confrontation with a redneck local, who started waving a knife. That's when George intervened.

'George head-butted the prick,' Loyde would later tell writer John Tait.

The knife-happy local wasn't the only one to spill blood during the trip. Easybeats drummer Snowy Fleet had a car crash; as *The Sydney Morning Herald* reported, 'There was a lot of blood and he'll have a nasty headache for a few days.'

George was consumed by his work with Stevie (and sometimes Harry). They wrote the songs, Ted Albert picked the hits, and the band ruled the charts like no other local act. In just one year, from June 1965, The Easybeats dropped an astonishing four hit singles, two EPs and two LPs. It was an incredible hot streak.

★

Within weeks of the explosion of 'She's So Fine', George and Stevie had another single ready to roll: 'Wedding Ring'. It was a catchy, energetic stomper, barely two minutes long, with an urgent vocal from Stevie layered on top of George's propulsive rhythm guitar and more livewire work from Harry. During their shared harmonies, George and Harry shouted their 'yeah yeah's and 'uh huh huh huh's like they were the most important lyrics ever written. The song hit number 6 on the charts during September 1965.

'Early as it was,' George would later admit, 'we went through that musicians' phase where we tried to get clever . . . to prove that you're more than just a three-chord rock and roll band. With that track we tried to be commercial, but at the same time, to be a bit different.'

Melbourne pop star Normie Rowe followed The Easybeats into the charts with a song called 'Tell Him I'm Not Home', but it was yet another cover, first recorded in 1963 by US R&B singer Chuck Jackson. Only the Bee Gees, whose 'Wine and Women' nudged the Top 30 in September 1965, seemed to have anywhere the same acumen as The Easybeats when it came to writing their own material.

The Easybeats' debut LP, simply called *Easy* and released in September, set them further apart from the pack. All fourteen tracks were originals: George wrote half of them with Stevie, three on his own and one with Harry, who contributed two songs—clearly his English was improving—and co-wrote another with Snowy Fleet. Included on the album was 'She's So Fine' but, curiously, not 'Wedding Ring'. Recorded over two nights in Sydney, with Ted Albert producing, the album hit a peak of number 4.

Writing in the pop-culture magazine *Everybody's*—the weekly that had let slip George's home address—Margaret Lindsay-Thompson gushed over the album. 'The Easybeats have a ball on this manna from record heaven for the fans,' she noted, and added—rightfully so—that it had 'a distinctively English sound with overtones of Merseyside'.

Chart domination was a decidedly fickle business, and another single, 'Sad and Lonely and Blue', was rush-released. It reached number 9 on the charts in December 1965, but didn't have the same impact as 'Wedding Ring' or 'She's So Fine'. Its relative failure gave George an indication of what the 'kids' were really after, as he told *Bomp* magazine much later. Admitting the track was 'a bit of a bomb for us', George recalled how the band thought, '"Bugger it! Let's go back," so we gave up all pretensions and gave the kids what they wanted—to dance and sing to good, happy choruses.'

George sat down with Stevie and, in what he later insisted was all of ten minutes, the pair wrote 'Women (Make You Feel Alright)'. George was true to his word—it was tailor-made for the kids who were more interested in their hips than their heads. Wright sang with a chuckle in his voice—he knew the lyrics were inane—yet regardless, or perhaps because of its simplicity, it reached number 1 in early 1966. It muscled aside another local artist, Ray Brown, with yet

another cover—his take on Patti Page's 'Tennessee Waltz'—
as it rocketed to the top of the charts.

All this success and ambition was heady stuff, but as
George later revealed, it was hardly a prosperous time for him
and the band. They were on a weekly wage of £5, and record
royalties, when they did appear, went back into the Alberts
coffers to keep the band running. (The average Australian
weekly wage at the time was just under £30.) And Australia
was a small market. So it was hardly surprising that the band
soon decided it was time to head offshore, where they knew
that the real musical action was happening. When 'Women'
hit number 1, George later said, 'it was the intention to get
to England'.

Ted Albert was in full agreement. Now all the band
needed was for Mike Vaughan to work out the details.

★

George later harboured a lot of regrets from his time with
The Easybeats, but perhaps the most deeply felt was that
he didn't involve himself in the business side of the band:
that was left to Vaughan and Albert. That's not to suggest
there was any impropriety on the part of either, but Vaughan
wasn't an experienced manager, Albert had the family business to care for, and things were moving incredibly rapidly.
The Easybeats were the first Alberts act to break open the
charts with their own material, and the first Alberts act with
the potential to match The Beatles. There was no existing
business plan for what was happening with the band.

George came to believe that 'the group should have been
making tons of money, but it wasn't'. He felt that Vaughan

didn't market them properly; no doubt he would have seen the proliferation of Beatles' merchandising—everything from wigs to boots—and figured they'd missed out on a very lucrative earner.

In later years, George indicated that his faith in Vaughan was one reason he and the band didn't inquire about their finances. 'The manager to us was father and God rolled into one. Nobody questioned him,' he later acknowledged.

'We were heavily managed,' said George. 'We had everything done for us, we practically had our arses wiped. The management excuse was that we were so busy being The Easybeats, we had no time for anything else.' A rumour circulated that Vaughan would 'fine' the band if they behaved in a manner not befitting solid-gold pop stars.

Vaughan's control of the band extended into their personal lives: drummer Fleet had trimmed seven years off his age for public purposes, and his wife, Maureen, and their child weren't spoken of publicly. George clipped a year off his birth date, as did Dick, while Harry's marriage to Pamela was never mentioned in the media. As far as the public was concerned, The Easybeats were a happy-go-lucky bunch of swinging bachelors, barely older than most of their audience.

But George was a teenager when The Easybeats exploded, and still very green as far as the music business was concerned. Vaughan and Albert, for that matter, were still young men, too, both just 29 when the band decided to try their luck on the UK scene.

And there was barely a minute for George and the band to take a breath, let alone discuss a business plan or ask someone to take a look at the books. As soon as the hits started coming, there were always more shows to play, more

TV appearances to do, more new material to write, more eager women throwing themselves at the band. In rapid succession during early 1966, for instance, the band appeared twice on Channel 10 Sydney's *On the Town* and then on ATV-0 Melbourne's *Ten on the Town*, swiftly followed by spots on Channel 9 Sydney's *Saturday Date*, and *Club Seventeen* on Channel 7 Perth. Then it was back to Sydney for a spot on Channel 7's *It's All Happening*. In mid-March they made an appearance on *The Go!! Show*, which was filmed at the inaugural Australian National Record Awards in Melbourne, where the band ripped up 'She's So Fine', Stevie yelling himself hoarse as the kids in the crowd screamed like banshees.

George went along with it, but his distaste for their live performances grew with each show. 'Basically it became theatre, with Stevie doing his thing, the music became . . . can't say secondary, but it was pointless in a way, trying to be good musicians or good players, because it tended to be overshadowed by the screaming and the riots, that sort of stuff.'

Mike Vaughan, meanwhile, had set off for England and the US in February 1966. He had a relatively small budget of $4000 and limited time, but he was hell-bent on returning home with an international record deal.

*

The story broke in early April in *The Sydney Morning Herald*. The headline read: 'How The Easybeats got a big US contract'. But the band, despite their huge success in Oz, had been a tough sell in the States. Vaughan's ego, as well as his budget, took a battering as he tried to convince US record labels that there was an Australian rock-and-roll group worth signing. No Oz rock act outside of Johnny O'Keefe, who'd had a brief relationship with Los Angeles's Liberty Records in 1960, had ever been signed directly to an American label. Billed as the 'Boomerang Boy', O'Keefe spent a hitless year with the label, costing Liberty thousands of dollars due to failed, sometimes chaotic, promotions.

On what he intended to be his final day in the US, Mike Vaughan's last port of call was United Artists (UA), a label best known for easy-listening releases and film tie-ins—they'd released the soundtracks to the two Beatles films, *A Hard Day's Night* and *Help!* in North America. Their roster in 1966 was a musical allsorts, including actress/singer Patty Duke, and pop group Jay & the Americans. It was hardly Capitol Records, the home of The Beatles and The Beach Boys, whose headquarters, built to resemble a stack of records on a turntable, was one of LA's more prominent landmarks. But Vaughan had run out of options.

He spoke with Murray Deutch, the vice-president of UA's record division, a music man who'd helped discover Buddy Holly. Vaughan played his ace straightaway: the band he represented, he said, currently had a number 1 hit back home—'Women (Make You Feel Alright)'. He told Deutch that the band whipped up the same kind of hysteria as The Beatles. As Vaughan revealed on his return, that 'apparently made him think the group might have something, so he agreed to listen to their records'.

According to Vaughan, it was the fact that the band wrote their own songs—the very thing that set them apart in Australia—that sealed the deal. He extended his stay by several weeks to negotiate: 'My lawyer and theirs shouted at each other and wrangled over points in the contract.' UA agreed to a five-record deal, with US$25,000 reportedly committed to promoting the band. There was even a promise of a spot on the hugely popular and influential *Ed Sullivan Show*.

'I have not seen such excitement, such hysteria, about any artist since we first established our relationship with The Beatles,' gushed Murray Deutch when the deal became official. 'I have the same feeling I did when I first became aware of Beatlemania.'

It was the big time. George and the guys had come a long way from Villawood—and all in a mere three years.

But there was a caveat. United Artists weren't especially interested in the band's existing material, especially after the one song they did release—'Women', under the name 'Make You Feel Alright (Women)', to avoid confusion with a hit by Brit duo Peter & Gordon named 'Woman'—tanked in the US in July 1966. UA wanted new songs, new material, that would hopefully continue the momentum (and sales) of The Easybeats' string of Australian hits. This put huge pressure on key songwriters George and Stevie.

Many years down the line, George reflected on the agreement with UA, referring to it as a 'deal of sorts' but without any ironclad arrangements. 'There were no guaranteed releases and there was no guarantee that they were going to release any of the product that we had made in Australia,' George recalled. 'We would have to come up with some song that cracked the international market.'

★

A date was set in place for The Easybeats' departure from Australia: 14 July 1966. The plan was to base themselves in London, where they'd have fewer visa hassles than the US, and record at the fabled Abbey Road studios, home of The Beatles.

Before their departure, George and the band agreed to get something 'in the can' to help keep their local audience satiated in their absence. They returned to the studio with Ted Albert and emerged with yet another hit, 'Come and See Her'. This time around, stony-faced bassist Dick Diamonde was given the job of growling the title lyric in his booming voice, in much the same way Who bassist John Entwistle did on songs such as 'Boris the Spider'. In the background, George and Harry moaned and groaned their harmonies as the tempo quickened—the song couldn't have been any raunchier if they'd changed the spelling of 'come'. The trick worked; 'Come and See Her' reached the Top 5 soon after its April 1966 release. The record was preceded, by a month, by the release of their second album, *It's 2 Easy*, which included 'Wedding Ring', which had been left off their debut LP, as well as 'Sad and Lonely and Blue', 'Women (Make Me Feel Alright)' and 'Come and See Her'. The album, naturally, was a smash hit.

When the band played 'Come and See Her' live, audiences would get involved in an unexpected way. When Wright sang the line, 'Doctor, doctor, my baby's sick', cheekier punters dropped 'Come and see her'—which was the next line—and instead yelled out, 'Gonorrhoea'. A few years later, two of the bands that George mentored, AC/DC and The Angels, would inspire equally funny responses from their fans, the former during 'The Jack' and the latter when they played

'Am I Ever Gonna See Your Face Again'. 'Come and See Her' was a trailblazer.

And it was keeping some impressive company in the charts. When 'Come and See Her' hit number 1, it dominated a chart that featured new releases such as The Beatles' 'Norwegian Wood', 'Substitute' by The Who, The Rolling Stones' 'Fortune Teller', 'Shapes of Things' by the Yardbirds and Bob Dylan's raucous ode to high times, 'Rainy Day Women #12 & 35'. It was a stellar time for Anglo-American rock and roll—and George and The Easybeats were now competing with the acts they revered.

Yet George admitted that by then he'd stopped paying so much attention to these so-called rivals; he and the band were more concerned with their own music. And George was developing a strong cynicism towards 'the game'. 'At first we took a lot of notice of overseas trends in groups, but then it became apparent to us that was all just a money game,' he said. 'It didn't mean so much.'

Around this time, George and Stevie's hideaway was once again tracked down by zealous fans, and they were forced to move. It was the Burleigh Street riot all over again. The situation got so dire that Vaughan pleaded with the band's followers to allow them a little privacy. He persuaded Mike Walsh to publish his request in *The Sydney Morning Herald* in late May.

'Their manager, Mike Vaughan, appeals to these fans to allow The Easybeats and their families some privacy,' wrote Walsh, 'and I'm sure Georgie [*sic*] and Stevie will think this far more devoted of them.'

Soon after, in June, Vaughan broke an even bigger story in the press—Beatles producer George Martin had personally requested that the band get to London ASAP in order to record with him. ('Beatle man sends for The Easybeats' was the headline, although the truth was that Vaughan had reached out to Martin via a mutual acquaintance at EMI.) This would be followed by a lengthy tour of England and Scotland arranged by Brian Epstein, The Beatles' manager, said the press report. Brian Sommerville, who had handled The Beatles' PR and currently worked with The Kinks, would be The Easybeats' press agent; he'd been recommended by Martin. The band didn't even have a dedicated press agent at home—Vaughan usually worked the phones and hoped for the best—so this was another step up the ladder. It would be first class all the way in the UK.

'We're delighted,' said Vaughan, in what might have been the understatement of the year. 'George Martin has asked us to come sooner and we are going to come as soon as humanly possible.' And the tour? 'We are gambling everything that we'll be a success. I think we've got a good chance.'

*

As always, there was no shortage of business to attend to at home before they started rubbing shoulders with pop royalty. There were several weeks of touring; the rush-recording of a new EP, *Easyfever*, and an album (the imaginatively titled *Volume 3*, which would give their fans some new product while the band was overseas); and a round of TV appearances including a 'farewell' show on Channel 9's *Bandstand*, which was filmed on 19 June.

In his awkward intro, *Bandstand*'s bespectacled host, Brian Henderson, didn't seem to quite know what to make of George and the others. He spoke about the new bands in 'the Rolling Stones style' that were 'springing up right across the country. Suddenly they're everywhere . . . They seem to appear fully fledged, able to play guitar with what even professional musicians consider reasonable skill'. In a nod to his audience's parents, 'Hendo' admitted that 'the long hair can be a bit off-putting', but accepted that musical invasion was not going to stop. 'And that's why The Easybeats are starring in this *Bandstand*; they're head and haircut above all the rest.'

The stage design was quaint: the band played while perched high on a platform as a team of shapely go-go dancers shook and shimmied around them on the studio floor. All five 'Easys' wore turtlenecks, with their dark jackets buttoned up high—they looked sharp, world conquerors in waiting. (For a performance of 'Come and See Her', they changed into more traditional suits and ties, which didn't look anywhere near as good.)

George couldn't suppress a grin as he and Harry chanted, 'Easy, easy', during a run-through of 'Easy as Can Be'; it was all a bit silly. Stevie Wright, however, was in his pomp, a true pop star, shaking his ass when the tempo was hot—his skinny legs seemed to have a life of their own—and then staring straight down the camera with big puppy-dog eyes when the mood turned sombre. A million hearts broke across Australia.

When George and Stevie were interviewed by Henderson in a break between songs, the host admitted to having a soft spot for 'In My Book', the tear-jerker that required Wright to do the old 'onion in the eye' trick.

'George, you write most of the songs, right?'

'In My Book' definitely wasn't George's finest moment as a songwriter, but he grinned for the camera and nodded in agreement, all the while looking hugely uncomfortable, a man eager to be elsewhere. Playing guitar was much easier than this.

George had a more enjoyable time during one of their other pre-departure TV spots. While banging out 'She's So Fine', he found it hard to keep his mind, or his eyes, on the job; he spent most of the shoot smiling broadly at the scantily clad dancers who flanked him. At one point he cheekily aped one of the girl's dance moves.

The job did have its perks, after all.

★

The Easybeats had one more TV commitment before departing, shooting another special, this time a Coca-Cola–sponsored program for Channel 7, where they mimed a twenty-minute set of their hits—'Women', 'Wedding Ring', 'Come and See Her' and 'She's So Fine' among them. Billy Thorpe hosted the show, which wouldn't air until October. George must have cringed when he and the band were forced to play nice with the show's sponsor by performing a cheesy ditty named 'Make Life Sweet (With Coca-Cola)'.

But it was the events that transpired immediately after the shoot that cast a long, dark shadow over the band.

George and Harry were the most enthusiastic about heading overseas. It was an odyssey for them, a great adventure. But the others had their reservations: Stevie was uneasy about leaving his new girlfriend, Gail Baxter, and wasn't as motivated as George and Harry—he enjoyed being a big fish in the small pond that was Australia. Snowy had his wife and daughter to consider—was it fair to leave them behind? Dick's devout parents, meanwhile, were convinced that he was going straight to hell the longer he continued with rock and roll—it being the devil's music, after all—and he was racked with guilt.

The situation became even more complicated when Mike Vaughan made it known that they were on a tight budget; the only non-band members travelling would be Vaughan himself and George's brother-in-law, Sam Horsburgh, their roadie. No girlfriends, no wives, no children.

The morning after filming the Channel 7 special, Harry Vanda's wife, Pamela, was found dead at their home. She had taken an overdose of sleeping pills. At an inquest almost a year later, Harry admitted that his wife had been depressed, particularly by the fact that she wasn't going to accompany Harry to the UK.

'Tragedy struck The Easybeats on the eve of their departure for England,' reported *The Australian Women's Weekly*, 'when the wife of guitarist Harry Vanda died of an overdose of sleeping tablets. Few people knew that Harry was married.'

It was tragic that probably the first mention of their marriage in the media was during the report of her death. (George, too, was in a serious relationship, with Sandra, which hadn't yet been 'exposed' in the press.) It typified the sort of subterfuge that bands such as The Easybeats agreed to in order to maintain their public image as young, available bachelors. Changes of name and birth dates, the denial of serious relationships, let alone marriage—this was all part of 'the biz'. And sometimes the consequences could be devastating.

Vanda was shattered but decided to continue with the trip. 'Being in a band is like being part of a family,' he said, and opted to lean on his bandmates for support and bury himself in the work. He and George were growing especially tight. 'Don't worry, Harry,' George told him. 'You're with me for life.' A grief-stricken Harry sent his five-month-old son to live with his parents in the Netherlands.

On the following Thursday, 14 July, The Easybeats, Vaughan and Sam Horsburgh flew out of Sydney for London. Each band member had $250 in his pocket. They were sent off into the blue yonder by around 500 screaming teenage fans—'dressed in miniskirts and armed with banners', noted *The Sydney Morning Herald*—while more forceful fans managed to break the police line and race onto the tarmac in the general direction of the band's Qantas flight.

'Qantas officers and customs men quickly forced the dejected fans back to the overseas terminal,' reported the *Herald*, 'and the police closed their ranks.'

The entourage didn't even manage to get out of the country before more chaos ensued. Sitting on the tarmac during a stopover at Perth Airport, having just waved goodbye to another 4000 fans, the band, along with 100 other London-bound passengers, were quickly hustled off the plane—someone had phoned in a bomb threat, and they had to evacuate. Now!

In what was not the best spur-of-the-moment decision ever made, the band was told they were to give an impromptu performance on the far side of the airport and were driven to an enclosure. Not surprisingly, the big crowd that had gathered started to push forward, and for a moment it appeared as though the mesh fence that separated band from fans would give way. The performance was quickly cancelled. Then the group discovered that someone had punctured a tyre on the police vehicle used to transport the band from the plane, while fans had stomped all over two other nearby vehicles, damaging them badly.

The Easybeats limped back to their flight and slumped into their seats, quietly hoping that all this mayhem wasn't a taste of what lay ahead.

4

Saved by The Swingle Singers

Flower power was never going to be an easy fit for someone as strongly grounded in reality as George, yet he and The Easybeats arrived in London on the cusp of the city's psychedelic awakening. The Beatles were about to jump headfirst into acid-pop with their next LP, *Revolver*. Carnaby Street would soon be awash with paisleys and vivid colours, while The Byrds' 'Eight Miles High' and Donovan's deeply dippy 'Sunshine Superman' captured the mood of the moment. The UFO, the underground club that would launch Pink Floyd—and probably its fair share of acid casualties—was about to open its doors. Yet none of this meant much to George.

'The flower children thing,' George admitted, 'was really a drag for us.' The number 1 hit in the UK was Chris Farlowe's 'Out of Time', which may as well have been written for the recently arrived group of hostel lads from Sydney.

The first band that George and the others caught in London was The Move, fronted by gifted singer, guitarist and songwriter Roy Wood; their drummer was Bev Bevan, who'd go on to fame and fortune with the Electric Light

Orchestra. George and Harry were knocked out by The Move, who fused together elements of soul, blues and psychedelia, and could be just as anarchic on stage as The Who. Vanda admitted that he almost felt like 'packing up and heading home again'.

George's immediate plan was clear in his mind, as he later told Australian *Rolling Stone*. It was all pretty straightforward. 'We had figured on staying there three or four months, doing a bit of recording, hopefully getting a single out, hopefully getting it on the charts, and make ourselves a lot of dough working through Europe and America.'

If only it was that easy.

George, Harry and all The Easybeats moved into a flat in working-class Willesden Green, a relatively short trip from the city on the tube. While hardly the most affluent or chic part of London, Willesden would leave its mark on at least two prominent songwriters, being cited by both Ray Davies of The Kinks ('Willesden Green') and, much later, The Clash's Joe Strummer, in the song 'Willesden to Cricklewood'. British loons The Bonzo Dog Doo-Dah Band also name-checked Willesden in their song 'Shirt'. With its broad ethnic mix—immigrants from the Caribbean and the subcontinent had started moving into an area that already had a sizeable German, Polish and Austrian population—it must have reminded George of Villawood.

It was a tight fit at Easybeats House: the seven men shared three bedrooms, so privacy was hard to come by. (Ten years later, George's brothers, Malcolm and Angus, would settle into a similarly cramped band house 30 minutes away, in Bayswater.) George gravitated to the Cromwellian Club in the city, a three-storey venue housing a casino, bar and discotheque. Owned by entrepreneur Tony Mitchell—with a little help from four well-known British wrestlers, who each had a stake in the club—it was fast becoming the hangout for London's 'in crowd', even though George and the band were far from that. But it was a great place to scope out the opposition—it was there, in the basement band room, that George and the others caught sets from Rod Stewart and blues guitarist Peter Green, who were soon to join Small Faces and Fleetwood Mac, respectively. On another night, George checked out guitarist Jeff Beck, whose hit single 'Hi Ho Silver Lining' was part of one of the first musical 'care packages' that George sent to his brothers, Malcolm and Angus, back in Burwood.

London was bursting at the seams with new music, and the album charts were also awash in great records: *Pet Sounds* by The Beach Boys, The Rolling Stones' *Aftermath*, *Small Faces* and the ubiquitous Beatles, whose *Rubber Soul* still clung to the Top 20 eight months after its release, alongside new album *Revolver*. The Stones, The Beatles and The Who had recently shared a bill at the *New Musical Express* poll winners' show in London—a remarkable line-up, even then. Soon after, The Beatles appeared on *Top of the Pops*, performing 'Paperback Writer' and 'Rain', again moulding the pop form into a strange and exciting new shape, challenging everyone to try to keep pace with them.

All of this action was a handy reminder that George and the band needed to get back to work. Another reminder was their limited resources—they had a start-up budget of AU$20,000, which explained why they were sharing such cheap digs. Even though talk of working with Beatles producer George Martin seemed to have stalled, everything was in place for their tilt at the international market. Ted Albert, who agreed to continue producing the band, flew out in August to join them. They were to record at Abbey Road, which impressed George hugely.

'We all felt chuffed about the fact that this was it,' George told Jane Albert. 'You're in the place where all these great records were being made.'

The Beatles had spent time at Abbey Road putting the finishing touches to *Revolver*, while The Hollies and the evergreen Cliff Richard had also worked there of late. But something didn't click when George and the band reconnected with Ted Albert; the songs weren't flying in the same way that they had back in Sydney.

Two tracks were recorded—'Baby I'm a Comin''" and 'Mandy'—but neither were destined to become Easybeats classics. The first was a mid-paced ramble with weather-obsessed lyrics (it had been a very cold summer, even by British standards); the latter was equally uninspired, a song in search of both hook and melody. Both lacked the red-hot energy of their Australian hits; their pace seemed sluggish, insipid. In George's words, 'They weren't very good.'

This failure, and the lack of response to the one old single released in the UK—'Come and See Her' backed with 'Make You Feel Alright (Women)'—meant that serious changes needed to be made. Ted Albert had been a master at capturing The Easybeats' raw energy back in Australia, but it was clear, at least to United Artists, that the band needed to work with a new producer. And Albert, as George would acknowledge, was busy with the family business back in Sydney; he was thinly stretched and agreed to step aside. (In what was a textbook instance of deja vu, George would find himself in the same situation with AC/DC a decade later.)

Brian Sommerville, the band's PR guy, knew American producer Shel Talmy, who was currently working in the UK. The ambitious Talmy was very much the producer of the moment, having hit paydirt with The Kinks' 'You Really Got Me' and its scratchy, driving guitar sound, and The Who's incendiary 'My Generation'. George loved both songs: '[They] were straight out of the box, the black hole in space . . . the sound was so exciting.' Talmy agreed to meet with George and the band.

Talmy, like George, wasn't much for hype—he firmly believed that The Who's notoriously erratic manager, Kit Lambert, was 'certifiably insane'—and he connected with The Easybeats, describing them later to writer Richie Unterberger as 'a good bunch of guys'. He could also see that George and Harry were interested in how the studio worked. 'They certainly were alert to what was going on.'

Talmy began recording with The Easybeats at the IBC Studios in London's Portland Place during September. George could see that Talmy understood the studio: 'I thought he was a terrific producer.' George also hit it off with Talmy's English engineer, Glyn Johns, a man who could have passed for a rock dandy himself with his long hair, piercing eyes and sharp dress sense, a cigarette never too far away from his lips. He and Talmy were the A-team. (Johns would go on to work with The Beatles and The Rolling Stones.)

Yet once again, the songs weren't falling from the sky, despite another huge change, this time initiated by George. He believed that his writing partnership with Stevie Wright was at an end. George wanted to push himself more creatively, and didn't think that Stevie was up for that. Though a great frontman, Stevie was only a competent lyricist at best, and his lack of presence at Willesden Green—he'd taken to the London nightlife like a fish to water—also pushed George and Harry together as creative partners.

George's decision to write with Harry crushed Stevie, according to Michael Chugg, who later managed Wright as a solo act. 'He could never live with the fact that George stopped writing with him,' Chugg told Jane Albert. Wright's biographer, Glenn Goldsmith, had a different take: he felt that Wright wasn't as motivated as George and didn't appreciate the suggestions made by United Artists, who regarded his lyrics as dated. 'He told me that the idea of starting again with his lyrics under the microscope was too much. He preferred to hang out and smoke hash.'

George began writing with Harry, but none of the songs they presented to Talmy at that first session—among them were 'Remember Sam' and 'Pretty Girl'—struck the producer as hits-in-waiting. But there was one riff that George was tinkering with that grabbed Talmy's attention, even if the song wasn't complete.

'Harry and I had been messing around for a couple of months with this idea and that idea,' George said in the documentary *Friday on My Mind: The Story of The Easybeats*, 'and getting nowhere.'

But Talmy sensed something. 'Go away and work on that,' he told George.

George had to act fast, because the band was now out of money and Vaughan had been forced to wire home for more cash. Frustrated and still searching for a hook, George and Harry went to the movies. Slacking off proved to be the defining moment in the career of George Young and The Easybeats.

*

The Swingle Singers were—and still are—a French vocal group, formed in 1962, with a flair for pop, jazz and the classics: they could put a dazzling a cappella swing on such austere pieces as Bach's 'Fugue in G Minor'. George had never heard of them until he and Harry drifted into a cinema while still trying to figure out what to do with their latest work in progress. The Swingles featured in a documentary that ran before the feature, and George was struck by their vocal gymnastics. As he recalled, 'They did a whole lot of doo-doos and daa-daas and woop-woops. It was quite clever.'

That night, back at their flat, George returned to his musical idea but with a much clearer plan. 'Some of those doo-doos from The Swingle Singers made [their] way into the idea. So, I suppose, in a fashion, The Swingle Singers were responsible for it.'

That song became 'Friday on My Mind'.

When George and Harry brought it into the studio, the track came together in near-record time, 'about three or four hours', as George remembered it. Harry added a distinctive Eastern-influenced guitar part—tricky enough to be the curse of legions of future guitarists—while drummer Fleet, with a little help from Shel Talmy, added the signature drum break in the finale (it later inspired Meatloaf, a big Vanda/Young fan, for the big moment of his song 'You Took the Words Right out of My Mouth'). Stevie sang his heart out, even though the song was at the top of his range, and a classic was born.

The lyric for 'Friday' was a reflection of the band's hard-scrabble life before fame. Friday was the one day of the week that every working person looked forward to, a chance to break loose, party hard and forget about the week that had just passed, or the one up ahead. Yet when young Aussie filmmaker Peter Clifton visited the band in London, George spoke with him and downplayed the suggestion that the song was some kind of anthem. It was merely a reflection of the world he knew. He told Clifton, 'It's understandable why "Friday" can be seen as an ode to the working class given the weekly grind of the average punter. But it has more to do with our outlook on the world than any class statement.'

'Friday' also vindicated George's decision to write with Harry rather than Stevie. 'Made My Bed, Gonna Lie In It' was picked as the B-side, making it the first time the Vanda/Young team had 'owned' both sides of an Easybeats single. It was a huge leap forward for the fledgling songwriting team, and their first great record.

★

As good a song as 'Friday on My Mind' was, selling it was going to be a big challenge. The Easybeats had no track record in the UK and, despite the obvious appeal of 'Friday on My Mind', commercial radio wouldn't touch them. Being top of the pops in Australia meant nothing in Swinging Sixties London, where you couldn't walk 100 metres without bumping into another rock-and-roll superstar. Fortunately, as it turned out for The Easybeats, there was a mutiny happening on the high seas around the UK, with some fellow Aussies at the helm.

'Pirate radio' was a reaction to the conservative playlists of the various BBC radio services, which would typically air less than an hour of new music each day. Radio Caroline was the first pirate station, established in 1964, and it broadcast from a ship anchored off the coast of Essex. Because the 'pirates' broadcasted from international waters, they were not deemed to be breaking the law. Within a few years, Caroline's audience had grown to somewhere around ten million listeners and the total 'pirate' radio audience to about 25 million.

Radio Luxembourg, which would prove to be very Easybeats-friendly, was another key pirate station. Expat Aussie DJ Alan 'Fluff' Freeman worked on Radio Luxembourg and took to 'Friday' immediately upon its mid-October release. Freeman had been in Olympic Studios during the song's recording, clicking his fingers to the playback and nodding his approval. As George recalled, 'The pirate radio stations, who had Australian DJs, would slip in the record even though it wasn't programmed.'

Radio London was another big advocate of the song; their on-air staff included expat Aussie Ian Damon, while his colleague Pete Drummond had also spent time in Australia. Other on-air talents such as John Peel, who had great taste, and the madcap Kenny Everett were hugely influential figures. When The Easybeats visited one of the pirate stations for a 'meet and greet' session, they came away a vivid shade of green: the North Sea waters could get extremely choppy.

'Friday on My Mind'—which swiftly caught the ear of London hopeful David Jones, about to morph into the androgynous David Bowie—kept some great company after its release. There were new releases from The Beach Boys (the masterly 'Good Vibrations'), Motown's Four Tops

('Reach Out I'll Be There') and The Supremes ('You Can't Hurry Love'), as well as 'Stop Stop Stop' by The Hollies, among others. More than 60 new singles were released at the same time as 'Friday'. By the first week of November, with the high demand on pirate-radio airplay forcing the more commercial stations to play the song, 'Friday' began to climb the UK Top 40. It reached number 33 in mid-November and was number 20 a week after that.

Much to George's bemusement, the band was suddenly in demand. According to manager Vaughan, they were 'turning down offers of £300 and £400 a week to tour'. Prior to 'Friday', George had felt that the local media regarded him and the group as 'a bunch of Aussie hicks', something that 'didn't go down too well with us'. Now everything had changed. He said that the song's success was 'one in the eye to everyone who thought we wouldn't make it'.

During November, there was a run of dates with the Four Tops, including two gigs at the Saville Theatre in London, whose landlord happened to be Beatles manager Brian Epstein. Looking on each night were some Beatles, Rolling Stones Mick Jagger and Charlie Watts, as well as Georgie Fame and Eric Burdon. These were A-list shows. (A year later, Epstein's Beatles shot their burlesque 'Hello, Goodbye' film clip at the theatre.)

George referred to the gathering a bit dismissively, describing it as 'the usual assorted glitterati of the pop world', but he couldn't deny that he and the band were catching the eye of all the right people.

A photo shoot followed with photographer Caroline Gillies, the band looking every inch the pop act on the rise: Dick wore a sharp striped jacket, Harry a cream coat, while George stared intently down the barrel of the camera, his hands in the pockets of his snug white trousers, which he teamed with a purple shirt and short black jacket. The combined look was 'effortless cool' (and probably a tad cold). The same couldn't be said for the shots Gillies took of the band in a nearby kids' playground: George was wedged into a swing, the look on his face less than impressed. He was, most likely, already thinking about the follow-up to 'Friday'.

The band made two appearances on the hugely influential (if cheesy) TV show *Top of the Pops*, which had an audience of several million viewers. The first Easybeats spot was on 24 November, and they returned two weeks later. Both times they performed 'Friday', which by early December was now sitting just outside the UK Top 10, having shot past The Hollies and The Kinks' 'Dead End Street' during its run up to the business end of the charts. They also performed the song on TV's *Ready Steady Go!* during November, and on *The Rolf Harris Show* soon after.

George didn't mince words when the *New Musical Express* dispatched their writer, Keith Altham, to talk with him and Harry, for a piece that ran on 3 December. As George absent-mindedly scattered sugar all over a coffee-shop table, he was asked how it felt to have his songs compared with maestros Lennon and McCartney.

'We're flattered,' he accepted, 'but it's annoying. We never intentionally went in to copy anyone. However, comparison with The Beatles is more of a compliment than most. We're already thinking about the second disc, and we intend to be very careful that there is no similarity with the next one.'

Typical George—no bullshit.

Altham's read on Vanda and Young was accurate: 'George

is short, dark, assured . . . in contrast to Harry, who is tall, fair, unsure and desperate to be helpful.'

The title of the article—'Easybeats didn't copy The Beatles'—neatly summed up the pair's mindset. They'd finally had some success beyond Australia, which was fantastic, but they didn't want to be seen as imitators, some sort of 'Antipodean Fab Five'.

★

Mike Vaughan had been drip-feeding the Australian media news of 'his boys'—he'd even let slip their first London address, on Teignmouth Road in Willesden Green, in the hope their Oz fans might drop them a line and tell them they hadn't been forgotten. But once 'Friday' broke, it was the press that was suddenly pursuing Vaughan.

'Now The Easybeats are poised for the big time . . .' was the splash in 13 November's *The Sydney Morning Herald*. The *Herald*'s journo, Allan Veitch, reported from London that the single was climbing several key charts—those of Radio London, the *New Musical Express* and *Melody Maker*. By then, 'Friday' had sold 25,000 copies in the UK. Manager Vaughan admitted that if the single hadn't connected, the band would have been forced to slog it out on the British club circuit (though the absolute truth was that they probably would have returned to Australia).

'It would have been a bit of a setback to us if this record hadn't gone over well,' said Vaughan, proving he was a dab hand at understatement.

The band had recently shifted from Willesden Green to slightly more upscale digs—a two-storey house a few minutes' stroll from Wembley Park station, at 18 Barn Rise, the former home of American-born pop singer P.J. Proby. P.J.'s career momentum—he had four UK Top 10 hits between 1964 and 1965—was interrupted when he developed a nasty habit of splitting his pants on stage; his wardrobe malfunctions became a scandal. He was banned by the prominent ABC theatre chain and by the BBC, and his career slid downhill from there. The Easybeats had toured with Proby in Australia in 1965, although they kept their distance, as Wright had told *Go-Set*: 'We were told not to go to him until he came to us as big stars don't like crawlers or hangers-on.' When George moved into the Proby house, he laughed about its notorious former occupant: 'You can still see the stains.'

Mike Vaughan said that it wasn't the decor that concerned them but the neighbours. 'We figured [they] wouldn't be too happy with another pop crowd coming in . . . [but] after P.J. Proby we'd sound like chamber music.'

George made it very clear, when he spoke with *Herald* journo Veitch, that this was no party house; it was a place of business. 'We're there strictly for work,' George said, 'and we've really worked since we've been here. We're either writing songs or rehearsing all the time, day and night.'

Stevie Wright backed this up when he spoke with *Beat* magazine. 'Harry and George are always writing songs. They never stop. They start to record on the stereo tape, upstairs, late at night. They work right through until early morning.' Most nights, as Wright settled into bed, he could hear George and Harry working away on another new song.

Vaughan had been doing his best to create a smokescreen for George and the band, to continue presenting them as 'those nice boys from Oz'. Yet when director Peter Clifton visited The Easybeats' house, the first thing that struck him was that 'there were girls everywhere—young, pretty and willing to please'. Clifton didn't witness any drug-taking, but noted that 'everybody smoked like chimneys'. Clifton learned one other crucial fact during his visit, as he shot a documentary on the band: 'Harry Vanda and George Young were the heart and sound of The Easybeats.'

A very clear hierarchy had been established, with the band's hitmaking duo at the top. This extended into their live performances, too, as they played one-off gigs in regional centres Morecambe, Stevenage, Coventry, Margate and Grimsby into early December. George's rhythm guitar assault formed the backbone of the band's sound, while Harry's lead guitar provided the colour. Out front, Stevie performed the role that George's brother, Angus, would later take on with AC/DC: he was the livewire, the human dynamo. But George's insistent rhythm playing was the core of the band, its pulse.

Lobby Loyde, whom George had saved from an angry redneck back in Australia, was one of many peers who understood this. 'George was always the fucking engine room,' he told writer John Tait.

Back in Oz, the band's latest single, 'Sorry', released in late October, had raced to number 4 in the charts, while the pre-recorded *Coca-Cola Special* had screened on Channel 7 and rated highly. 'Friday' dropped on 23 November and by January had become their fifth number 1 in Australia; it would stick to the charts like glue for sixteen weeks. In the UK, it reached its peak of number 6 on 15 December. Fellow Aussies The Seekers were three spots ahead of them, with 'Morningtown Ride', but, unlike The Easybeats, The Seekers had recorded a cover.

Yet it was a different Australian chart hit that opened a new door for George—as a songwriter for hire. While still on the road in Australia, George and the band had been in Perth, preparing for a TV spot on local show *Club Seventeen*. The show's host was an aspiring pop hopeful named Johnny Young, born John de Jong, the son of a Dutch–Western Australian farming family. During a break in shooting, he brazenly asked George if he would write a song for him. George happened to have a song in his head, and began strumming it on his guitar.

'Stevie'll add some words,' he told Johnny.

A very eager Johnny Young fronted up at the band's motel room the next morning, expecting a finished song. Instead, he witnessed what he described as 'about a dozen girls sprawled out around the place; it was very rock and roll'.

But a song did come out of the debauchery, with lyrics by Stevie as promised. It was called 'Step Back'.

Backed by his band Kompany, Young cut the song and it became a local hit in Perth. It was nine long months before it became an Australia-wide hit. But it did eventually hit hard, reaching number 1 across the country in September 1966 and staying on the charts for the better part of six months, in the process transforming Johnny Young into Australia's newest pop idol. 'Step Back' was the first hit composed by George but not recorded for release by The Easybeats. Almost by accident, he'd now begun a parallel career.

At the time, though, George's mind was on more pressing matters: trying to conjure up a sequel to 'Friday on My Mind'. It was driving him quietly crazy.

5

The Young Millionaires

By mid-January 1967, George, Harry and the band had returned to work with Shel Talmy, but without the serendipitous inspiration of The Swingle Singers, the next hit just wasn't coming. They had three songs in recordable shape—'Happy is the Man', 'You Me, We Love' and 'All Gone Boy'—which were all Vanda/Young co-writes. Yet none of these songs was considered an adequate follow-up to 'Friday on My Mind', which by now was well on its way to selling one million copies worldwide.

When Bill Harry, a writer from the *Record Mirror*, sat in on the recording session for the follow-up single, he heard Talmy announce 'Take twenty' from the booth, which wasn't a great sign. Manager Vaughan pulled the journalist aside and told him that they had initially booked the studio for three hours, thinking that would be ample time, but he'd just rebooked the studio from midnight.

'They only had a short time to write this number we're recording,' said Vaughan. 'It's essential that we get this record cut as soon as possible.'

The song that George and Harry had presented to Talmy was called 'Who'll Be the One', and it lacked the energy, passion and melodic strength of 'Friday'. George sensed that it was not the right song to follow such a massive hit. 'It wasn't even on same planet' as 'Friday', he later admitted. 'It was rubbish, absolute crap.' But several months had passed since their debut UK hit, and George and Harry had no option but to pump out something—anything—to stay in the game, because the competition was so fierce.

In 1967 alone, The Beatles delivered John Lennon's spell-binding 'Strawberry Fields Forever' and Paul McCartney's equally wonderful 'Penny Lane', certainly their most auto-biographical, and perhaps most brilliant, double A-side single. In their spare time, they completed their masterpiece *Sgt. Pepper's Lonely Hearts Club Band* and the oft-overlooked *Magical Mystery Tour* soundtrack, a six-track collection that included 'The Fool on the Hill' and 'I Am the Walrus'. The Who, meanwhile, hit big with landmark singles such as 'Pictures of Lily'—a sly ode to masturbation—and 'I Can See for Miles'. The Stones released the suggestive 'Let's Spend the Night Together' and the aching ballad 'Ruby Tuesday'. Procol Harum cut the epic 'A Whiter Shade of Pale', while The Doors ('Light My Fire') and Jefferson Airplane ('White Rabbit') also released career-making tracks.

Yet George and Harry struggled to come up with just one song to maintain their momentum. George, when he spoke with a writer from the *New Musical Express*, did have a rough idea—but only of what he *didn't* want to do. 'We are hoping to ease in with some simple musical ideas which have no pretentions to being instructive or progressive but are simply entertaining. Our second disc should prove whether we are going to make it or not.'

Stevie also chewed this over when he spoke with Brian Matthew from the *Top of the Pops* radio show. 'We didn't want to follow it, as most groups have done, with another "Friday on My Mind".'

'Who'll Be the One' was released in mid-March and went absolutely nowhere.

It didn't help George's state of mind that he'd become entangled in a classic case of tall poppy syndrome. He told a *Melody Maker* reporter that the band stood a better chance of developing in the UK, as it was 'more musically aware and in touch' than Australia. His comments were undeniably correct—what musician wouldn't have wanted to be in the UK in 1967?—but it stirred up a hornet's nest of resentment back home. 'EASYBEATS KNOCK AUSTRALIA' screamed *Go-Set*, in blazing upper case, which left George compelled to talk it out with a writer from *Everybody's* magazine.

'I love Australia,' George insisted, 'the people, the attitudes and the country.' Snowy Fleet had a small Aussie flag on his drum kit, just to remind everyone where their roots lay. Even when it was pointed out to the group that they comprised a Scot, two Poms and two Dutchmen, they insisted that they were an Australian band. This misunderstanding hurt George deeply.

And The Easybeats were hardly a lone antipodean act seeking their fortune in the Old Dart. George hosted a conga line of expat Aussies at the band's digs in Wembley, where he and Harry had installed a small studio. Normie Rowe, M.P.D. Ltd, The Twilights and Johnny Young—the fortunate recipient of 'Step Back'—all worked on demos at Wembley as they had their own bash at the UK charts.

It wouldn't have escaped George's attention, either, that fellow expats the Bee Gees, who'd left Australia six months after The Easybeats, were poised for a golden run in the UK charts and then in the US. Between April 1967 and the end of the year, the toothy siblings had hits with 'New York Mining Disaster 1941', 'Massachusetts'—their first UK number 1—and 'World'. The Gibbs, like The Easybeats (bar Snowy), were little more than kids—Barry Gibb was just two months older than George, twins Robin and Maurice were seventeen—but they already seemed able to pump out hits with a Beatles-like consistency.

Stevie Wright was certainly aware of the Bee Gees' progress, as he admitted to UK writer Penny Valentine. 'I don't mean to sound nasty,' he said, 'but you can't help getting a bit envious when another Australian group come to Britain after you and have such luck.'

Part of the Bee Gees' success was due to the marketing savvy of their manager/mentor Robert Stigwood, a canny entrepreneur who made Mike Vaughan look like, well, a former Sydney real estate agent. When he felt the time was right to introduce the US to the Bee Gees, Stigwood hired a launch that sailed grandly around New York Harbor. The Bee Gees hadn't even released a song in the US, yet there they were, surrounded by local press, looking very much like pop royalty. The Gibb brothers were soon earning so much money that Maurice could afford to buy John Lennon's bespoke Mini Cooper S. 'Mo' even scored a seat on the Magical Mystery Tour bus; spots were reserved strictly for Beatles insiders. George and the band, meanwhile, were stuck in their share house in Wembley, arguing with the neighbours about the noise.

★

That's not to say that George and the band didn't have their moments breathing rarefied air in the wake of the success of 'Friday'. In late January 1967, while his younger brothers, Malcolm and Angus, were merely faces in the crowd at a Yardbirds show back in Sydney, George and the band were invited to a party at Brian Epstein's home. There, George met Paul McCartney and controversial gay playwright Joe Orton, riding high on the success of his play *Loot*. Orton confessed that he was a big fan of 'Friday'; he even wrote about the encounter in his diary, sounding like a loves-truck schoolboy. He described the band as 'five very young and pretty boys . . . In a way they were better (or prettier) offstage than on'. (A few months later, Orton would die a grisly death, murdered by his lover, Kenneth Halliwell.)

The band also had a private sit-down with McCartney, who invited them to his digs in St John's Wood. Fellow Liverpudlian Snowy Fleet bonded most strongly with the Beatle. 'I think we drank him dry,' Fleet recalled.

There'd been a recording of 'Friday' at legendary London club The Marquee, for German TV show *Beat Club*. Then they travelled outside the UK for the first time, playing dates in Germany in late January 1967. They treated themselves to new bespoke suits, pairing candy-striped jackets with neatly tailored blue trousers and shiny leather shoes. George appeared to live in his jacket; he wore it pretty much any time he posed for a photographer. The band's other go-to uniform matched dark twin-buttoned suits with shiny silvery shirts and ruffles, worn with suede shoes. They weren't quite dandies of the calibre of Small Faces or Brian Jones from the Stones, but they still looked pretty damned good for a scruffy bunch direct from the Aussie suburbs.

Yet the heat was still very much on George and Harry to write another masterpiece. George would admit to being under 'a lot of pressure' to rewrite 'Friday', 'which was pretty much impossible . . . there is no way you can duplicate it style wise or musically and achieve the same success'.

Part of the problem, as George would gradually come to understand, was that 'Friday' wasn't a typical Easybeats song: 'It was such a departure from the kind of band that we were.' But it took a lot of striving—and failing—for George to realise that The Easybeats, at their best, 'were a three-chord pop-rock band'.

Things began unravelling with producer Talmy, who blamed it on 'management problems', as he told writer Richie Unterberger. The arrangement between Alberts and Talmy was for him to produce singles and then an album, and be paid a royalty on sales. But according to Talmy, Ted Albert tried to modify his royalty deal when 'Friday' became a hit, figuring that the producer was earning a percentage from sales of 'Friday' and—as Talmy said, allegedly quoting Albert—'now you can take less'. (There is no record of Albert making this statement.)

Talmy walked, leaving The Easybeats to work with his engineer Glyn Johns, who was still making his way up the production ladder. It was rumoured that The Easybeats' song 'Do You Have a Soul' was George and Harry's response to the problems with Talmy, though both kept shtum about the song's target.

George and the band escaped their studio travails by travelling to Europe for a run of shows opening for The Rolling Stones, over three weeks in late March and April 1967.

George and Harry were big fans of the Stones—Harry had stated that The Easybeats 'were into stuff by the Pretty Things and the Rolling Stones'. They'd played a number of Stones songs in their first audition for Ted Albert, so touring with them was a thrill.

The tour took them through West Germany, Italy, France, Switzerland, the Netherlands—where they played in Harry's hometown, The Hague, with Harry and Dick introducing all their songs in Dutch—as well as Greece and even Poland, where they rocked the Palace of Culture and Science in Warsaw. Then in early May they undertook their own tour of Belgium.

Europe would become a happy hunting ground for the band; in George's opinion, it had a lot to do with Wright's frenetic stage presence, which rivalled even that of Mick Jagger. 'They had never seen an act like ours that jumped around so much,' said George. 'Friday' had made serious inroads into various European charts, hitting number 1 in the Netherlands—much to Harry and Dick's delight—as well as number 10 in Germany and the Top 20 in Austria.

On their return to the UK, Vaughan had some positive news for George and the band: 'Friday' was charting in the US. By mid-May, it had climbed into the Top 20 of the *Billboard* singles chart. George knew his pop history well enough to know that the US was the promised land—even The Beatles admitted that it was only when they played *The Ed Sullivan Show* that they felt they'd hit the big time.

But before The Easybeats could head stateside, they had a situation that needed to be addressed immediately: a homecoming tour of Australia. It wasn't a move that thrilled George and the band hugely, but they were swayed by a 23,000-signature petition pleading that they 'Please Come Home'. And that recent loyalty imbroglio lingered in George's mind. This was his chance to quash it once and for all.

★

'The Easybeats are coming home—in triumph', announced *The Sydney Morning Herald* on 7 May. Manager Vaughan, who'd flown back ahead of the others, said that the band was 'a bit homesick' and revealed that they'd stay in Australia for a month, playing shows in most of the capital cities.

'It's amazing what one record will do,' Vaughan said of the success of 'Friday'. 'Things have never looked better.'

The group flew back into Sydney on the morning of 12 May. 'Suddenly they were here,' gushed a *Sydney Morning Herald* journo. 'Australia's five triumphant Easybeats blinked in the warm autumn sunlight as they bounced off their plane at Mascot.' Everyone had grown their hair out considerably since their departure; they were the very model of a happening 1960s band. George was dressed like he meant business in suit and tie.

George and Stevie—whose father had just returned from a tour of duty in Vietnam—sat down with reporters at the airport. Stevie wore an embroidered red-and-gold Chinese-style jacket, which he'd snapped up in Hong Kong.

'How much of your act is music and how much of it is your appearance?' they were asked. 'Hair, and fancy clothes, a good publicity agent and so on.'

'The lot,' replied band spokesman Stevie, who appeared much more willing than George to play the media game. 'The lot makes up a good group.'

'Do you think you can be tone-deaf, and still . . .' continued the reporter, but George and Stevie cut him off before he had the chance to add '. . . be in a successful group?'

'No, no, no,' they said in unison. The muso in George felt compelled to answer that question at least.

'What do you wear this wild gear for, Steve?' asked a clue-less scribe, casting an eye over his ruffled collar. 'Is it being worn on the streets of London by a lot of teenagers?'

'Oh, hang on a second,' flashed Stevie, feigning offence and gesturing to his clothes. 'Not as wild as these!'

George, who'd changed into his favourite blue velvet coat, looked away—Stevie could handle the press.

When the band stepped onto the Festival Hall stage in Brisbane on 13 May, they found that the noise level of their fans hadn't abated one bit. Of course, that also meant that George's old bugbear—that they couldn't be heard beyond the screams—remained. He didn't stand there and pick his nose as he'd once threatened to do, but he must have been tempted.

The band had recently introduced Ike and Tina Turner's urgent, epic 'River Deep, Mountain High' into their set, after hearing it on a massive sound system in a club in Germany, when they were 'all rotten drunk', according to George. 'We'd never heard anything so huge and exciting before.' The band had mastered its layered harmonies and tricky guitar parts, which proved just what good players they'd become—it'd taken the full might of producer Phil Spector's Wall of Sound to create the original—but their Australian fans hadn't come for that. Each of them simply wanted to profess their love for their favourite Easybeat.

On 15 May, they packed the Sydney Stadium, the former boxing venue that had hosted The Beatles in 1964. 'Last night,' stated one reviewer, 'The Easybeats made a triumphant return to Australia.' Frontman 'Little Stevie', not surprisingly, was the recipient of most of the kudos; he was praised for his 'infectious dynamism'. But the rhythmic assault of George and the band wasn't overlooked; their 'musical sophistication . . . could be discerned even through the barrage of screams'.

George wasn't crazy about big gestures, but while in Sydney he and the band were given a civic reception and the keys to the city, along with a gold record marking one million sales of 'Friday'. Their host was the Lord Mayor of Sydney, John Armstrong. To George, this gesture was one of the high points of the band's career. They were officially the first Australian rock-and-roll band to crack it overseas.

'We were genuinely pleased that we had done it,' he said. 'We didn't come back with the standard excuses [of other Australian bands] for failure . . . there was no bullshit, it was real.'

A photo of George with his parents, sharing a bottle of champagne, was splashed across the front page of the *Daily Mirror*. 'The Young Millionaires', read the headline. George was brought back to Earth when he and the others left the reception and were mobbed by overzealous fans.

The Australian immigration department also jumped on The Easybeats bandwagon in its *Good Neighbour* bulletin, reporting that 'five young immigrants known as the "Easybeats" have made a million dollars in the past year'. What the public didn't know, but George understood only too well, was that whatever money they had made was sunk back into the band, helping to keep them on the road and in the studio. Their overheads were huge, and they were deep in debt to Alberts, who were about to sever their financial lifeline to the band. George and the others were as good as broke, getting by on $10 a week. This was, perhaps, George's biggest problem with The Easybeats: 'Nobody was making any money out of it.'

Nor did anyone know that this tour would be the last go-round for Snowy Fleet. He deeply missed his wife, Maureen, and his five-year-old daughter, Mandy, whom he hadn't seen for twelve months. Fleet wanted to settle down in Oz for good. He'd had enough of the peripatetic life of a rock and roller.

★

The response of their Australian fans, and a bit of downtime, offered welcome respite for George and Harry, who were still struggling to come up with another three-minute miracle to rival 'Friday'. But within days of their return to the UK in June 1967, they were back in London's Olympic Studios with Glyn Johns and their problems continued.

Earlier in the year, before their homecoming tour, film-maker Peter Clifton had recorded the band working with Johns on the song 'Heaven and Hell'; the footage only surfaced in 2012. George spoke about the track with Clifton. 'We had a hellish chord on the guitar; it sounded just like hell. So we decided it would be a good title . . . And we found another chord—another couple of chords—that signified heaven, that sounded like heaven. So "Heaven and Hell" was a good title.' Clifton also filmed George talking the song through with Stevie. 'Try and make it sound beautiful,' he requested.

In a very candid moment, George spoke about the group and their future. 'The band will probably last for three more years . . . and in the future I'd like to have my own studio.'

'Heaven and Hell' was a potentially great song; it was catchy and dynamic and took some surprising turns. But it was almost too much—it sounded like two or three strong ideas shoehorned into a single song. Upon reflection, George, as much as he liked the record, felt that it 'lacked a strong melody; we tried to cram a lot of musical experimentation into a three-minute commercial single, but it didn't work. It never does.'

When it was released on 23 June in the UK, 'Heaven and Hell' created a whole new raft of problems for the band, and was proof that they couldn't take a trick. The BBC refused to play a song that featured such racy lyrics as 'discovering someone else in your bed', and when it was released in the US, the use of the word 'hell' in the title put the fear of God into radio stations in the Bible Belt, who wouldn't play it. It fizzled on both sides of the Atlantic and then faded into obscurity.

'Trouble for The Easybeats', noted *The Sydney Morning Herald* when it reported on the problem with the song's lyrics. This was putting it lightly; two flops on the trot was the kiss of death for a pop band. Their UK-release album *Good Friday* (released as *Friday on My Mind* in the US) had dropped in May but hadn't set the charts alight either, failing to reach the UK Top 40. George's prediction that the band would probably last three more years couldn't have been more prescient if he'd been gazing into a crystal ball when he'd spoken. He knew they were adrift.

And yet they continued the slog, more out of desperation—and obligation—than hope. A month-long, 27-date US tour, opening for pop crooner Gene Pitney, began in early August; Pitney was best known for his versions of story songs such as 'Twenty Four Hours from Tulsa' and '(The Man Who Shot) Liberty Valance', and he shared a booking agent with The Easybeats. But rather than hit the key music centres of LA and Chicago and New York City, the tour stopped in outposts such as Commack in Long Island, Roanoke in Virginia and Terre Haute in Indiana. This was hardly the high life. Buffalo Springfield were part of the troupe but pulled out after Neil Young briefly quit the band, apparently because he didn't want to 'sell out' and perform on *The Johnny Carson Show*.

Before the tour began, The Easybeats pre-recorded two performances for broadcast on the syndicated US music program *Upbeat*, which would be their only American TV appearance. Their fellow guests were an impressive bunch, among them Motown masters Stevie Wonder and Smokey Robinson, as well as legendary drummer Gene Krupa. Introduced by host Don Webster as 'the pride of Australia, singing their new hit single "Heaven"!', they lip-synced their way through a now retitled 'Heaven and Hell' and also performed 'Friday on My Mind'. The band wore their matching black suits, except for new drummer Tony Cahill, who wore a white T-shirt. On set, Stevie Wright was so animated, so dynamic, that the director stopped shooting close-ups and instead switched to long shots for the remainder of the performance. But as far as the US was concerned, The Easybeats were a one-hit wonder.

'The audiences found us weird,' George said in 1976, 'strange as it may seem, because the American bands we toured with, including Pitney, were just MOR [middle of the road] schmaltz.'

Drugs had now started to work their way into the band's lifestyle. 'By that time,' George told Glenn A. Baker in 1978, 'the band was stoned off their nuts most of the time.' Stevie Wright was probably the biggest partaker; in a few years, Wright would descend into a drug hell that dogged him for the rest of his life. 'The general lethargy of the band was due to the dope thing,' George said.

George smoked his share of dope, too, until he had a bad experience and hid in the bathroom, crying, according to his friend, Brian Lee. 'Sandra told me that George freaked out, from smoking too much; he was crying, really upset about something. Mike Vaughan took him in for a few days. It was then he decided to give up drugs.' (The next time George saw Lee, he gave him a block of hash. 'Take it,' George said, 'I don't want it.')

In keeping with their habit of connecting with expat Aussies, when they reached New York George and the band found a true believer in the form of seriously well-connected writer Lillian Roxon. She was a great person to befriend— known as the Mother of Rock, Roxon was the New York correspondent for *The Sydney Morning Herald* and had helped Helen Reddy get started in the US, as well as advocating for just about every Aussie who washed up in the Big Apple. (She'd hosted Mike Vaughan when he was 'shopping' The

Easybeats to US labels in early 1966.) Roxon held court in the back room of Manhattan club Max's Kansas City, along with the 'superstars' from Andy Warhol's Factory and every musical A-lister in the city. It was *the* place to be seen. Roxon recognised immediately that George was the creative soul of the band; at the same time, his cut-the-crap nature rubbed her up the wrong way. 'George was a bit rude, as I learned he always was,' she wrote, 'but it doesn't matter because he's a genius.'

The Pitney tour did open George up to some new sensations. He was introduced to ska, in particular an album called *Club Ska '67*—which George described as this 'blue beat/reggae thing'—which would have a big impact on his future work. George and Gene Pitney bonded over seemingly endless games of cards on the tour bus. George dubbed Pitney 'the great gambler'. The tour itself was a financial success, grossing some US$200,000, though little trickled back to George and the band, as it was a package tour with as many as five bands playing some nights.

The band also undertook a recording session while in the States, in what George remembered as 'an old studio in New York that was no longer operating'. (It was actually A & R Studio on West 48th Street.) There, they cut the widescreen, and self-produced, 'Falling Off the Edge of the World' and even took a crack at Jimmy Webb's equally melodramatic 'MacArthur Park'. (A minister's son, Webb wrote huge hits such as 'Up, Up and Away' and 'Wichita Lineman'.)

Lillian Roxon introduced her friend, Lou Reed, to 'Falling Off the Edge of the World', which was rush-released on 4 September while The Easybeats were still in the US. Reed was so moved that he called it 'one of the most beautiful records ever made'; he'd stand at the Max's jukebox, pumping in coins, playing it repeatedly. Despite Reed's devotion and a favourable review in *Billboard*, where it was described as 'a powerhouse rocker [that] should put the group back in the "Friday on My Mind" selling bag', the song didn't put a dent in the charts.

Their first and only US sortie ended in the worst possible way—they were late in applying to extend their work visas and were given 48 hours to leave the country. George departed the country with a curious memento: a souvenir T-shirt from the Joliet Penitentiary in Illinois. (Years later, when he left London for good, he brought home a shirt from The Beatles' short-lived Apple Boutique.)

Come mid-September, George and the band were back in London, with no touring commitments for the rest of the year. George started spending time at London clubs such as Bag O'Nails and Rasputin's. 'They play a lot of ska music,' he explained, 'which we all dig.'

George took some time out to speak with a journalist, touching on subjects as broad as the differences in ages between pop fans back home and in the UK—'Fans here seem to be much older. The other day I got a letter from a girl of 22!'—and the life expectancy of the average pop star. 'When a pop singer reaches 25,' said twenty-year-old George, 'he must feel ridiculous and look ridiculous. He should pack it in.'

What about the band, he was asked. How long would The Easybeats last?

'We shall stay together as long as we are having a laugh and making a living, but I can't see us stretching it out until people call us old men.'

Before they got too old, though, they returned to the studio where they cut the terrific 'The Music Goes Round My Head', a nod to George and Harry's new interest in blue beat. George felt it was their attempt to 'combine ska, pop and psychedelia in one song'; to him, he said, it sounded like 'reggae flower power'. Like 'Heaven and Hell', it was too clever for radio, bearing little resemblance to their signature song, 'Friday on My Mind'—and it stiffed on the charts when released in December 1967. They also cut a second, more cinematic track called 'Come In You'll Get Pneumonia', an attempt to emulate what George called the 'big ballad', best heard in the massive hits of tuxedoed crooners such as Tom Jones and Engelbert Humperdinck. 'Music' and 'Pneumonia' were produced by Vanda and Young.

But nothing was going right for The Easybeats, and inertia began to creep into the band.

'That,' George would eventually admit, 'was when the rot set in.'

6

'We Tried to Get Clever'

Family was important to George. His mate from the hostel, Brian Lee, guessed that George's family connections were so strong because, outside of music, 'he never really had a chance to make any friends'. George regularly sent home packages of records and press clippings to his younger brothers, and encouraged their musical development. In early 1968, news broke of a family reunion between George and his brother, Alex, the black sheep of the Young family, who'd chosen a life in music over relocation to Australia, much to the dismay of his parents.

Alex may not have matched his younger brother's success with The Easybeats, but he'd done well enough, first in Hamburg with the Bobby Patrick Big Six and, more recently, with a group called Grapefruit. When Alex reconnected with George, Grapefruit had just been signed to Apple Publishing by Terry Doran, a Beatles insider, who also managed Alex's band. Various Beatles would be very hands-on when Grapefruit eventually got into the studio— Alex was a good friend of the Fab Four. John Lennon even named the band, with a nod to a book of the same name by Yoko Ono.

George and Alex shared a boozy night out and bonded strongly, although George vowed not to let his mother know about their catch-up. 'When Mum reads this, she'll probably go mad at me,' George confessed.

The truth is that there was a fair bit of spin to the 'long-lost brothers' angle of the reunion story, reported in the *Disc and Music Echo* as 'Reunited—Grapefruit and Easybeat brothers'. At least a year before, in early 1967, Alex had turned up at The Easybeats' share house to work on some saxophone parts for the band, so clearly he and George were in touch. And George, in dark shades, and his partner, Sandra, in chic miniskirt, were seated in the front row in a clip of Grapefruit playing 'Deep Water' in 1968, so clearly it wasn't a one-off. As for the notion of Alex being some kind of family rebel, he was in his twenties when the Youngs left for Australia; he had been an adult and had made his own decisions.

The Easybeats were now working with a new PR firm called Masterplan, who were of the 'any publicity is good publicity' school. Or, as George put it: 'As long as they got us a few lines in some paper, it didn't matter how daft they made us look.'

This 'siblings reunited' story was a classic example of their dark art, as was the scheme of having the band, in rented top hats and tails, pose for a photographer outside the grounds of Buckingham Palace. George was snapped in the midst of 'storming' the palace gates in an attempt to gatecrash the Queen's Garden Party. 'Naturally we're disappointed that we didn't meet Her Majesty,' said Stevie, playing along with the ruse. The band also agreed to have their name associated with a breakfast cereal (Nabisco Rice Krinkles), along with the more traditional instrument endorsements—in their case, Maton guitars and Beverley drums.

George and Alex had something to celebrate aside from their so-called 'reunion': The Easybeats' most recent single, 'Hello, How Are You', another widescreen ballad fit for hitmakers like Jones and Humperdinck, had snuck into the UK Top 20. It was a long overdue return to the charts, their first Top 20 hit in the UK in almost eighteen months—and their last. Reaching one spot higher the following week was George's gambling buddy, Gene Pitney, crooning 'Somewhere in the Country'.

But George hated 'Hello'; he felt it was another wrong move for the group. 'It was a classic mistake from our point of view; we were a rock 'n' roll band and what was a rock band doing with this cornball schmaltz shit? We shouldn't have done it.'

Over time, George accepted that he was more guilty than anyone in the band for pushing them in the wrong direction. 'As I was doing most of the writing, it fell on me. We . . . tried to get too clever.'

On the B-side was the even soggier 'Come in You'll Get Pneumonia'. Alex Young helped out on the track, as did nineteen-year-old pop hopeful Olivia Newton-John, friend of Sandra Young from the days of Beatle Village, who sang backing vocals.

In strictly commercial terms, George was right: by mixing up the band's sound and style, they continually missed the mark (and, more often than not, the charts). But he wasn't giving himself due credit for imagination. He and Harry were proving how versatile they were becoming as songwriters and musicians, seemingly able to write in any form, be it teary ballads, ballsy rockers or epic constructs such as 'Hello, How Are You'. This was something that was beyond even The Rolling Stones, who, after dabbling with psychedelia (badly) on their *Satanic Majesties Request* album in late 1967, swiftly got back to what they knew best—bluesy rock—and continued to do so for the next 50-odd years.

★

In a move that was as much about survival as anything else, George and Harry had formed their own production company, which they named Staeb Productions ('Beats' spelled backwards). Manager Mike Vaughan continued supplying the Aussie media with news, and in mid-February 1968 there was a report about Staeb, noting George and Harry's plans to work with various bands, including a Scottish act named My Dear Watson. Vaughan had brought My Dear Watson to George and Harry's attention, so he was effectively Staeb's A&R man.

George and Harry were also having some success pitching their songs, with acts such as Spanish band Los Bravos (who'd record 'Bring a Little Lovin''), Jamie Lyons from The Music Explosion (who had toured with The Easybeats in the US), Amen Corner (they cut 'Good Times', a song that should have been a monster for The Easybeats) and The Tremeloes all agreeing to record Vanda/Young tunes. More would follow.

The deal they had in place for Staeb was sound. George and Harry would be paid from a small recording budget, and also earn royalties, if they were forthcoming. Accordingly,

George ensured that a Vanda/Young composition made it to the flipside of their first production, with My Dear Watson. That song, 'The Shame Just Drained', came with an intriguing backstory.

In June 1967, just after The Beatles had unveiled their long-playing masterpiece, *Sgt. Pepper's Lonely Hearts Club Band*, The Easybeats had gone into London's Olympic Studios with producer Glyn Johns, along with two additional players: drummer Freddie Smith, who had played with Alex Young in the Bobby Patrick Big Six, and renowned keyboardist Nicky Hopkins. George's plan had been simple—a new Easybeats album. He and Harry had come up with some great material, including the ballsy rocker 'Good Times', which was much closer to George's vision of The Easybeats as a simple, punchy rock-and-roll band. (He'd later regret that they hadn't written the song as a follow-up to 'Friday'.) 'The Shame Just Drained' was another standout track from those sessions.

But a business conflict arose while they were working with Johns. One version has it that when The Easybeats first signed with Alberts in 1965, they'd inked a worldwide deal for their music and publishing. This meant that when Mike Vaughan set up the deal with United Artists in 1966, he needed to create a lease agreement between Alberts and UA, a five-year deal with a subsequent yearly renewal option. This was fine at the start, but in the wake of the success of 'Friday', the band felt short-changed: a percentage of their royalties were already being deducted by Alberts, and now more would go to UA. Another possibility is far less complicated: perhaps the band simply neglected to pay their Olympic Studios bill, which would have come due while they were out of the country, resulting in the tapes being 'held hostage' by the studio until their debt was paid.

George simply described the backroom dramas as 'contractual problems'.

Whatever the cause, their new work—which could have resulted in The Easybeats becoming legitimate contenders as an 'album band', a handy accolade in the time of *Sgt. Pepper's*—was shelved, even though the songs had been recorded and mastered. They'd already come up with a cover image and track listing for the proposed record, which over time became known as the 'lost album'. Only two tracks, 'Good Times' and the psychedelic 'Land of Make Believe', were released during the band's lifetime. Almost everything else languished in the vaults until 1977, while songs such as 'The Shame Just Drained' were recorded by other acts. Two songs—'Bad News', a final Young/Wright co-write, and 'I Know'—have never seen the light of day.

It was the latest cruel blow for George and the band, another tough lesson learned: even when dealing with a mentor such as Ted Albert, very much an Easybeats advocate, the business side of music making sometimes intervened. It eventually got to the point where George and Harry were forced to write under the pseudonym 'Brian Russell', when they signed a publishing deal with a company called Shaftesbury Music in 1969, to get around an ongoing publishing relationship with Alberts.

George held no hard feelings towards Mike Vaughan, but admitted that his manager was in over his head. 'He was the first Australian manager to go [overseas] and he had to fight it out by himself,' George acknowledged; although successful in Australia, Vaughan was 'small fry' abroad.

Jeff Apter

Another of the songs from the 'lost album' sessions, the catchy if trite 'My Old Man's a Groovy Old Man', eventually caught the ear of one Ronald 'Bon' Scott, who was at the time sharing vocal duties in an Australian pop group named The Valentines. The band and Scott—who'd immigrated to Australia from Scotland in 1952, at the age of six—were a vision in their matching red velvet suits, several layers of make-up hiding the tattoos that Scott had acquired as a wild teenager in Fremantle (tattoos then being the domain of bikers, ex-cons and sailors). Scott and The Valentines would reach the Australian Top 20 with 'My Old Man' in August 1969, their biggest chart success.

It would take a few more years for the paths of George Young and Bon Scott to eventually intersect—but when they did, the results would be remarkable.

★

Staeb Productions needed a base, and George and Harry found a small four-track demo studio in London's West End at 9 Denmark Street, known as Central Sound Recording. It'd be the pair's base through the latter part of 1967 and all of the following year.

Denmark Street had its share of musical history. At its peak in the 1950s, it was known as the British Tin Pan Alley, home to music publishers, music stores and recording studios; the West End theatres, big buyers of sheet music, were nearby. The Rolling Stones had cut their debut album in Denmark Street, while The Kinks, Small Faces, David Bowie and many others rehearsed and/or recorded there. Music industry hopefuls sipped cappuccinos and chain-smoked in the cafe

Giaconda, sniffing out their big break. Elton John and Bernie Taupin worked as songwriters for hire at Denmark Street while George and Harry were bunkered down in Central Sound. John and Taupin wrote the song 'Bitter Fingers' about their time toiling on London's Tin Pan Alley. Dick James, The Beatles' publisher, was also based in Denmark Street.

In the wake of The Beatles, most acts were now writing and recording their own songs, which was slowly rendering institutions such as Denmark Street obsolete. But Central Sound was perfect for George and Harry, who were incredibly prolific, cutting as many as seven demos a week. Their approach was simple: they'd lay down backing tracks in the afternoon and vocals the next day. If the song they were working on was in too high a register for Stevie, George would sing the vocal.

Those songs that didn't suit The Easybeats were shopped to others: a band called Pepper cut 'We'll Make It Together', while The Bubblegum recorded 'Little Red Bucket'. 'Good Times' was not only cut by Amen Corner but also by Black Claw, Cliff Bennett & His Band, and Pussyfoot. In Australia, Mike Furber recorded 'I'm on Fire' and 'Watch Me Burn'; in the US, Jennifer's Friends recorded 'Land of Make Believe' and the Jamie Lyons Group released a version of 'Good Times' (retitled 'Gonna Have a Good Time'). Numerous foreign-language versions of George and Harry's songs were also recorded, mainly in Europe.

None of these cuts were big hits, but the experience was invaluable. George and Harry seemingly had songs on tap. Writer's block meant nothing to them.

★

Meanwhile, The Easybeats were stuck in neutral. There were two BBC Radio appearances—one for the Jimmy Young show, another for Pete Brady—that aired in late January and early March 1968. They played numerous UK club dates through April and May—in London, in regional venues such as Burley's White Buck Inn and the Shrubbery Hotel in Ilminster, and further north at the Top of the World in Stafford and the Hawick Town Hall—but they were hardly high-profile gigs. No wonder George and Harry busied themselves at Central Sound—it was a bleak time for The Easybeats, with one exception—a spot on the bill at the Sounds '68 concert at the Royal Albert Hall, alongside The Byrds, The Move, Joe Cocker—and brother Alex's band Grapefruit. But their lost album, meanwhile, remained just that.

Then in June, after another run of UK dates, a 'new' Easybeats LP did emerge, their second and final album for United Artists. Titled *Vigil*, it was a strange brew, a patchwork quilt of a record that mixed the big ballads 'Hello, How Are You' and 'Come In You'll Get Pneumonia' with a re-recorded 'Falling Off the Edge of the World', as well as some covers. Among them was 'Hit the Road Jack', a nod to George's renewed interest in the music of Ray Charles, and their take on 'I Can't Stand It', originally recorded by The Chambers Brothers, another act that George greatly admired.

Covering other people's songs was something The Easybeats had avoided in the past, because it was so commonplace in Australia—and done so amateurishly. But this was different. They weren't trying to remake hits; they were simply paying some dues while having a blast.

'We really enjoyed it,' George said. 'It was a light relief from the pressure of turning out our own stuff, a bit of a laugh. It showed that we weren't above appreciating other styles of music.'

Vigil also included two songs rescued from the lost album, the roaring 'Good Times' and 'Land of Make Believe'. 'Good Times', which included lively backing vocals from Small Faces' Steve Marriott—a partying buddy of Stevie Wright and a good friend of the band—did get some radio airplay when it was released in the UK during September 1968. It was good enough to hit Paul McCartney with such force that, after catching the song by chance on the BBC, he pulled off the road, dashed to a phone and demanded the station play it again. Yet even with Macca's support, the single somehow stiffed on the charts—as did *Vigil*.

'By this time, everybody in the band was pretty jacked off,' George later told *Bomp* magazine. 'Bands have to have some sort of musical identity, and . . . people didn't know what to make of us.'

The band no longer shared the one house. Harry, Dick and drummer Tony Cahill lived at 'Kangaroo Vale', at 4 Old Manor Yard near Earl's Court station, while Stevie had settled down—as much as someone like Stevie could— with his Aussie girlfriend, Gail Baxter, and they had moved into a place nearby. George and Sandra were living above a Chinese restaurant in Holland Park; recent occupants of the flat-cum-studio had been Anglo-American supergroup-in-the-making (David) Crosby, (Stephen) Stills & (Graham) Nash. George upgraded the two-track recording device in the house to a four-track and buried himself away, rarely stepping outside. He boasted that he could complete an entire track in an hour. It was no idle boast. Harry would soon move in.

Their star may have well and truly faded in the UK and the US, but demand for The Easybeats in Europe remained strong, and on 12 October they made another appearance on German TV show *Beat Club*. It was a vastly different-looking Easybeats to the band that had rocked West Germany some eighteen months earlier. The candy-striped matching outfits were long gone, replaced by street clothes. The band looked wild and unfettered, their hair long and shaggy, the energy level incredibly high, sweat flying.

In what was probably the most animated Easybeats performance captured on film, the band tore up 'Good Times'. Stevie was at his Jagger-esque best—no, he was better than Jagger—as he pulled off an impressive knee drop, his body in constant motion. The handsome Harry flailed away at his guitar like a fair-headed Pete Townshend, while George even had a spell on an upright piano, tinkling away with his guitar slung behind his back. Tony Cahill, meanwhile, pounded the drums caveman style. For a band that was coming undone, they looked fantastic, very much alive, if only for a few minutes. Only bassist Diamonde wasn't bursting with life, but that was hardly out of character.

After a mid-November gig at the Marquee in London, George and the band shut down for the year. 'That was when we decided to pack it in,' George said a few years later. But the band did have one more killer song in the works, a late-career reminder of how great The Easybeats could be when they stripped everything back to rock-and-roll basics.

★

It was while tinkering away in the Moscow Road studio that George and Harry came up with 'St. Louis', a soulful rocker to rank with 'Good Times'. Their deal with United Artists had been wound up, so the track would be their first release for Polydor.

In April 1969, a jaded Easybeats assembled in Olympic Studios to record the song with Ray Singer, a former comic best known for producing Peter Sarstedt's folksy hit single 'Where Do You Go To (My Lovely)'. This made him an unlikely ally for The Easybeats, but George and Harry had decided it would be good to work with an outside producer again. (Harry once admitted that 'songwriters are their own worst producers'.)

What ensued was a spirited few minutes of gutsy—and timeless—rock and roll. George and Harry had a habit of producing classic songs when times were tough, as they'd proved with 'Friday', and 'St. Louis' was released as a single in the UK in June. But it had been a full nine months since 'Good Times', which was a lifetime in the helter-skelter pop world of the 1960s. The Beatles, in roughly that same passage of time, had recorded and/or released 'Hey Jude', 'Get Back', 'Let It Be', 'Something' and numerous other standards. The competition remained fierce.

A review of 'St. Louis' in the *New Musical Express* captured the essence of the song. 'It drives along at breath-taking pace and will knock you into submission so you'll be forced to buy it. I hope.' It was a forlorn wish; the song didn't chart.

What George and Harry didn't know was that Polydor was quietly assembling an 'album', of sorts, from the single and assorted Moscow Road demos that had never been intended for release, songs that George hoped to pitch to other bands. The end result, *Friends*, was another mess of an LP, made even messier by a typo that credited the songs to 'Leon Russell', rather than George and Harry's current pseudonym, Brian Russell. This generated plenty of confusion in the press when the album was released in August 1969: Leon Russell was a musical everyman from Oklahoma, best known for his mad hair, top hat, and inspiring work with Joe Cocker and George Harrison.

'I don't know if it is the same Leon Russell,' noted one reviewer, 'but the songs are crummy enough to be his.'

George and Harry played almost everything and sang vocals on all but two of the tracks—'St. Louis' and 'Tell Your Mother'—so it was much more a Vanda and Young record than an Easybeats album.

And George's assessment of *Friends*?

'That was a fuck up. The *Friends* album was basically just songwriting demos—they weren't even done in a studio, just upstairs in my flat in London.' The only track that passed the test for George was 'St. Louis': he called it 'a good, straightforward rocker'.

★

Just prior to the release of *Friends*, word reached the Australian press of another homecoming tour. The response was far less feverish than it had been in 1967. Details of an upcoming show in September at Sydney venue the Trocadero were buried away in a *Sydney Morning Herald* column titled 'Glitter: The young scene', in which updates on The Dave Miller Set, Jeff St John & Copperwine, and 'The Sherbet' were deemed far more newsworthy.

The report was brief: 'The Easies, once the kings of the Australian pop scene, are being brought out by Coca-Cola and Lufthansa. The revived fan club is holding a get together . . . on Sunday August 10.'

If that wasn't sufficiently humiliating, a European tour in August that preceded their Australian visit was a disaster from go to whoa, as George recalled: 'We eventually got to the last gig and of course [the promoter] vanished and we were left high and dry in Vienna.' The band limped back to London in a beaten-up van on the cross-Channel ferry. 'We were penniless,' said George. 'We thought, that's it. We can't go on like this, time to call it a halt.'

The seventeen-date, five-week Australian tour was designed to offset some of the debts that the band still had with Alberts. George, Harry and the others knew it was the end of the line, and the response to their arrival at Mascot Airport on 23 September said it all: barely a dozen fans turned up to greet the band, who had just endured a 45-minute search by Customs officials. ('They even unscrewed the backs of the guitars,' reported Stevie Wright.)

'Sedate welcome for The Easybeats,' reported the Sydney press, which pretty much said it all.

The troublesome subject of money arose when the band hosted a press conference at Sydney's Caesar's Palace. 'In Europe, it's ridiculous,' said drummer Cahill, his eyes hidden behind dark shades, looking not unlike Black Sabbath's Ozzy Osbourne. 'There's like eight, nine guys between you and the cash, all copping their whack. So sooner or later you think "Well, this is a bit stupid, man."'

George dragged on a ciggie, looking cool if exhausted as he reclined in a chair.

He was asked how the band's 'trip' had been. 'It was really nice,' he replied, a tad unconvincingly.

Stevie Wright, also sporting sunglasses, turned a bit prickly when asked the simple question: 'How have things been?'

'Being in England we've taken in a lot of influences,' he replied. 'Alcohol.' When he removed his shades, he revealed what could best be called midnight eyes; he was a different character to the effervescent 'Little Stevie' who had been the poster boy of Easyfever.

George was asked about the company he'd formed with Harry (presumably Staeb): was it a management company for Australian acts in the UK?

'No, it's managing anybody with talent,' George clarified. 'Good songwriters, groups, singers that have a lot of talent but never get the chance to get somewhere.'

'I've got talent,' Stevie said to George. 'Will you sign me up?'

What about 'Peculiar Hole in the Sky', they were asked, an older song that had just been released in Australia? Was it typical of their current sound?

'Nup,' Stevie replied.

Harry agreed. 'No, it's not typical of our sound today,' he said, scratching his head.

And that was it. Press conference over. Dick Diamonde, typically, barely uttered a word.

George and the group had returned to a vastly different Australia, musically speaking. One of the biggest recent hits had been Russell Morris's 'The Real Thing', a madcap seven-minute psychedelic symphony, complete with explosions, wild sonic effects and the recording of a Hitler Youth rally.

The song was written by Johnny Young and produced by Ian (later 'Molly') Meldrum. Billy Thorpe, who only a few years back had been sporting a neat suit and tie when he politely introduced The Easybeats on their TV special, had grown his hair, discovered LSD and transformed his band the Aztecs into a furious, bluesy beast, the loudest band in the land. Progressive rockers Tamam Shud had soaked up the sounds of Jimi Hendrix, Pink Floyd and others to emerge with a distinctly Aussie spin on psychedelia, as had Sydney band Tully, who were booked on the Easy's upcoming tour. And here were The Easybeats, having emerged from the other side of their own period of indulgence and experimentation, trying to revert to being a straight-ahead rock-and-roll band. George knew immediately that they were an uneasy fit.

'Australia was into this flowery musical thing,' he said in 1976, 'and by this time we were back to where we were before—a rock band . . . Here was us, a brash, couldn't give a shit rock and roll band, coming along and spoiling all their beautiful flower thing, which had, of course, died in England by that time. So we died a death twice.'

One bright moment from the tour was a party staged for them at a Kings Cross hotel. George's parents were in attendance; it was their first get-together with George for some time. His father smiled broadly for the camera, yet George's mother looked directly at him, concern in her eyes. 'We miss George,' she told a reporter at the event, 'but we go along with what he wants to do.' Stevie Wright, meanwhile, was photographed with his parents at the same party: his staff-sergeant father was in full military uniform, a strange sight amid all the long hair, shades and bell-bottoms. As for Dick Diamonde, his parents made it very clear that they disapproved of his career choice. 'We never encouraged him to follow this life,' stated his mother. 'We are worried. It is not right the children idolise him.'

Touring with The Easybeats was The Valentines, who shared George's dislike of psychedelia. They were a pop/rock band, Perth-born, who'd recently been the first Australian group to be busted for dope—or at least to make it into the papers after being busted. The 'real' Bon Scott had recently emerged from beneath a veneer of red velvet and Max Factor; he and the band now wore denim and T-shirts, casual gear. And Scott knew a good Vanda/Young song when he heard one, The Valentines having cut several—aside from 'My Old Man's a Groovy Old Man', they'd also recorded 'Peculiar Hole in the Sky' and in 1967 the Young/Wright song 'She Said'. They, too, were on their last legs as a band and would last barely another twelve months.

The tour dragged along into October, stopping in at rooms of renown such as the Yellow Submarine Disco in Rockhampton and Toowoomba's Koala Motor Inn. On 12 October, their visit to Sydney's Trocadero was dubbed 'Easybeats Day' by the press, although the band had to work hard for the title: they played two sets, the first at midday, the second at 3 p.m. It was a heavily stacked bill, including acts of the moment such as The Flying Circus and Doug Parkinson in Focus, as well as fair-haired pop idol Johnny Farnham. It was proving to be a tour of finales: the Trocadero would close its doors within eighteen months, making way for the Hoyts cinema complex.

During a sit-down with a Sydney reporter, George admitted that Tony Cahill had plans beyond The Easybeats. He was asked if the drummer was leaving.

'Yes, he probably will,' George replied.

George spelled out the band members' various creative pursuits: Stevie 'is writing short stories for various mags and moving into the acting bit'—the first and last time that was ever mentioned—while Cahill was 'doing stacks of session work'. As for him and Harry, '[We] have a production company and recording studio going.' George also revealed that soulful duo Delaney & Bonnie, an act touted by Eric Clapton, were 'the current rage' in London, and that Jimi Hendrix had cut off all his hair. But he didn't let it slip that the band was on the verge of breaking up.

The local press seemed more interested in the private lives of the band than in their career situation. *The Australian Women's Weekly* revealed—with due dismay—that possibly as many as three Easybeats were engaged: Harry to 21-year-old Melburnian Robyn Thomas, whom he'd met in London, and Dick Diamonde to a vivacious African-American singer named Charlene Collins, who had appeared in the Sydney production of *Hair*. They'd met just a few weeks earlier in New York. Stevie's partner, Gail Baxter, had also been spotted wearing what looked suspiciously like an engagement ring. ('Actually, I've been engaged for several months,' Stevie eventually revealed.)

George had already married Sandra, a fact that seemed to slide underneath the *Women's Weekly* radar. They now had a baby daughter named Yvette, known as Evie.

'St. Louis', meanwhile, didn't quite break the Australian Top 20, hardly a fitting farewell for a band that had set the charts ablaze during 1965 and 1966.

Go-Set's review of The Easybeats' Melbourne concert captured the strange mood of the tour. 'There is almost dead silence in the hall as they start to play . . . At the end of the first number the audience seems puzzled . . . They're not sure whether to scream or clap or what.'

After another run of Sydney shows in the last week of October, that was it: the show was over. A brief report of the band's split ran in the *Daily Mirror*, beneath the far bigger news regarding Mr and Mrs E.O. Smith of Castle Hill, who'd just won a local gardening competition. *The Sydney Morning Herald*, meanwhile, reported that 'members of the group were millionaires'. That couldn't have been further from the truth—the band was $85,000 in the hole to Alberts. Mike Vaughan's final gesture as manager was to present George and the others with cheques for $800, their payments for the Oz tour. Then he moved to New York.

The five Easybeats gathered in late October at Sydney's Wayside Chapel for Diamonde's wedding to Charlene Collins. The entire band wouldn't occupy the same room again for seventeen years. Stevie Wright was set to resume working at upscale Sydney menswear store The House of Merivale. He'd had enough of music for the time being; in his own words, he'd realised that 'I'm never going to achieve the kind of success The Easybeats had'. Drummer Cahill was joining a band called Python Lee Jackson and then would 'disappear off the face of the Earth', as George later put it. Diamonde's marriage ended quickly enough, and he, too, would fade away. 'He went off the deep end,' said George.

A few weeks after the final tour, news trickled through from the US: in a stroke of irony that wasn't lost on George, 'St. Louis' had begun to chart, long after he and the now defunct group had given up on any dreams of conquering the States. It reached number 100 in mid-November, their only American chart entry since 'Friday on My Mind'.

By that time, however, George was on his way back to London. He was about to begin what he would later call his 'four-year binge'.

7

Down and Out with the Glasgow Mafia

George's reunion with Sandra and Yvette in late 1969 was about as glamorous as The Easybeats' farewell tour of Oz. First there had been the long flight, roughly 30 hours, with half a dozen stops between Sydney and London; George was wedged in a middle seat all the way. He had two gifts with him: a teddy bear for his daughter and a bottle of whisky. When he finally reached home and rang the doorbell, he dropped the whisky, which smashed at his feet—so much for the booze. At least he still had Yvette's teddy bear. George checked his pockets and counted the money he'd brought home with him—he had all of nine shillings.

'That was it,' he told Jane Albert. 'That was the grand total of what I came out of The Easybeats with.'

Harry and his partner, Robyn, soon rejoined George in London, and the duo, now using the name Shock Productions, got to work in the four-track studio in the flat on Moscow Road. Their plans weren't especially grand:

their first priority was to make enough money to pay the rent. George and Harry intended to write and record demos, using any number of made-up band names, and hope a label would show enough interest to finance a proper recording. And if the song had some success, then—and only then—they would form a band. That way, they could eliminate the need to support a group between recordings, which had been one of The Easybeats' biggest burdens. They'd turned the typical rock-and-roll band concept on its head: try and score a hit first, *then* form the band. In theory, it was a masterstroke.

George and Harry assembled a solid team of musicians. There was George's big brother, Alex; drummer Freddie Smith, who they'd worked with back in 1967; Scottish vocalist/bassist Iain Campbell—'an amazing singer, one of the unsung heroes of western rock and roll', according to George; as well as drummer Eddie Sparrell and saxophonist Howie Casey. The latter's claim to fame was being the leader of Howie Casey and the Seniors, the first Liverpool group to ever record an LP; entitled *Twist at the Top*, it was released in February 1962.

The ensemble was nicknamed the Glasgow Mafia, a hard-drinking bunch who were as much on the hustle as George and Harry.

Singer Campbell was a larger-than-life character, 'a rogue Scotsman' in the words of Brian Lee, who spent a lot of time with him while visiting George in London. 'Campbell lived with nothing. He'd go back to Scotland once a fort-night to sign for the dole, then head back to London and George. It was nothing for him to arrive in a sports car with a big blonde woman, some important movie-star type.'

Campbell would openly proposition women as he walked down the street. Lee was taken aback. 'Why are you doing that?' he asked.

'It's just a question of numbers, Brian,' Campbell replied, with a wink.

That entire four-year stretch, from late 1969 to the end of 1973, was marked by an 'anything goes' approach, whether in George and Harry's esoteric selection of band names, or in their broad musical styles and releases on various labels in any number of regions. (And it became an absolute goldmine for future Vanda/Young trainspotters, who'd spend the next 40-odd years trying to document their Rubik's cube of releases.)

George enjoyed the idea of being an anonymous studio musician; in fact, he described the entire period as 'just having a laugh'. A story emerged that he and Harry would pop down to their local for a few beers and ask if anyone would be willing to be photographed for the cover of their next release. The cover of the German release of one of their groups, named Paintbox, featured a shot of five African-American soul brothers, which was about as far from the identity of the players involved—George, Harry and Alex—as genetically possible.

★

'Paintbox' was credited as the band on the very first Shock release. The track was called 'Get Ready for Love' and was released on 5 June 1970. Alex Young wrote the A-side, while George and Harry contributed the B-side, a twangy rocker called 'Can I Get to Know You'. The single was released on the Young Blood label, which was run by Miki Dallon, who'd gotten to know George when The Easybeats were still living at the share house in Wembley. Dallon would also release music by Python Lee Jackson, Tony Cahill's new band.

Two weeks later came 'Lazy River', a Vanda/Young co-write credited to an act called Moondance—basically George and Harry's studio team, with George singing the vocals. It was a smart pop song that could have passed for an Easybeats track. On the flipside was an Alex Young song called 'Anna St. Claire', simply credited to 'Alexander' (he was now using the professional name George Alexander). The A&M label in the UK released the single in mid-June 1970, and it went absolutely nowhere, chart-wise, apart from in Sweden. It also had a belated release in Oz, under the Vanda and Young name, in November 1971.

George may have had little chart success, but there was enough support for his and Harry's work to keep the releases rolling. There was a series of recordings with John Miles, a UK singer with a powerful voice, who cut a rock-solid version of the Vanda/Young tune 'Why Don't You Love Me', released in September 1970 (even though the song was credited to 'Errington', it was written by George and Harry). George recalled in 1976 that this song was 'about the first thing we did' in England, so despite its release date, it may well have been the first Shock production. It, too, went nowhere, chart-wise. Another recording with Miles, a Vanda/Young song called 'The World Belongs to Yesterday', stayed unreleased for the time being.

There was also an act they christened Tramp. An Alex Young song called 'Each Day' was originally chosen as the A-side. On the other side was a Vanda/Young song called 'Vietnam Rose', which caused a fair bit of head scratching when it was released. George laughed when asked if he'd written a political song, this being the time of war in South-East Asia. Not quite.

'Vietnam Rose,' he explained, 'meant a dose of the clap.'

Young Blood's Miki Dallon liked it enough to flip the record and make 'Vietnam Rose' the A-side; it appeared during July 1970, but again without any chart success. A few months later, 'Vietnam Rose' was recorded by an English outfit named Whichwhat, whose entire reputation was based around being very big in Nottingham. Their version also kept its distance from the charts.

One of George and Harry's next releases was called 'Children', which, allegedly, was recorded by a real flesh-and-blood singer named Eddie Avana. The song was co-written with British actor and pop hopeful David Hemmings, a former boy soprano and child actor who'd recently been seen in the sexy Jane Fonda cult classic *Barbarella*. George and Harry met Hemmings through a contact at Chappell Music; Hemmings introduced himself and showed them some lyrics he'd written. (Harry Vanda later said that Hemmings' lyrics were 'heavily vetted' by George.)

The Young Blood press release for 'Children', dated 27 November 1970, provided some biographical detail for Eddie Avana: 'Eddie is 23 years old. American born and an artist who could have a big future.'

The truth was that Eddie Avana was Harry Vanda in disguise, who felt relieved when the single flopped—otherwise, he explained, 'I would have had to go on *Top of the Pops* looking like a complete twat.'

Oddly, no one seemed to question why the Eddie Avana on the B-side of the single sounded very different to the

Eddie singing 'Children'; it was Alex Young singing this time. 'Children', or *'Kinderen'* in its translated form, was later covered by Belgian crooner Louis Neefs.

*

But in the wake of all these flops came some good news: there were developments taking place in Australia that would have a huge impact on George's future, and on Harry's. After years of issuing records through the Australian branch of Parlophone, in late 1970 Ted Albert took the plunge and established his own in-house label, which used the same name, Albert Productions, as the company he'd set up in 1963. He planned to hire a studio to record and produce the label's music. Artists were also encouraged to sign with J. Albert & Son, their in-house publishing arm, which George and Harry soon did, and their relationship with Alberts shifted back to what it had been in 1965: a true partnership. (Albert wrote regularly to George in London; they were never out of touch.) Albert had plans to build his own studio, which would make the company even more self-contained.

Alberts hit paydirt with its first release, 'Falling in Love Again'—written, fittingly, by George and Harry, and performed by Ted Mulry.

Ginger-haired 23-year-old Mulry was another Ten Pound Pom, with working-class roots in Oldham, Lancashire. He was currently holding down a job driving a bulldozer. Although he'd develop into one of Australia's favourite pub rockers, Mulry began his journey as a balladeer. He did it well, too; 'Julia', his debut single, had hit the Sydney Top 10 in May 1970. 'Falling in Love Again', however, was a career-maker; its unashamedly lush production made it a song for young lovers everywhere.

'It was deliberately schmaltzy,' George told writer Debbie Kruger. 'Those type of songs tend to get covers more easily.'

The music press was hugely underwhelmed by the song when it was released in January 1971. Writing in *Go-Set*, Stephen MacLean stated: 'I wouldn't have it for a gift.' But this was a song for the mainstream, not the counterculture, and 'Falling' hit a national peak of number 11 in June, charting for six months. George and Harry finally had their first hit as songwriters for hire.

'Falling' was entered in the World Popular Song Festival, the Asian answer to Eurovision, staged in Tokyo at the Nippon Budokan arena, where The Beatles had played in 1966. Although Mulry's nerves got the better of him at a crucial moment in the competition, 'Falling' did reach the final 20 out of some 44 songs from 37 different countries. George and Harry, having never been to Japan before, took advantage of the all-expenses-paid return trip to Tokyo and travelled with Mulry. While there, George made some handy connections, which led to a German version of 'Falling in Love Again'—aka *'Wieder verliebt zu sein'*—being recorded by Daliah Lavi, a sometime-actress who'd appeared in the James Bond spoof *Casino Royale*, alongside Peter Sellers.

As Mulry's song climbed the Australian charts, a still very broke George remained bunkered down in his London studio, continuing to write prolifically with Harry while dreaming up new band names. Another co-write with the 'heavily vetted' David Hemmings, called 'Pasadena', surfaced in late January 1971; George sang the vocal on the demo. The released version was sung by Phil Pickett, using the band name Buster. The German-born, British-based 25-year-old Pickett briefly worked at E.H. Morris, one of the publishers to whom Vanda and Young pitched their songs, which was most likely how he'd heard the demo.

'Pasadena' was a terrific song: a few melancholy minutes of pristine pop, flavoured by a singalong chorus, chiming pedal steel guitar and a neat change in tempo as it headed off into the sunset. Once again, the song didn't chart, though it was destined for a second life back in Australia, as well as becoming one of Vanda/Young's most covered songs. Phil Pickett, meanwhile, would soon enough hit the jackpot with a band called Sailor, best known for their jaunty dress sense and frothy 1970s hits 'A Glass of Champagne' and 'Girls, Girls, Girls'.

George and Harry's next production was a 'message' song dealing with black consciousness entitled 'Beautiful and Black', recorded by a band called Heavy Feather, also sung by Pickett, and released in March 1971. It would be a stretch, though, to categorise it as 'soul'; it had more in common with the rustic folksiness of early Hall & Oates. It didn't matter greatly, because 'Beautiful and Black' was yet another commercial flop.

Alex Young's band Grapefruit, meanwhile, despite their impressive connections, had fallen apart, so George and Harry teamed up with Alex to record Grapefruit's swansong, a track called 'Sha-Sha', which emerged in September 1971. Another chart failure.

It seemed that George and Harry were destined to have more success in Australia. And there was one local singer, in particular, who was poised to begin a long and fruitful association with Vanda and Young. George wouldn't be broke for too much longer.

★

John Young—no relation—had grown up only a few streets away from George's family in Glasgow; he and his three siblings, his parents and his aunt Rita had shared a one-bedroom flat. They'd bathe once a week at his grand-mother's house (she was a mother of twelve). John's father, Jimmy, was a stonemason who moonlighted as a bouncer and an air force reservist. When the family migrated to Australia in 1962, John spent his first two years in the same migrant hostel as Snowy Fleet, in East Hills on the banks of the Georges River.

By day, John—a handsome 21-year-old with a cheeky smile, long flowing hair and a reputation as a very useful pinball player—worked as a sheet-metal worker at a company called Commonwealth Engineering, and by night he sang with a band named Elm Tree. He was known to his band-mates as 'Mungy'. For a time, a singer named Andy Imlah shared vocals with Young in Elm Tree, but Imlah left to join Sydney group Velvet Underground (not to be mistaken for Lou Reed's American band of the same name), where he played with George's younger brother, Malcolm.

Ted Albert at the time was being helped out by an Englishman named Simon Napier-Bell, a bon vivant and music industry all-rounder, who was on an (accidental) working holiday in Sydney. Napier-Bell had originally come to Oz strictly for a vacation but had befriended Ted; they bonded over long lunches of grilled cheese sandwiches and red wine in Albert's office (until Albert's father walked in on them one day and they changed their routine to dinner). Among various impressive achievements, Napier-Bell had co-written the huge hit 'You Don't Have to Say You Love Me', Dusty Springfield's first number 1.

A product of London's upscale prep school Durston House, Napier-Bell was a smart operator with a sharp sense of humour; he once said of T. Rex's Marc Bolan, whose career he set in motion, 'It took me a month to persuade him that he wouldn't become an instant superstar simply by announcing that he existed.' Napier-Bell had formed a production company named Rocking Horse with Ray Singer, who'd produced The Easybeats' 'St. Louis', so he unknowingly had a connection with George.

Albert commissioned Napier-Bell to produce some songs, and he was immediately struck by George and Harry's 'Pasadena'. For one thing, it featured a drum loop, created by George—a rarity in the early 1970s. (A drum loop is a short recording of a groove that has been edited to repeat continuously, creating the illusion that the performance was much longer. It was a handy tool for a record producer.)

'I thought it was a hit so long as we got the right voice,' Napier-Bell told Jane Albert.

Ted Albert approached Ted Mulry about recording the song, but it came to nothing. Then, in November 1971, Napier-Bell found himself at the Liverpool Masonic Hall, watching, of all bands, Velvet Underground. Impressed by Andy Imlah's voice, he spoke with the singer and the rest of the band, asking if they'd be keen to record 'Pasadena'. The band passed—Malcolm Young thought that the song was far too pop for the group, despite it being co-written by his brother.

Instead, Velvet Underground's drummer Herm Kovac recommended 'Mungy'—John Young—to Napier-Bell.

Napier-Bell met with Young and invited him to Alberts' King Street office, and he turned up the next afternoon, fresh from the day shift at the factory in Fairfield, in Sydney's southwest. He was wearing blue overalls, his long hair tied back in a ponytail. 'I swear,' Young said, 'Ted looked at me and thought, "Jesus Christ, where have they dug this one up from?"'

Regardless of his appearance, Young got the gig and flew to Armstrong Studios in Melbourne, where Napier-Bell asked him to sing directly over the top of George's vocal on the demo (although traces of George's voice made it into the final recording). 'Pasadena' became a hit in this second incarnation, reaching the Australian Top 10 in January 1972. Young duly signed a five-year deal with Alberts. Elm Tree folded.

Back in London, George was hugely impressed by Ted Albert's ability to spot a hit; clearly, he hadn't lost the knack he'd demonstrated time and time again during the heady days of The Easybeats. The success of 'Pasadena', George said, 'did keep us going. We were pleased to be eating.'

During his stint in Sydney, Napier-Bell conjured up another hit with a song George wrote with Harry called 'Superman', which was recorded by a soulful Sydney vocalist named Alison MacCallum and reached number 12 nationally in May 1972. This was one of George's favourite versions of a song he'd written 'because it was so different', he said in 1978. He'd recorded the demo at Abbey Road; George's friend, Brian Lee, had contributed some handclaps.

As for John Young, he would soon change his name to John Paul Young so as not to be confused with Johnny 'Step

Back' Young, another singer who owed a debt to George. Post-'Pasadena', he set off on a 30-month stint in the Australian production of *Jesus Christ Superstar*, alongside none other than Stevie Wright—and numerous Oz pop luminaries-in-the-making, such as Jon English, Marcia Hines, and Air Supply's Graham Russell and Russell Hitchcock.

But in due course, George and John Paul Young would work together again, to everyone's immense gain.

★

Back in the UK, new works by George and Harry appeared at regular intervals, with almost invariably the same insipid commercial response. Another version of their 'Lazy River' emerged in May 1971, this time recorded by Durham-born singer Tony Williams. Despite being BBC Radio 2's pick of the week, 'Lazy River' Mark II did no better than the first version. In 2007, singer Williams, quoted on an Easybeats online forum, suggested that it failed because a certain BBC DJ wasn't 'rewarded' sufficiently for his support and refused to play the song at a time when one spin would have led to an appearance on *Top of the Pops*.

'Needless to say,' Williams wrote, 'he is not on my Xmas card list.'

However, Williams, like many others who recorded George and Harry's songs during their 'binge', soon found his feet, joining a band named Stealers Wheel. They'd become best known for their Dylan-esque hit 'Stuck in the Middle with You'.

The next Shock Productions release was 'I Can Try', credited to an act named Shortcakes, which most likely comprised (again, details are sketchy) George, Harry and their usual 'Glasgow Mafia' studio consorts. The wonderfully named Katie Kissoon, a Trinidadian, sang the vocal; she would go on to have an impressive studio career, singing with everyone from Van Morrison to Eric Clapton, Roger Waters to Pet Shop Boys. As for 'I Can Try', it was released in May 1971 and went into extinction soon after.

Not long after, another take on George and Harry's ode to STIs, 'Vietnam Rose', appeared, this time recorded by Belgian act The Spotlights. The most interesting part of the release was the misspelling of Harry Vanda's name on the credits: the song was billed as the handiwork of 'Banda-Young'. (In February 1972, another Vanda/Young song, 'Life is Getting Better', by sister act The Hendrys, was credited as written by 'Vander-Young'. The guy couldn't win.) A few months later, in mid-August, Australia's reigning King and Queen of Pop, Johnny Farnham and Allison Durbin, cut George and Harry's sweetly melodic 'Come on Round to My Place', but it was purely an album track, buried away on their co-release *Together*.

★

George was beginning to think about moving his family back to Australia. He and Sandra were growing tired of the lack of space for their daughter, Yvette. Their home was comfortable, spread over three floors with a studio at the top, but it was nothing like a typical Australian house.

'Where we lived in London,' said George, 'the only backyard that [Yvette] could actually play around in was a six-foot square slab of concrete at the back of this terrace house. It's not exactly the best place to bring up a kid.'

One day, Yvette came home and told her father that she'd volunteered his services at school. George was to come in and play a song for the class. George was enthusiastic, at least until Yvette informed him that the song he was to play was her current favourite, the very cheesy 'Chirpy Chirpy Cheep Cheep'. George was appalled—it may have been Yvette's song of the moment, but he hated it—yet he still carried out his fatherly duties.

Back in Australia, Malcolm and Angus Young were slowly emerging from the large shadow cast by George. It had become clear early on that a life in music was the only thing that would sustain both of them, because they weren't built for academia. On his first day of high school, Angus was caned purely because he was Malcolm's younger brother. When asked about his time at Ashfield Boys' High, Angus once said: 'I think they hung up garlic cloves to keep me out.'

Seventeen-year-old Malcolm, who'd left school to work in the Berlei bra factory briefly, had been recruited as rhythm guitarist by Velvet Underground in the summer of 1970. The band, who'd formed in 1967 and worked regularly up and down the east coast of Australia, had been playing in Toowoomba, opening for former Easybeat Stevie Wright, when talk turned to their need for a guitarist.

Wright told them about Malcolm. When they found out Malcolm was George Young's brother, it pretty much sealed the deal. It didn't hurt, either, when they learned that Malcolm's current guitar, a Gretsch, was a Harry Vanda hand-me-down from his Easybeats days. Surely that was a good omen.

Wright wrote down the Youngs' Burwood address (they didn't own a phone).

When the band—drummer Herm Kovac, singer Andy Imlah, guitarist Les Hall and bass player Steve Crothers—rolled up to the house in Burwood, probably the most fabled suburban three-bedder in Australian rock-and-roll history, all eyes turned to the gold record for 'Friday on My Mind', which sat alongside the usual family snaps on the mantelpiece. (One day, Malcolm couldn't resist: he took the record down and played it on the family stereo, just to see what would happen. The recording, though barely audible, was of 'Sorry', not 'Friday on My Mind', bizarrely.)

Kovac, as soon as he met Malcolm, could sense a little of George in the way he confidently carried himself. Malcolm wasn't one for fucking about. 'I didn't know if it was a self-aware thing,' Kovac said. 'I got to see it hundreds of times over the next 40 years: the look on his face and spring in his step was always the same.'

Angus, too, had taken to rock and roll like a zealot, and he was intent on proving to the guys in Velvet Underground that Malcolm wasn't the only guitar slinger in the Young household. He cornered Kovac and showed him all his tricks, jumping from bed to bed as he played his Gibson SG guitar like a pint-sized madman. Kovac looked on, maintaining a perfectly straight face.

'What do you reckon?' Angus asked him at the conclusion of his one-man show.

'Do you know any chords?' teased Kovac.

Angus became a regular at Velvet Underground gigs, but only after his sister, Margaret, gained an assurance from Kovac—forever after known as Uncle Herm—that he'd keep an eye on Angus. The kid was, after all, barely fifteen years old. Angus, in return, made the entire band mugs of

Ovaltine when they adjourned to the house in Burwood after gigs.

Ted Albert occasionally checked in with the Youngs; on one visit, when he heard Malcolm and Angus playing somewhere in the house, he asked William Young, 'Pop', to ensure that if they intended to follow in George's footsteps, he'd best let Ted know. 'If they ever want to do anything,' Albert said, 'send them to me.'

Albert may not have realised it at the time, but he was on track to reunite George with his two younger siblings—and change their lives forever.

8

Back to Oz

George described his London stretch as a 'four-year binge' for good reason: he was incredibly prolific. Recording for numerous labels in a maze of deals and contracts, he was working with enough artists (some real, some imagined) to fill several football teams.

Well into 1972, the third year of their binge, George and Harry were pumping out material in London, working on records with acts such as Worth, Fluff, Tina Harvey and a number of others, none of whom emerged from pop obscurity. They even cut a song for an ad in late 1972, for the sticky-sweet chocolate Toblerone. Phil Pickett had a crack at another Vanda/Young song, this one called 'Bluebird', using the name Mosaic. There was also George, Harry and Alex's own outfit, Band of Hope. They had a deal in place with Decca Records that also fizzled out, apart from one unreleased single, a song called 'Working Class People', which did nothing apart from become a very collectible 7-inch.

There was even a strange moment in early 1972 when The Easybeats existed briefly again, at least contractually. An

American named Marc Gordon worked with Motown out of Los Angeles and had scored heavily with The 5th Dimension, purveyors of what was known as 'champagne soul'. He now had his own label and signed George and Harry to a deal that was announced in *Billboard* on 8 April 1972. 'Three new acts have signed with Rocky Road Records,' read the report. 'They are singers Colin Areety and Irma Routen, and the Easy Beats [*sic*].'

Nothing came of this, as intriguing as it is in hindsight. It seems likely that the new 'Easy Beats' would have only featured George and Harry, and probably Alex, given that two of the former members were either busy elsewhere— Tony Cahill was still playing in Python Lee Jackson (now managed by expat Aussie provocateur Richard Neville, the co-founder of *Oz* magazine), while Stevie Wright was trying to resurrect his career in *Jesus Christ Superstar*. Dick Diamonde had disappeared after his marriage collapsed.

In fact, Diamonde's disappearance worried his parents so much that they asked George's old friend from the hostel, Brian Lee, who was on his way to see George in London, if he could help find Dick. They hadn't heard from their son for months and thought that he may be in the Netherlands. They told Lee that they'd pay for Dick's return to Australia. When Lee reached London, George told him that Dick had recently visited; he was in London.

Lee had barely been at George's for a day when there was a knock at the door.

'Lo and behold,' said Lee, 'I looked out the window and saw that it was Dick. He was a bit off his face.'

'I just thought of you,' Diamonde said to Lee, speaking as if they'd been apart for days, not years. 'I saw a truck with

127

tomato sauce and it reminded me of a tale your mother had told me that you wouldn't eat anything without tomato sauce.'

'I knew that his intuition was working,' Lee recalled. 'I told him of his father's offer and he accepted immediately. He went home and stayed home.' (Diamonde settled in Lismore, in northern New South Wales, on a property owned by his psychiatrist.)

George was pleased to see his old friend Lee, so much so that he insisted that Lee cancel his hotel booking and bunk down with him and Sandra. They had plenty of room.

Lee noticed the impact that the tough past few years had had on his friend. 'George had grown up more; he was world wise. He told me about all the buggery in the business, how they're all rip-offs, how it's not a very nice business.'

Just as it had been during his Easybeats days, George had few friends outside of 'the biz'. He spent most of his time in the studio with Harry and the 'Glasgow Mafia', or at home with Sandra and their daughter. Ted Mulry, who was trying to make his way in the UK, was one of the very few visitors from Oz. He recorded a Vanda/Young song named 'Ain't It Nice' under the name Steve Ryder.

Lee was surprised, when he arrived, to learn that George had married Sandra, who'd been with him since the days of Beatle Village. 'George was secretive,' said Lee. 'I didn't know that he'd married Sandra. I knew her well from Australia and didn't expect to see her leaning out the window when I arrived in London.'

George had known what it was like to lose one's privacy when he was in The Easybeats. Now he reclaimed it with a vengeance, to the extent of not mentioning the small matter of his marriage to one of his oldest friends.

While Lee stayed with George, they worked on a small business that kickstarted George's interest in collecting art. Lee had commissioned a graphic artist to draw images of typical UK tourist spots—Anne Hathaway's Cottage, Hampton Court Palace and the like—that he then had reproduced. With George's backing, Lee would sell these lithographs door to door; he'd also place them in shop windows, selling them for 'whatever you could get; they were only worth threepence'. Lee gave the originals to George, who had them framed and hung them in his house.

'I'm going to collect art, Brian,' George told his friend. Lee would later connect him with a friend, artist Kevin Oxley, and George's collection grew from there.

Fate finally intervened for George in the shape of another Vanda/Young production, a song called 'Shot in the Head'. It was sung by Iain Campbell, the 'rogue' who'd worked on the earlier Paintbox recordings and who was one of George's favourite vocalists.

'Shot in the Head', first released in 1971, was perhaps George's pick of his entire binge; he described it as 'very down home dirty'. At the time of its recording, George and Harry had been approached by a whisky company named Haffy's, who were bringing out a new mixed drink called Haffy's Whiskey Sour, a name that to George conjured up 'a southern American moonshine image'. To him it was the perfect band name to go with 'Shot in the Head'. It didn't really matter to George that it failed to chart; it was still 'one of my favourite tracks that we ever did', he said. English band Savoy Brown cut the song in 1972; George felt that they 'covered it real nice'.

More importantly, the song would find a place on an album that would feature no less than three Young brothers.

And it was this recording that would eventually convince George, and Harry, to return to Australia.

★

Though no official record exists, it's very likely that Ted Albert met with George and Harry in London in July 1972, and floated the idea of the two becoming more formally involved with the label he had recently established in Australia (when he wasn't successfully racing his Dragon-class yacht, *Rawhiti*, around Sydney Harbour, a vessel that George, too, would come to enjoy). Albert had one-stop music powerhouses such as Motown in mind; he wanted to make Alberts into a label that could scout out its own talent, create and record its own music and then, with the distribution and marketing muscle of a major label, get its work out to the listening public. As songwriters, musicians and producers, George and Harry would be invaluable assets, and their longstanding relationship with Albert, despite the odd bump in the road, made them perfect partners. And they'd already scored in the Australian charts with Ted Mulry and John Paul Young, which was two more hits than they'd had during their entire period as freelancers in the UK.

While Albert's pitch was still percolating, George had been approached by a friend named Wally Allen (aka Wally Waller), who'd played bass in The Pretty Things—a UK band that had recorded one of the first rock operas, 1968's *S.F. Sorrow*—and was now producing records for EMI. He wanted George and Harry to do some recording with him in Abbey Road studios.

As George said in 1976, 'He would supply the booze, we would supply the music. So we went down to Abbey Road and knocked out about four or five tracks on the spur of the moment.'

Among these was a song called 'Natural Man', which was released as a single in August 1972 under yet another nom de plume, Marcus Hook Roll Band—which had nothing whatsoever to do with the town of Marcus Hook in Pennsylvania. The name simply sounded good to George, and it stuck. Roughly the same amount of contemplation went into the raw and rocking B-side, written by Allen, which George sang. It was called 'Boogalooing is for Wooing'.

Thinking that it was nothing more than the latest in a seemingly endless list of one-shot productions, George departed on a long-overdue visit back to Australia over Christmas 1972 and into the new year. While there, he was surprised to get a call from Wally Allen, who told him that EMI in the US was very interested in hearing more from this mysterious Marcus Hook Roll Band.

'We got word that America was very hot on this,' said George, 'which we thought was hilarious—it was just a joke to us.'

But not for long, because Allen told George that EMI had agreed to bankroll the recording of an entire album. And so the Marcus Hook Roll Band album was born. George refused to cut short his Australian holiday, so Allen booked a flight to Sydney. Sessions were set to begin in July 1973.

Needing musicians, George decided that it was time to initiate Malcolm and Angus into the ways of the studio. Harry, who'd had some visa issues but was back in Australia by early 1973, would also play a big part.

Malcolm, now aged twenty, had continued playing with Velvet Underground, having packed in his day job at the bra factory. On occasions he'd be part of the backing band for Ted Mulry, even though the role of support act wasn't something that the ambitious Malcolm craved. He was now the proud owner of some impressive new gear, which he'd bought, with the help of drummer Herm Kovac, from a Sydney music store that offered a 'trust you once' payment scheme. Kovac introduced Malcolm to the store owner as a friend—this qualified him for 'trust you once', which required $100 monthly repayments—and Malcolm walked out with a brand spanking new Marshall amp and Quad box. The rig was huge.

'Mal looked like a pixie next to his tower,' said Kovac.

As for eighteen-year-old Angus, he'd been involved with a couple of bands. Among them was a local group called Kantuckee, whose centrepiece was playing a live album from American rockers Cactus, *'Ot 'n' Sweaty*, in its entirety. Just like Malcolm, pint-sized Angus was dwarfed by his amplifier but was proving to be a quick study on lead guitar. He and Malcolm had taken a lot away from George's work with The Easybeats. It would help define their own playing styles—Angus on lead, Malcolm on rhythm guitar—as Angus noted: 'George had that very high rhythm and Harry provided the highlights, the colour.'

George, meanwhile, had no intention of treating the Marcus Hook Roll Band as anything more than yet another one-off project.

'We had Harry, myself and my kid brothers, Malcolm and Angus,' George said in 1978. 'That was the first thing that Malcolm and Angus did before AC/DC. We didn't take it very seriously, so we thought we'd include them to give them an idea of what recording was all about.'

That also included introducing them to the requisite in-studio boozing. Old Grand-Dad bourbon was their tipple of choice. 'We all got rotten, except for Angus, who was too young'—and a teetotaller—'and we spent a month in there boozing it up every night.'

'Shot in the Head', the song that George ranked as the pick of his binge years, was one of several tracks recorded during July and August 1973. The finished album, which was christened *Tales of Old Grand-Daddy* in honour of the bourbon they'd quaffed during the sessions, was more than some throwaway record, even though George refused the US label's request to tour and promote it. (George and Harry were forced to buy back the masters and organise their own Australian release, which is why it didn't surface until 1974, and then only brushed the charts.)

The playing throughout the album was solid, the song-writing smart. In particular, 'Shot in the Head' was a standout. It was George's acerbic take on the pitfalls of the music biz: 'I spent 22 years in a rock-and-roll band,' he sang, 'and all I've got to show is a hole in my hand/Where my money has burned me through.' George was writing directly from personal experience, and he wasn't holding back.

While working in the EMI studio in Sydney, George and Harry came to a realisation. 'After a while,' George said later, 'the thought of going back to England wasn't very exciting, so we decided to stay on here.' This was the moment, George told Australian *Rolling Stone* in 1976, that 'Harry and I decided we'd had enough buggering around and decided that we may as well get back into some serious work'.

So, at the end of 1973, the four-year binge was over.

Ted Albert sweetened the deal when he helped both George and Harry buy homes in Sydney's suburbs. George and his family moved into a comfortable home in Ryde. George's daughter, Yvette, finally had the backyard he'd been hoping to provide for her—and a swimming pool as well. George bought a piano and positioned it near his and Sandra's bed, just in case inspiration struck at an odd time.

Albert told George that he had plans to build a studio inside Boomerang House, the King Street building in Sydney, owned by the Albert family, that was the base for Albert Productions. George would have his own sonic playground. This had to be better than being back in London, bouncing between labels and artists and projects, trying to scare up a living. Ted Albert had provided him with a lifeline.

George, Ted and Harry would strike up a deal known as the AHR agreement: the letters represented Ted's surname (Albert) and Harry and George's middle names (Hendrikus and Redburn). George and Harry would develop songs, acts and productions in exchange for a good chunk of royalties from the acts they brought to Alberts. It promised a lot more security than George had experienced at any time in his career. He had so much trust in Ted Albert that no contract was ever drafted. It was a handshake deal—one that stayed in place for almost 30 years.

It was time for George and Harry to get to work. Stevie Wright had recently signed to Alberts, and he would be the first act that George and Harry would produce under their new arrangement with Albert. But a lot had changed for Wright since the end of The Easybeats.

★

134

Wright hadn't been doing it so easy since the 1969 demise of the band that had made him famous. After dabbling with a couple of local groups, and his brief return to a 'straight job' selling menswear, in May 1972 he took on the role of Simon Zealotes in Harry M. Miller's big-budget production of *Jesus Christ Superstar*, pocketing a handy $130 a week. His partner, Gail Baxter, was pregnant with their first child. The production was a huge success, running for more than two years, but it would prove to be the undoing of Little Stevie Wright.

Wright had never dabbled in hard drugs during his time with The Easybeats, but he was fond of the fast life. During the *Superstar* production, he noticed a musician tinkling away on a piano, completely lost in music, his eyelids heavy.

'It was fabulous piano playing that was out of this world,' Wright said later, on the ABC's *Australian Story*. 'And I couldn't believe it. And I said, "What's with him?" And somebody said, "He's on heroin."'

Wright tried the drug, which at first made him violently ill. But he was determined to beat the nausea that heroin induced and tried it again.

'But by the time I'd beaten it,' he said, 'it had me.'

He would become so consumed by heroin that his relationship with Baxter ended. 'My concern was that [our son] wasn't safe in that house with syringes around, loaded syringes,' she said on *Australian Story*.

Fifa Riccobono, who was involved in practically every part of the Alberts business, asked Stevie what the appeal of the drug could possibly be; its users looked wasted, half-dead (sometimes completely dead). Why put yourself through that?

'Why?' Stevie replied. 'That one high can make up for ten lows.'

It's unlikely that George knew about Wright's heroin problem, or even thought it his business. He was more concerned about getting his old bandmate's career back on track and having him record 'Hard Road', a song he'd written with Harry. Ted Albert had played it to Wright in demo form, among other Vanda/Young tracks, and felt that the song was a perfect fit—a roaring rocker with a lyric that picked apart the often tough life of a career musician.

George was confident that Wright could do the song justice (as Rod Stewart did, when he recorded the song in late 1974). 'Stevie was still a great performer, still a great singer,' George told Jane Albert.

George made a rare TV appearance with Wright in early June 1973 on ABC's *The Aunty Jack Show*, playing rhythm guitar on 'Hard Road' roughly a year before it was released. As usual, George looked impossibly cool, even in an era of dangerously wide shirt collars and even wider jacket lapels. Also in the makeshift band, named Cool Bananas, was Rory O'Donoghue, who played *The Aunty Jack Show* character Thin Arthur—and also played a mean lead guitar. Wright was in great form, his pencil-slim body constantly moving, his shaggy hair falling around his shoulders. He looked every inch the rock star, with no obvious signs of his drug addiction. It was his best TV appearance since 'Good Times' on German TV back in 1968.

George was hell-bent on finding the proper representation for Wright. He and Harry turned up unannounced at the Sydney office of the Sunrise agency. It was run by 26-year-old Michael Chugg, who was stunned: this was Vanda and

Young from *The Easybeats*. Chugg, a former race caller, had been a huge fan. He'd grown up in Tasmania reading about the band in magazines, completely starstruck. Now the two key players were here in his office. *What was going on?*

'We'd like you to manage Stevie,' George told him.

Chugg couldn't agree quickly enough, although, as he'd one day admit in his memoir, *Hey, You in the Black T-Shirt*: 'Had I known then what I was getting myself into, I would have told them in words of one syllable where they could stick the devious little bugger.'

There was a selection of songs in good shape for what would be Wright's debut solo album, some written by Stevie, others by Vanda/Young. Among them was the lengthiest and most ambitious piece that George and Harry had ever attempted, entitled 'Evie', that played out like a modern tragedy. (George's wife, Sandra, had a friend in London named Evie, who may have inspired the title; George's daughter, nicknamed Evie, was far too young for the events depicted in the song.) Originally written as three separate pieces, George decided to link them only when they began rehearsals.

'We found that each musical change flowed smoothly into the next,' he said. 'The changes felt natural and it would have been crass to spoil the mood.'

But the idea of an eleven-minute single was madness, especially when the pop charts in mid-1974 were dominated by three-minute ditties such as Paper Lace's 'Billy Don't Be a Hero' and Terry Jacks' 'Seasons in the Sun'. George had an inkling, though, that modern radio stations such as Sydney's 2SM would play the rockier 'Evie (Part 1)', while more conservative stations would reach for the slower 'Evie (Part 2)'.

It may have defied all the rules of radio, but 'Evie' was a remarkable piece of work, one of the greatest songs in the Australian rock canon. Wright sang every word as though he was reading from his personal diary, while George on bass, and Harry and Malcolm on guitars, truly brought the song to life. Malcolm, his confidence growing thanks to George's encouragement, boldly tackled the guitar solo in the first part of the song—gutsy stuff for a studio neophyte who preferred to play rhythm. Harry played the aching closing solo.

With 'Evie' and the accompanying *Hard Road* album in the can, Wright needed to get back in front of an audience. Michael Chugg set up a series of three live performances with Wright, among them a show at the Sydney Opera House on 9 June 1974. Stevie was backed by an impressive band with the equally impressive name of The All Stars; George and Harry played, as did Malcolm. John Paul Young helped out on backing vocals.

And the opening act was an up-and-coming outfit by the name of AC/DC.

George had seriously underestimated the impact of the Opera House show. It was the first time since 1969 that George, Harry and Stevie—a rare sighting of three Easybeats—had played live together, a real event. 'Scramble to see Easybeats', reported *The Sydney Morning Herald* on the day of the show. The capacity for the gig was around 2500, but some 10,000 fans had to be turned away, although most stayed and listened to the concert from the Opera House steps. It was a mob scene, reminiscent of the heyday of Easyfever.

'The kids [in the audience] didn't really care much about our presence,' said George, referring to his and Harry's role, 'but the industry was all interested and they got a kick out of it . . . Stevie loved it.'

'Evie' was released as a single in early June 1974. Neither George nor Wright could believe their luck when some DJs opted to play the lot—all three sides and eleven minutes of 'Evie'—rather than opt for whatever 'part' best suited their station's format. Trevor Smith, program director at 2SM, was a key swayer of opinion—his DJs played the song every hour, a bold decision given that it consumed so much airtime. 'Evie' was that good. It didn't hurt that 2SM was fast becoming the most popular, and influential, pop radio station in Sydney. The timing of 'Evie' was perfect.

By the end of the month, 'Evie' was rising fast in the national Top 40, hitting number 16. Suzi Quatro, later to cover 'Evie (Part 1)', was on top of the charts with 'Devil Gate Drive'. Four weeks later, 'Evie' had reached number 4; Wright's *Hard Road* album, meanwhile, was also in the Top 10 (it would chart for 32 weeks). 'Evie', which eventually did hit the top position, charted for a mammoth 26 weeks. It was the longest song to ever reach number 1 anywhere in the world, and had a good four minutes on The Beatles' 'Hey Jude'. Queen's six-minute epic 'Bohemian Rhapsody' was still a year away.

It was a remarkable return for Stevie Wright, but an equally big accomplishment for George and Harry. It was their first number 1 hit since 'Friday on My Mind' and their first as Alberts' in-house songwriters/producers. It wasn't a bad start for AHR.

Although invited to tour with Wright, possibly as part of a re-formed Easybeats, George had no interest in going down that road. He admitted that by the time of his third Sydney concert with Wright, it had become 'a drag'. 'There was a lot of pressure to re-form the band, but we didn't want to know about it—that was all history.'

Instead, the studio was calling George. In the wake of the success of 'Evie', new projects were starting to pile up. Among them was working with his brothers' band of reprobates, AC/DC.

★

Malcolm and Angus had decided to join forces in late 1973. They were reluctant at first, because sometimes the wrong type of sparks flew between them, as is the case with most strong-willed siblings. When they told their father of their plans to form a band, Pop just laughed.

'It'll last a week,' he said. He'd seen what happened when they disagreed with each other; it could get ugly.

But, like George, Malcolm and Angus were pragmatic types: they knew each other well, which would make it easier when disagreements happened, and their playing styles were complementary—Angus wanted to breathe fire on lead guitar, while Malcolm felt that he was more suited to the precision of rhythm guitar, just like George. His right hand was part jackhammer, part metronome. 'I love rhythm,' said Malcolm.

Malcolm's tenure with Velvet Underground had ended in early 1973 when he refused to continue supporting Ted Mulry. 'We shouldn't be backing Ted,' Malcolm told his friend, Herm Kovac. 'It makes us look like a backing band—and we should be the stars.'

Angus's bands had also folded, and would soon be little more than footnotes to his career. So, they figured, why not work together? Had to be better than a proper job. And given that neither had finished high school, they were hardly the most employable pair.

Malcolm was once asked whether he had a grand plan for the band when he brought it together. 'Yeah, there was a vision—that was basically that we didn't have to have day jobs and could get out and play guitar for a living . . . We were just working-class people, and we were just glad you could enjoy yourself making money, even if it was 50 bucks a week.'

As for the make-up of AC/DC, by early 1974, when they played some 'coming out' shows at Sydney venue Chequers, it was still a work in progress. Lanky, glam-rock–loving Dave Evans ɪwas the vocalist; the drummer was Colin Burgess, who'd been in The Masters Apprentices, one of many local bands that had followed The Easybeats to the UK (and duly fallen apart). Rob Clack played bass. All three were considerably older than the Youngs. Sometimes, George would sit in with the band; he even took over one night at Chequers when Burgess's drink was spiked and he did a header into his drum kit.

Ted Albert had signed AC/DC to his fledgling label, so it was logical that George should produce the band's first recording session, which took place during January 1974. They cut a number of songs, including 'Can I Sit Next to You, Girl?', which would become their debut single. Harry co-produced.

George sensed that his brothers hadn't yet mastered the craft of songwriting—'I was not hearing any great musical ideas,' he remembered—but they did have an identifiable sound, which was where George had gone wrong with The Easybeats, who had been too experimental for their own commercial good. 'The very first recordings had the guts of what became known as AC/DC,' George later recalled. 'They had something more than the germ of a style, which is crucial for a band.'

Beyond the songs, it was the wisdom George shared with his brothers that left the strongest impression at this nascent stage of their careers. George had a clear-cut policy: if the song that Malcolm and Angus brought into the studio could be played on the piano, it was fit for recording.

And if it didn't work on the piano?

'You can't polish a turd,' George told his brothers. That was hard to argue with.

George's ability to 'read' a song impressed Angus in particular. George could hear a rough demo and quickly come up with ideas to make it better. 'It was like he had it all in his head,' Angus said.

George, over time, would also advise his brothers on the business of music; he was determined that AC/DC wouldn't repeat the mistakes he'd made with The Easybeats. He'd sit in on most of the band's early discussions; he even met with Melburnian Michael Browning before he got the job as the band's manager, sizing him up. George wasn't just their co-producer—he was their mentor.

During an interview with Sydney's Double J, Chris Gilbey, who had been Alberts' A&R man at the time, made it very clear how important George was to the band: 'I think in the early period of time George was a far greater controlling influence on the band than any of the members of the band. Because George was the big brother and he'd been there with The Easybeats, he knew the ropes, he'd gone to England, he'd had hit records.'

'I think he imparted a very strong ethic as to what the music business was about, what music was about and staying close to the roots. He was the band's éminence grise.'

Back in the days of The Easybeats, Ted Albert had shared some of his own wisdom with George regarding production. 'Get it right, get the song right, get the music right, get the mix right,' Albert told him. 'And only then, when you are happy that you have the absolute best out of the song, out of the record, out of the mix, then you release it.'

This provided George and Harry with a mission statement: the song came first. That philosophy would prove incredibly handy during their work with AC/DC and others. And Ted Albert would remain George's sounding board, an essential third set of ears. When he and Harry had a track that they thought might work as a single, they'd head upstairs to Ted's office and play it for him. Then they'd gauge his reaction.

'If Ted sat up in his chair,' said George, 'you knew, "Hey, we're happening!"'

George, Harry and Ted had big plans—not just for AC/DC, but for their production enterprise. They needed to build their own studio, and now Albert, thanks to a recent business deal, had the $100,000 they needed to make that a reality.

9

'Fuck Me, George. I'm White, I'm from Kurri Kurri and We're a Rock Band!'

The project that would christen the new Alberts studio when it opened for business in late 1974 was a relatively straight-forward affair: the completion of the debut Ted Mulry Gang album, *Here We Are*. It would launch a studio that would soon become known as 'the house of hits'—even though its official title was Studio 139, over time simplified to Studio 1.

The studio was built in a warehouse space one floor below Ted Albert's office in Boomerang House. It wasn't the most sophisticated set-up—Albert basically divided one large room into two and hung up some speakers—but to George and Harry it was paradise.

The space was dark and downbeat, painted black—apart from one white wall, which quickly filled with graffiti—while the low-slung lights that hung from the ceiling were matched with orange lampshades. Some ageing green curtains were set up so that they could be moved around the room to deaden the sound. A grand piano added a touch of class to the very utilitarian set-up.

The control room—George and Harry's domain—looked straight through to the main recording space. It was all very basic, but it was also highly functional.

As George recalled, there wasn't much thought given to 'acoustics, acoustic shape or acoustic design', but that became part of the studio's charm. 'Because it wasn't acoustically designed, it had its own unique sound. But it was [a] pure fluke,' he said.

There was ample space on the recording console for the cans of KB lager that George and Harry consumed as they worked; the ashtrays overflowed with cigarette butts— George smoked Benson & Hedges, Harry preferred Drum roll-your-owns. Harry kept a 'secret' bottle of vodka stashed away in an air-conditioning vent. Dope was openly smoked inside the studio. It was down home, very funky, more like a rumpus room than a formal studio.

The plan had been for George and Harry to co-produce the Ted Mulry Gang record, and it seemed like a natural fit: the Ted Mulry Gang was signed to Alberts, George and Harry had had success with Mulry back in the time of 'Falling in Love Again', and his new group was a tight rocking three-piece, raised in the pubs. George knew this type of music inside out.

The sessions actually began in EMI Studios, as the King Street studio wasn't yet ready. Drummer Herm Kovac— who'd moved on from Velvet Underground with guitarist Les Hall and joined forces with Mulry—remembered being awestruck during his first encounter with George and Harry.

'I could not believe they had just shaken my hand,' Kovac said later. Les Hall felt the same.

Once Kovac's drum sounds were fine-tuned, and his nerves settled, it was time to try to record something. George suggested that they attempt a song called 'I'm on Fire', which they'd nailed in rehearsal. That was when things started going awry.

George had an idea for the band. 'Think dance,' he said. 'Think black.'

Several heads were scratched in unison. *What did he mean?*

George stood in front of Kovac. He then broke into an improvised dance as the drummer looked on, trying to work out what the hell to say.

'You are kidding me, right, George?' Kovac asked. 'Is this a wind-up?'

'No, 'Erman,' George replied, his Scottish brogue growing more and more dense, 'jooost watch and groove it up like the black cats play.'

'Fuck me, George,' Kovac said. 'I'm white, I'm from Kurri Kurri and we're a rock band!'

Kovac couldn't believe that he was arguing with one of his heroes. But George's idea was crazy; they were about as funky as Norman Gunston.

'He's right, you know,' said Mulry, coming to Kovac's defence.

It was agreed that they'd shut the session down and try again the next day. But Ted Mulry had other plans. He went straight to Ted Albert—who he cheekily referred to as 'Dward', a play on 'Edward'—and told him that it wasn't working out. An engineer named Bruce Brown was brought in, and the album proceeded without George and Harry. They'd been sacked.

'To their credit,' added Kovac, 'I think they admired that we stuck to what we believed in. George ended up becoming a mentor and encouraged me to follow my path as a producer.'

It wasn't, however, the end of George's association with the Ted Mulry Gang, or the album (which was mixed at Alberts). There was one track, 'Only Love Can Make It', that Ted Albert felt would benefit from the Vanda/Young touch.

Herm Kovac was surprised to learn that there had been no hangover from their sacking. 'George and Harry arrived full of enthusiasm, raring to go. They admired the fact we stuck to our guns and they were all for helping out.'

Harry quickly came up with an idea to layer instruments, à la Mike Oldfield's hit instrumental album *Tubular Bells*. George agreed that it was a great idea. George then got to work on the song's vocal parts, 'teaching' Mulry and Harry as they stood around a single microphone.

'Hearing the track today,' said Kovac, 'you can hear the genesis of their big songs like "Love is in the Air". We didn't know it then, but we were witnessing the hallmarks of the great Vanda and Young productions.'

As Kovac summed it up: 'Ted Mulry wrote the song, TMG played it, but Vanda and Young made it.'

★

Ever since the days of the mysterious Eddie Avana, George had harboured dreams of producing a pop star, to tap into what Joni Mitchell, in her 1974 song 'Free Man in Paris', had called 'the star-maker machinery behind the popular song'. George didn't just want to write and produce the songs; he wanted to devise the 'concept', the whole shebang, right down to suggesting what the star wore on stage. George and Harry had already come up with the perfect song, an infectious stomper called 'Can't Stop Myself from Loving You'. All they needed was 'the talent', someone who could easily be moulded into a pop idol.

Sydneysider John Cave was a suburbanite who lived with his parents, proprietors of a fruit and vegetable shop. Cave had flyaway hair and a shop-soiled weathered face, and he looked older than his 25 years. But he could sing, in a distinctive falsetto. He'd been the vocalist with a Sydney 'Beat' band called The Amazons, which released one single, in 1966, called 'Ain't That Lovin' You Baby'. When that band split, he continued playing clubs and pubs, despite recurring problems with his mental health. Depression and panic attacks were not uncommon for Cave.

Desperate for a big break, Cave had auditioned for AC/DC. He maintained that he had been offered the job but his manager had advised against it, saying, 'Well, do you want to sing in a bloody pub band all your life or do you want to be a star?'

'I want to be a star,' Cave replied, and passed on the offer.

Cave was in the studio when Stevie Wright was attempting to sing 'Can't Stop Myself from Loving You'. But Wright struggled; it was simply too high for his vocal range to handle. Cave volunteered his services to George and Harry, making it clear that he could hit the notes that Stevie couldn't manage. George discovered that this was true, and offered him the song, but his image definitely needed some work.

George Redburn
Young at the Young
family home in
Burleigh Street,
Burwood, May
1966.
Mitchell Library, State
Library of New South
Wales and Jill Molan,
PXE 1626

Three Easybeats outside the Young house in Burwood, May 1966.
From left: Dick Diamonde, Stevie Wright and George Young.
Mitchell Library, State Library of New South Wales and Jill Molan, PXE 1626

George with his sister, Margaret, a major influence on his musical tastes.
Glenn A. Baker

George meets his fans, suburban Sydney, May 1966.
Mitchell Library, State Library of New South Wales and Jill Molan, PXE 1626

George makes his
way through the
screaming masses
at Sydney Stadium,
1966.

On stage with The Easybeats at the Coca-Cola Teenage Fair,
Yennora, Sydney, May 1966.

The Easybeats in Regent's Park, London, 1967. *From left*: Dick Diamonde, Harry Vanda, Stevie Wright, George Young and Snowy Fleet.
Colin Beard

The Easybeats arrive in the Netherlands, January 1967. George is at far right.
Ben Merk/Anefo/National Archives of the Netherlands

George (far left) and his fellow Easybeats performing on Dutch TV, August 1968.
Anefo/National Archives of the Netherlands

George's brother, Alex, aka George Alexander (seated, far left), with his band Grapefruit (seated) and friends, London, January 1968. *Back row from left*: Brian Jones, Donovan, Ringo Starr, John Lennon, Cilla Black and Paul McCartney.
PA Images/Alamy

The Easybeats in the Netherlands, August 1968. *Clockwise from top left*: Tony Cahill, Stevie Wright, Dick Diamonde, Harry Vanda and George Young.
Anefo/National Archives of the Netherlands

The Easybeats try (and fail) to gatecrash a garden party at Buckingham Palace, London, 1968.

The final Easybeats show: the Trocadero, Sydney, October 1969.
Philip Morris

George (left) and Harry Vanda plotting their future, Sydney, October 1969.
Philip Morris

The soon-to-be-no-longer Easybeats on set at TV station CBN-8/CWN-6 in Orange, New South Wales, October 1969.
Stephen Fleay

George (far left) on stage with, from left, Malcolm Young, Harry Vanda and Stevie Wright, Sydney Opera House, June 1974.
Philip Morris

Harry Vanda (left)
and George at work
in Sydney's Alberts
studio, the legendary
'house of hits', 1975.
Philip Morris

Harry and George on a video
set, in character as Flash and
the Pan.
Glenn A. Baker

George (left) and Harry Vanda making magic with John Paul Young, Alberts studio, 1975.
Philip Morris

George (in Angus cap), Harry Vanda and their families, Victoria Park, Sydney, September 1975.
Philip Morris

George (in AC/DC T-shirt) backstage with brother Malcolm, Sydney, December 1976.
Bob King

The Angels' Doc Neeson recording the *No Exit* album at Alberts, early 1979.
Philip Morris

A rare live appearance from George (right), jamming with Malcolm and AC/DC at Sydney's Strata Motor Inn, February 1979.
Philip Morris

George with his mentor, Ted Albert, during the Easybeats reunion, November 1986.
Bob King

From left: Stevie
Wright, Dick
Diamonde
(reclining), Snowy
Fleet, Harry Vanda
and George, Sydney,
November 1986.
Bob King

Rose Tattoo's Angry
Anderson, Sydney's Hordern
Pavilion, December 1977.
Bob King

Actor Will Rush portraying George Young in the TV mini-series *Friday on My Mind*, 2017.
Tony Mott

The 'band' in the studio with Ted Albert (actor Ashley Zukerman) in *Friday on My Mind*, 2017.
Tony Mott

George Young (1946–2017), the legend who helped to create the Great Australian Songbook.
Philip Morris

What kind of a pop star was called John Cave, especially in the time of glam rockers with names like Gary Glitter and Alvin Stardust?

During a lively conversation with George in the studio, in which they discussed possible names, a frustrated Cave said, 'Oh for fuck's sake, I might as well call myself bloody William Shakespeare.'

George's eyes grew wide. 'That's it.'

'It's an unusual name, isn't it, William?' joked ocker comic Paul Hogan, when the singer appeared on Hogan's TV show to perform the song.

The newly christened William Shakespeare soon had 'Can't Stop Myself from Loving You' done and dusted, but his wardrobe also needed a major overhaul. His manager, Rod Thomas, and Alberts' Chris Gilbey took him to see a dresser of Kings Cross drag queens—who dabbled in cross-dressing himself—and Shakespeare emerged with some of the most outrageous looks ever devised in Oz pop. He sported more glitter and satin than all the members of Sherbet combined, while his sleeves billowed out like the sails of a boat—a strong wind could have blown him all the way across the Tasman. The cream of the crop was an outfit with a pair of diamante-encrusted 'wings'; he seemed to be part dinosaur, part transvestite. It was impossible to look away.

The song hit number 2 in October 1974, charting for a staggering 32 weeks—much of it while Stevie Wright's 'Evie' was still charting highly. George said that it was a 'star-making exercise that worked'—well, at least for a time, as fate would prove.

★

AC/DC's debut single, 'Can I Sit Next to You, Girl?', produced by George and Harry, was finally released in July 1974. Although it charted modestly, it was enough to secure them the support slot on New York shock-rocker Lou Reed's Australian tour. Admittedly, the band wasn't a hard sell to local promoters when they learned that Malcolm and Angus were George's brothers. The Easybeats were Oz rock royalty, after all.

Lou Reed had swooned over The Easybeats' 'Falling Off the Edge of the World' when Lillian Roxon introduced him to the song back at Max's Kansas City. But it was unlikely that he knew there was a connection between that soaring ballad and the spindly-legged guitarists—one wearing satin, the other a school uniform—of AC/DC, his opening act. In any case, Reed was too busy sparring with the local press, who had no idea how to deal with the media-baiting Andy Warhol protégé, currently sporting hair the colour of custard.

'Why do you want people to take drugs, Lou?' asked one reporter.

'Because it's better than Monopoly,' Reed replied, sipping something orange through a straw.

'Are you a transvestite or a homosexual?'

'Sometimes.'

When the Reed tour reached Melbourne, George got a call from his brothers. There was a problem. Their band was being forced to play at a low volume, so as not to show up the neurotic headliner. George didn't hesitate for a moment: he caught the next flight to Melbourne, took a cab to Festival Hall and confronted Reed's crew.

'You give these boys'—he gestured at AC/DC—'the fucking lot.'

That wasn't the end of it. George spent the entire set standing by the mixer, ensuring that his brothers' band got 'the fucking lot', casting wary looks at the sound guy. As Dave Evans said at the time, 'Nobody fucks with George Young, man.'

It reinforced the belief that George was much more than AC/DC's co-producer: he was their guardian, their muscle.

George wasn't the only Young with a take-no-prisoners attitude. After an AC/DC gig at Sydney venue Chequers, Malcolm and the band got into a squabble with another group. When Malcolm was confronted in the back alley behind the venue, he picked up a broken piece of pipe and chased away his would-be assailants.

★

John Paul Young was always going to be a more marketable pop star than William Shakespeare: he was better looking, for one thing, and was a better singer. But although *Jesus Christ Superstar* had been a career maker for Jon English, Marcia Hines, Reg Livermore and many others, and generated a handy windfall for producer/promoter Harry M. Miller, the box office takings didn't trickle down to the principals. Both Stevie Wright and John Paul Young were broke when the production wound up in February 1974, after more than 700 performances.

Young—or 'Squeak', as he'd soon be dubbed by Sydney power publicist Patti Mostyn—was considering a return to the factory floor when he got a call from George. It was time to get back to work; after all, he did have a contract with Alberts.

'Come into the studio,' George said. 'We've got a bunch of songs for you.'

Among these songs was something called 'Bad Trip'. George told John that the demo was the first track they'd laid down in the new studio. This may have been a good omen, but the song wasn't long for either the Vanda/Young or the JPY canon when it appeared in March 1974.

It was a peculiar song, a melodic pop confection with a provocative lyric—'I'm on a bad trip'—that was destined to encounter the same kind of censorship that had cursed George and Harry's 'Heaven and Hell' in 1967. Not only was it banned but, as 'Squeak' recalled, the radio DJs 'just didn't play it'.

George had another, much better song in mind for Young, with a lyric that drew on his heady experiences with The Easybeats and the aftermath (although he never revealed this to Young). It was called 'Yesterday's Hero'. But before George and Harry could get to work on that track, they needed to co-produce AC/DC's debut album.

★

Bon Scott had undergone a series of big changes since the days of The Valentines. For a time he'd swapped the red velvet for hippie beads, sprouted facial hair, smoked some herb and got back to basics with Adelaide-based band Fraternity, who modelled themselves on Americana icons The Band. He even took up playing the recorder. The group lived communally on a property in the Adelaide Hills, getting in touch with nature and their inner feelings, and wrote music based on the experience. At least, that was the plan. The truth was that bassist Bruce Howe ruled the band, and Bon, who'd joined the group in late 1970 and harboured plans to write songs, was at the bottom of the Fraternity hierarchy.

Fraternity won the 1971 Hoadley's Battle of the Sounds competition and followed in the footsteps of The Easybeats by basing themselves in London. But like so many Australian bands of the time, their dream was snuffed out in the highly competitive UK music scene, and Scott limped back to Australia in late 1973. On the mend from a horrific motor-cycle accident that had nearly killed him, and his two-year marriage to Irene Thornton almost at an end, Scott was hanging up posters around Adelaide, helping out his former Valentines partner Vince Lovegrove at his booking agency. He feared that his music career was over.

That's when George Young called Lovegrove. AC/DC's original lead singer, Dave Evans, hadn't been a good fit; he was too glammy, a little too camp for a red-blooded rock-and-roll band. (Perhaps even a bit too tall; the Youngs, after all, were pint-sized rockers.) Malcolm wanted to get rid of him, and he'd asked George for advice.

'My brothers' band is looking for a singer,' George said to Lovegrove. 'Know anybody good?'

Lovegrove knew just the guy.

George would have known Scott via The Valentines, who'd recorded several Vanda/Young songs and had been on the bill during The Easybeats' final Australian tour. But it's unlikely they'd spent any time together.

Scott was now 28 years old, a veteran in comparison with Malcolm, who was 21, and nineteen-year-old Angus. He wasn't convinced that AC/DC 'understood' rock and roll; after all, they were just kids. But a jam session with them at a party in Adelaide on 20 September, and a long chat with Angus and Malcolm about their shared Scottish roots, were enough to convince Scott that they were the real deal.

He also didn't lack self-confidence. 'I can sing better than that drongo you have at the moment,' Scott said, glancing towards Dave Evans, who was duly sacked.

*

In November, AC/DC returned to Alberts studio to work with George and Harry on their debut album. George took a moment to give the new recruit the once-over: with his tatts, shark-tooth earring and broken teeth, he looked a lot older than 28.

'He's been around the block a few times,' George said, nodding towards Scott, who was settling into the vocal booth.

George, however, was no wowser; he knew enough about the business to understand that Scott had a certain bad-boy appeal. And when he heard Scott sing, George realised that his brothers had gotten very lucky.

'He's your man, no doubt about it,' George told Malcolm and Angus. 'You're a rock-and-roll band now.'

All the songs on the *High Voltage* album, bar a roaring cover of the old blues standard 'Baby Please Don't Go', were written by Bon, Malcolm and Angus. The brothers had not only found a great frontman, they'd also unearthed a creative collaborator.

Despite the addition of Scott, AC/DC hadn't yet settled on a permanent line-up. They didn't currently have a rhythm section, so George sat in on bass (not for the last time) and

Sydneysider Tony Currenti was brought in to play drums. The group accepted George and Harry as surrogate band-mates: they dubbed George the 'gorgeous Glaswegian', while Harry was the 'Dutch damager'.

George developed a very precise approach while working with Angus on his lead guitar solos, which were recorded separately to the basic tracks (as were Scott's vocals). He'd talk through a riff with Angus, and the two of them would then play it repeatedly, until Angus knew it inside out. After perhaps twenty minutes of this, George would nod towards Harry, who'd go into the control room to record Angus's final version of the solo. Then George and Angus would move on to the next solo, and the process would begin all over again.

The volume inside the studio was deafening; other workers in the King Street building had a simple measure to tell whether the Youngs were at work in Studio 1: if they were in the house, the lift well would be shaking.

One thing that had surprised George and Harry when they returned to Australia in 1973 was the 'thinness' of local recordings. It struck them as the exact opposite of what they were hearing in the pubs and clubs that were now the heart and soul of the live scene. As John Paul Young recalled, 'They basically came up with the opinion that there were some great bands out there playing some great music but it wasn't being transferred onto record. So they made it their job to make it happen.' Singer Angry Anderson of Rose Tattoo, who'd later work with George and Harry, said they were 'magicians' at capturing that wild sound.

This was what they were seeking to achieve with *High Voltage*: to reproduce the primal, sweaty—and very loud—roar of what would become known as Oz rock, a wall of sound that could compete with the tone-deadening carpets and brick walls (and drunken punters) of the typical beer barn. Their approach clearly worked, because many of the songs on *High Voltage* would remain in AC/DC's set list for the next 40 years.

★

Just prior to *High Voltage*'s February 1975 release, the band received a last-minute request to play at the Sunbury Festival, outside of Melbourne, on the Australia Day long weekend. The promoters were concerned that British band Deep Purple, the headliners, might not play, so they needed an extra group to pad out the bill.

It was a high-profile gig, in front of some 15,000 punters. George, who'd just played bass with AC/DC at a Melbourne pub gig, travelled with the band. George didn't own a road case, so he slung the bass over his shoulder and carried it to the site. During their mile-long trek to the band area, after being dropped off nearby, a flotilla of Rolls-Royces breezed by them, raising dust, chauffeuring the members of Deep Purple to the gig. Clearly they were going to play after all.

Backstage, it was very clear that Deep Purple had the run of the event: they had their own trailer, which dwarfed the other caravans on site. The local bands on the bill— Sherbet, Skyhooks, Daddy Cool, Stevie Wright and about 30 others—shared very basic facilities, and split a paltry $27,000 in appearance money between them. AC/DC were to be paid $300; even the high-flying Skyhooks were to receive just $400. Deep Purple were being paid $60,000.

AC/DC were told that they could still play, but after Deep Purple, at 9 p.m. Their roadie, Tana Douglas, a teenage escapee from a Queensland private girls' school, began setting up their gear. Deep Purple's roadies intervened, telling Douglas to stop. She reported this to George and the band, who instructed her to try again. Again, she was told to stop—Deep Purple wanted to 'break down' their gear first, after their set was over. But this was a continuous festival, where one band ended and the next plugged in and played, so it wouldn't work; there would be too long a delay.

When Douglas tried one more time to set up—and failed—George, Malcolm, manager Michael Browning and others stepped in to sort out the problem. George was approached by one of Deep Purple's roadies who, in a threatening manner, said George had better be careful, because this roadie was from New York.

'Fook that,' George replied with a shrug, 'I'm from Glasgow.'

And with that, he headbutted his would-be attacker and a brawl erupted, in full view of the crowd. Browning clipped the chin of Deep Purple's manager, Bruce Payne, drawing blood and knocking him on his backside, while Tana Douglas, who was no shrinking violet, got in a few good shots herself. Bon Scott grabbed the nearest person and fixed him in a headlock. There was a flashpoint when parts of the crowd near the stage were ready to jump into the melee, egged on by Angus Young, but eventually some sort of order was restored.

The promoter said that AC/DC could play next—a lot of the crowd were keen to check them out. But again, Deep Purple's crew insisted on breaking down their gear before

Douglas could set up, and a second brawl broke out. That was it for George and the others, and they left. They made the right decision, because the festival's promoter, a company called Odessa Promotions, soon went into liquidation without paying any of the Australian acts on the bill. Sunbury '75 was a financial disaster, and the festival was never staged again.

This was a turning point for AC/DC. Malcolm Young, like George before him, had a strong drive to get his band out of Australia and take on the world. If this was how they were to be treated at home, then it was time to start thinking seriously about heading overseas.

The upside was that the following day's press coverage of the event focused on a bunch of feisty up-and-comers named AC/DC—and they hadn't even played a note.

★

It said a lot about George's anything-goes approach that he and Harry could switch from the hard-rocking *High Voltage* album to crafting another pop confection for William Shakespeare, who was in need of a follow-up to 'Can't Stop Myself from Loving You'.

The song they conjured up, 'My Little Angel', was more sugary than its predecessor. 'Angel' was a Christmas song; to the sound of chiming sleigh bells, John Cave half-sang, half-spoke the heartbreaker of a lyric, a conversation with his 'daughter', his little angel. (In short, some kids at school had teased a little girl, telling her that angels didn't really exist; waterworks ensued.) It was pure cheese, pop at its fluffiest, and it fairly galloped to the top of the charts in the early months of 1975. It charted for almost six months, and

William Shakespeare became just the third Alberts artist—after Ted Mulry and The Easybeats—to get an overseas release. In England, he'd be known as Billy Shake, so as not to offend lovers of the Bard.

With the success of 'Evie' and Shakespeare's first hit, 'Can't Stop Myself', George and Harry had two of the ten bestselling singles of 1974. 'My Little Angel' would make the list in 1975. George's decision to return home had been a winner; he was now on a roll. He and Harry were the most in-demand producers in the country.

Their timing couldn't have been better, either, with the advent of ABC's *Countdown*, which first aired in early November 1974 and was fast becoming a must-watch show for music fans right across the country. (It would run for an astonishing fourteen seasons and 563 episodes.) And the show's reach was crucial; an act like Shakespeare, who once might have been a purely Sydney phenomenon, was now recognised throughout Australia, even in places he'd never visited. *Countdown* was also one of the first Australian TV shows to be produced in colour, which only enhanced the recognition factor for the acts that appeared each week. Shakespeare's garish outfits really came to full and vivid life on the set of *Countdown*. He'd even been rumoured as a possible host of the show.

Countdown's groundbreaking use of video clips, which would prove to be incredibly useful promotional devices, was also crucial, MTV being still almost a decade away. Pretty soon George Young would take a very active interest in the world of video.

The Ted Mulry Gang, the first band to actually fire George and Harry, experienced the effect of *Countdown's* reach firsthand when they agreed to tour a more remote part of South Australia. They chose to do this more for the adventure than the benefits, because they figured no one would know who the hell they were.

But their shows were packed to the rafters, which prompted Herm Kovac to ask a local what was going on.

'How do you even know who we are?' he asked.

The reply was simple. 'We get *Countdown*, you know.'

10

The House of Hits

'Yesterday's Hero' was the most autobiographical song George had ever written. It was a snapshot of his helter-skelter days with The Easybeats and the strange after-effect of feeling washed up when he had barely reached his twenties. When John Paul Young sang 'Take a look at me, I'm yesterday's hero', the words could have come directly from George's mouth. It was also a really strong pop song with a very catchy chorus.

While recording the song, George thought that it needed a spoken-word passage, delivered in a newsreader style (a technique repeated several years later in John Farnham's 'You're the Voice').

'Do you know anyone who might be good for the part?' George asked Young.

He certainly did. He brought in two actors he'd met during his run on *Jesus Christ Superstar*. One was named Joe Dicker, who'd played King Herod. The other was budding thespian Michael Caton, formerly of Biloela in Queensland, who'd go on to enjoy a lengthy TV and film career, most notably playing the role of Uncle Harry in Channel 9's *The*

Sullivans and Darryl Kerrigan in the iconic Aussie flick *The Castle*. Alberts' Chris Gilbey read the opening line, 'Here is the news.'

Caton nailed his part, and another Aussie pop classic was born. Ted Albert confirmed this when George played him the end result—he immediately sat up in his seat, a telltale sign that the song was a winner. The connection between Albert, George and Harry was deepening with each new track recorded in the studio downstairs. 'With George, Harry and Ted,' said Alberts' insider Fifa Riccobono, '[they] could almost hear each other thinking . . . [they] just understood each other so well.'

The film clip for 'Yesterday's Hero' became another early Australian classic. A forlorn Young, his hands sunk deep into his pockets, was filmed walking the streets of Melbourne, with various members of the public shooting him 'Don't I know you from somewhere?' glances as he drifted by. It was intercut with studio footage of a very earnest and baby-faced Young performing the song, his hair perfect, wearing a shirt so vivid it would have made William Shakespeare blush. Some additional scenes of Young being mobbed by eager fans were shot in the ABC car park at Ripponlea in suburban Melbourne, where *Countdown* was produced.

'Yesterday's Hero' hit the national Top 10 in June 1975, keeping company on the charts with local hits such as Richard Clapton's 'Girls on the Avenue' and William Shakespeare's 'My Little Angel', which was still holding tight to the Top 40. In Melbourne, the song stayed at number 1 for six weeks.

Young was invited onto *Countdown*'s set to perform 'Yesterday's Hero' as it rose in the charts. He'd barely started to sing when the frantic (female) audience swallowed him up, stripping the shirt from his back and leaving him bewildered and bruised. A dazed Young swore blind that he'd had no idea he was going to get mobbed—it was an ambush—while *Countdown*'s host, Molly Meldrum, insisted that he had nothing to do with the crowd's reaction, despite whispers that he'd stage-managed the entire scenario. (Young wasn't yet such a big star that he would have attracted this kind of rampage.)

Because he was singing live, Young feared that the performance had been a disaster; the mob had yanked the cord from his microphone. He looked over at the floor manager, who had a simple direction: 'Keep fucking singing!' Young's other big problem, aside from not knowing what had just hit him, was losing his best shirt, which the mob had torn to shreds.

Young recovered sufficiently to become a regular on the set of the highly influential *Countdown*, whose audience built to around two million viewers a week. Occasionally, when Meldrum wasn't available, or not quite in the best shape, the affable Young would host the show.

'Yesterday's Hero' transformed 'Squeak' into a fully fledged pop sensation, the opposite of the washed-up character that George described in the song. By mid-1975, Young was a household name, and not just in Australia. 'Yesterday's Hero' did reasonable business in the US Cashbox charts, reaching number 42, the first song of George's to chart in the US since 'St. Louis'.

★

Hot off his and Harry's success with John Paul Young, George was keen to continue rebuilding Stevie Wright's career, which had been set in motion the year before with the epic 'Evie'. But it would prove to be a far tougher endeavour than George could ever have imagined.

George didn't know the full extent of Wright's problems when they commenced work in early 1975 on the singer's second solo LP. But something was amiss. During the *Hard Road* sessions, Wright had briefly regained his songwriting mojo, but for the new record he leaned more on George and Harry for songs—they co-wrote seven of the nine tracks recorded. They even dusted off 'The People and the Power' from the Marcus Hook Roll Band album.

'Guitar Band', a George/Harry co-write, had appeared in November 1974, well before the finished album. The track was ferocious; Harry unleashed a brutal guitar blitz, and Stevie capably delivered another of George's terrific story songs about a life in rock and roll, wailing: 'I'm gonna be a star/With my guitar/In a guitar band'. A rake-thin Wright, decked out in a red jumpsuit with a huge 'S' emblazoned on the front, put in an appearance on *Countdown* in early March 1975, ad-libbing badly over a recorded track of the song, dancing wildly among a crowd heavy with Sherbet T-shirts and mullets. The song hit number 13 in the charts, a peak Wright would never again attain.

The new album was recorded, then scrapped, then re-recorded. It took Stevie's manager, Michael Chugg, to expose George to the full extent of Wright's addiction. Chugg walked into the control booth at Alberts and motioned for George and Harry to come with him. There was something they needed to see.

Chugg took them to a part of the studio where they could see Stevie snorting heroin from aluminium foil.

'Look,' Chugg told them. 'That's what's really going on. He's a heroin addict.'

'They freaked,' Chugg said of George and Harry.

The situation got so bad that George and Harry were forced to promote the album, which was titled *Black Eyed Bruiser*, when it was released in August 1975. Wright had gone AWOL. Given George's wariness of the hype and the media, this must have felt like having sharp sticks poked under his fingernails.

'*Black Eyed Bruiser* is a thousand times better than *Hard Road*,' George told *Juke* magazine. That was a stretch: beyond 'Guitar Band' and the song 'Black Eyed Bruiser'—'a nightmare song about today's violent society . . . very violent and heavy', according to George, who rated it more highly than 'Evie'—the rest of the tracks were just not as strong.

George blamed the stop–start creation of the album on a couple of issues: 'Stevie went overseas [promoting the *Hard Road* album], then he was ill for a while.' George wasn't asked to go into details about Stevie's illness, but the singer's drug addiction was hardly a big secret.

Wright spoke with a reporter about why he took heroin. He explained that being a star at sixteen had been 'a high in itself', a feeling that he missed badly and had tried to reproduce. 'I thought, "[Heroin is] what I need. And what's more, I'm going to show the world this stuff's not what it's made out to be." But I lost the plot.'

It didn't help that Wright was also fast-tracking his way to alcoholism. At his worst, he'd polish off two bottles of Southern Comfort every day.

Black Eyed Bruiser didn't sell, scraping its way to number 61 on the national charts. It was a rare commercial misstep for George, though affected by circumstances way beyond his control.

Wright, to his credit, tried to get straight, but his problems intensified when he agreed to be a guinea pig for a radical new treatment known as 'deep sleep' therapy, at Chelmsford Private Hospital in the leafy Sydney suburb of Pennant Hills. (John Cave, whose career as William Shakespeare went into steep decline after a carnal knowledge conviction, underwent the same treatment.)

'Deep sleep' was the process of putting a patient into a coma via heavy doses of barbiturates, then zapping them with several thousand volts while they were unconscious, sometimes without their consent. Its leading proponent, Dr Harry Bailey, claimed that the treatment would 'cure' depression, and drug and alcohol addictions. The intention was to 'wake' the patient after a few weeks, freed from addiction, but the therapy was hugely controversial. More than twenty patients died either in the hospital or soon after their release. (Bailey committed suicide in 1985.)

Wright, who'd had fourteen ECT treatments in his two weeks at the hospital, left Chelmsford in a worse condition, psychologically and physically, than when he had entered.

A planned third Stevie Wright album with George and Harry didn't happen, and Wright's life, not just his career, went into freefall.

★

For George, working with his brothers, Malcolm and Angus, wasn't always easy—he still thought of them as kids, for one thing, even though he could see what good musicians they'd become—but it must have been a relief in comparison to working with Wright. George and Harry commenced work on the second AC/DC album in March 1975.

By this time, the demand for George and Harry's services was such that they would spend most days working with established acts such as Wright and John Paul Young, and then during the 'graveyard shift', when the demand for Studio 1 wasn't so high, they'd produce up-and-coming bands such as AC/DC. (The pile of beer cans and cigarette butts could grow very high during a long day's journey into night at Alberts.) George, Harry and Alberts put in place a system known as 'hot-bedding', in which one band would finish a session and another would come in and get started almost immediately, while the studio was still 'hot'.

There'd been a couple of changes on the AC/DC front since their first album. They now had a rock-solid rhythm section, having hired two street-smart Melburnians. Nineteen-year-old bassist Mark Evans came direct from the 'Prahran Hilton', a housing commission estate on the fringes of the city. Their new drummer was Phil Rudd, aged twenty, direct from his father's car yard. He'd played in a band called Buster Brown with singer Greg Anderson (soon to be 'Angry') out front. Both Evans and Rudd knew that they'd be breathing rarified (if smoky) air inside the Alberts studio. George and Harry were god-like figures in the local music world.

Mark Evans was struck by the physical differences between the Vanda/Young pair. 'George was a short, stocky, dark-haired Scotsman,' Evans wrote in his memoir, *Dirty Deeds*, 'while Harry was blond, fair and very tall—probably the best part of a foot taller than George.' Evans found their differing accents—George's Scottish burr and Harry's native Dutch—a challenge to comprehend. But everything started to make perfect sense when they got to work.

Evans was particularly impressed by George's habit of sitting at the piano in the studio and helping his brothers transform a sketch into a complete song—AC/DC didn't record demos, they simply came into the studio with ideas in their head. 'Malcolm and Angus would have the barest bones of a song, the riff and different bits, and George would hammer it into a tune.'

Evans was a studio novice, so much so that George played most of the bass on the finished album. But Evans was fine with that; the education he was receiving, courtesy of Harry and George, was invaluable. 'I learned as much as I could,' he wrote, 'between cups of tea, ciggie breaks and pizza.' George and Harry also sang all of the backing vocals needed for the record. George came up with the memorable chant of 'Oi! Oi!' during the track 'T.N.T.', which sounded like a cry from the terraces of a soccer ground.

One of George's more eccentric ideas was challenging his brothers to write a song using the chord progression A-C-D-C. 'That'd be a neat trick,' he told them.

Malcolm and Angus returned to the studio with 'High Voltage', a song destined to become an AC/DC classic.

Very early on in the sessions, which were slotted in between the band's hectic concert schedule during March and April and then July 1975, Malcolm pulled George aside. He was thinking about broadening the band's sound, taking in other influences besides flat-chat rock and roll.

'What do you reckon?' Malcolm asked.

George's reply was a firm no—this was exactly the mistake he'd made while in The Easybeats, when they'd branched into woozy psychedelia and bloated ballads. George believed that Malcolm and the band had gotten very lucky; they'd chanced upon their own sound early on—gut-level, straight-to-the-solar-plexus rock, the perfect soundtrack to boozy nights at the beer barns that were springing up in seemingly every suburb of Australia. With his brothers' dual guitar attack, Bon Scott's larrikin spirit and a powerhouse new rhythm section, George knew that AC/DC had everything they needed.

'That's your thing,' George said. 'Stick with it. Don't bastardise your sound.'

In short, don't fuck with the formula.

The band had brought a strong batch of song sketches into the studio. The pick was 'It's a Long Way to the Top (If You Wanna Rock 'n' Roll)', which featured Bon Scott's first great lyric, documenting his rough-and-tumble career to date, a time he'd spent 'Gettin' robbed/Gettin' stoned/Gettin' beat up/Broken bones'.

George spotted the song title in a notebook that Scott kept with him, in which he wrote a lot of his lyrics. He warmed to it immediately—the title alone sounded like a great rock song. And it was George who transformed the track into a stone-cold classic.

As Mark Evans recalled, the song 'was actually just one jam and George got the tape and cut everything in . . . The song was never played in one piece in the studio—it was all cut together from one big jam. That was George Young—the guy is a genius.'

The idea of adding a bagpipes solo, rather than the standard guitar break, was another of George's brainwaves. When George raised the idea, Bon Scott said that he'd been in a Scottish band during his early days in Fremantle. He could play the bagpipes. No problem.

What Scott neglected to tell George was that he had been a drummer in the Scottish band and had never played the bagpipes in his life. A hefty $435 was spent on a set of pipes, which everyone in the studio at the time struggled to assemble. 'Watching the Youngs at work [on the bagpipes],' said Mark Evans, 'was like a Scottish Rubik's Cube, with added swearing and shouting.'

What emerged, though, was memorable. Scott would blow the pipes convincingly on stage for the next few years whenever they performed 'Long Way to the Top'—not many people realised that he was playing to a backing tape. And no one really cared; it was great theatre.

George was also impressed by the lyrics that Scott had written for songs such as 'The Jack' and 'High Voltage'.

'He's a one-off when it comes to the double entendre,' George said of Scott.

He wasn't kidding; only Bon Scott could have described a sexually transmitted disease in quite the way he did in 'The Jack', where he snickered: 'If I'd known what she was dealing out/I'd have dealt it back'. The song fast became a crowd favourite. No one in the local rock scene came close to Scott and what he dubbed his 'toilet poetry'.

The *T.N.T.* album sessions were relatively calm, at least by Young family standards. There was just one flashpoint, when Angus became a bit stroppy, and George pulled him aside.

'Stop being soooch a foooking prima donna,' he snapped.

That was it; Angus saw red and leaped at his brother, fists flying. Despite the wrestling match that ensued, George wasn't in any danger. Angus was tiny. His punches were all air swings.

Soon after the record was completed, Bon Scott spoke with a reporter from *RAM* and was asked to define George Young's role. What did he mean to the band?

'He doesn't tell us what to do, just shows us how to get more out of the things we start,' said Scott, who could turn reflective when the situation demanded. 'He's like a brother—no, a father—to the group.'

★

Ted Albert was keen to sign more acts, with George and Harry helping as talent-spotters. In August 1975, with the *T.N.T.* album as good as done, Malcolm and Angus tipped George off to a new rock band in town, The Keystone Angels, who were playing a gig at Sydney venue Chequers.

Anybody who'd known the band back in their native Adelaide would have struggled to recognise them in 1975. They'd started out as a very different band five years earlier—the Moonshine Jug & String Band, to be precise—who'd play old chestnuts like 'Blues My Naughty Sweetie Gives to Me' at regular gigs such as the Modbury Hotel in Adelaide.

Their key members were the stern-faced Brewster brothers, John and Rick, and singer/bassist Bernard Neeson. Born in Belfast in 1947, Neeson was the eldest of six siblings. Like many post-war immigrants, Neeson had settled in the South Australian satellite suburb of Elizabeth when his parents immigrated to Australia. He had been called up for national service in the late 1960s, and served as an education corps sergeant in New Guinea. He'd studied film and drama at Flinders University and dreamed of directing movies.

'He was a total romantic and a bit sort of crazy,' said the band's manager, John Woodruff, a friend and former flatmate of Neeson's.

In 1974, the band changed both its name—to The Keystone Angels—and its style, going electric. Neeson, who was a good head taller than the rest of the band, had yet to develop his menacing stage presence, all crazy energy and theatrical flair, which drew on his love of cinema. But the character named 'Doc' would soon emerge, and he'd rival Midnight Oil's Peter Garrett and Bon Scott himself as the country's most dynamic frontman.

Unlike AC/DC, The Keystone Angels were a hit at the 1975 Sunbury Festival, eliciting a standing ovation. In April, they toured with American great Chuck Berry, perhaps their biggest musical hero. They played a run of shows in rural South Australia with AC/DC twice, in 1974 and then again in 1975. It was highly unusual for Malcolm and Angus to speak highly of another band; they felt everyone else was their rival. ('They hated everybody!' said guitarist John Brewster.) But The Keystone Angels were a rare exception, and they recommended the band to George.

It was an unnerving experience for the band when they plugged in to play at Chequers, knowing that out there in the darkness George and Harry were looking on. These were two guys who could shape their future. Despite playing to a near-empty room, something worked because George was sufficiently impressed to meet with them afterwards.

'Come to the studio at eleven tomorrow and we'll see what you got,' George said over drinks.

'It was a wonderful moment,' remembered John Brewster, who did admit that he was unsure as to what George saw in the band, because they were still a work in progress. Perhaps the duelling guitars of the brothers Brewster reminded George of another pair of sibling guitar-slingers currently making their way through the local ranks.

The audition itself was odd. The band came into Alberts lugging their equipment, but George pulled them up.

'You didna' need to bring your gear up,' he said. 'Here's a couple of acoustic guitars—let's hear your songs.'

George's response to their performance was brief: 'Okay, that's great, thanks for coming in, guys.' That was it.

But by late November 1975 they had a deal with Alberts. They also had a new name, courtesy of George: from then on, they were simply The Angels. 'It'll look better on your record and posters,' he figured.

Like so many acts that worked with George and Harry, The Angels were serious Easybeats fans. They knew that they'd gotten very lucky with their Alberts deal, which promised them the works: studio time, marketing support, and Vanda and Young as their producers, which they specifically requested be written into their contract.

'You're talking about [working with] two of the major songwriters from The Easybeats,' John Brewster told writer Jane Albert, 'and signing up to a company with the guy who actually produced The Easybeats!'

Ted Albert had just one request: he recommended that manager John Woodruff wear shoes from now on. That way he'd be taken far more seriously.

George, during his early sessions with the band, gave The Angels some advice very similar to that he'd given his brother, Malcolm. 'You're a rock band,' he told them. 'Play it like you do on stage. Be true to yourselves.' George referred to it as the 'KISS' principle: Keep It Simple, Stupid. His ability to cut through the crap was remarkable.

George also spoke with Neeson. He'd spotted the potential in Neeson's onstage persona, the enigmatic 'Doc', and wanted to help him develop it, in much the same way he encouraged his brother Angus to transform himself into the schoolboy guitarist from hell whenever he pulled on his Ashfield Boys' High outfit. These types of characters gave bands such as AC/DC and The Angels an edge, especially when playing live.

'Just do anything,' George told Neeson. 'I don't care if you throw a bucket of fish at the crowd, so long as you do something that will make them take notice.' (Neeson took George literally, but only once—the crowd threw the fish back at the band, and it stank up a storm.)

'He helped me feel free to build whatever character Doc has become,' Neeson said a few years later.

George also discouraged him from playing bass. He felt that Neeson would operate best as a frontman without the baggage of an instrument. They could find a new bass player.

The Angels had previously cut an original song called 'Am I Ever Gonna See Your Face Again' for major label EMI, but it had been rejected. George and Harry convinced the band to give it another shot, and it became The Angels' first release for Alberts, in March 1976. It wasn't a big hit, reaching only number 58 on the national charts, but it became an Angels live staple, eliciting the audience chant of 'No way, get fucked, fuck off' that would work its way into Oz rock-and-roll folklore. The Angels were on their way.

★

As George and Harry's hot streak continued through 1976, they juggled early sessions with The Angels with further John Paul Young recordings. 'Yesterday's Hero' had firmly established Young as one of Australian pop's leading 'spunks', a poster boy to rate with Sherbet's Daryl Braithwaite and Skyhooks' Graeme 'Shirley' Strachan. He was a darling of *Countdown* and the type of pop star everyone's mother would love. Decked out in a blue-and-white sailor's suit, his long hair shining brightly and a broad smile on his face, 'Squeak' had come a long way from the factory floor (although his love of fishing kept him both sane and grounded).

The next song that George and Harry had in mind for Young was called 'The Love Game', which packed more groove than pretty much anything they'd written before. George had tried the song out on various singers without success until Young sang the spots off it one day in the Alberts studio.

'That's my boy,' said George, and the song was Young's.

Young performed it on *Countdown* on 31 August with one eye on the audience, fearing a repeat of the 'Yesterday's Hero' carnage. Several members of Sherbet watched from the studio couch, glad it was Young and not them out there on the sound stage. This time, though, Young didn't lose his shirt.

Released in late August 1975—with Young's cover of the mighty 'St. Louis' on the B-side—it became his biggest hit to date, peaking at number 4 on the national list and charting for twenty weeks. It was also one of three Vanda/Young songs to rank among the year's top 50 bestselling singles. The others were 'My Little Angel' and 'Yesterday's Hero'.

Young, like so many others to work with George, was constantly surprised by his and Harry's ability to improvise in the studio. 'It wasn't uncommon for George and Harry to say, "Hang around a minute, we'll just finish the words."' George would wander off to a corner of the studio and return a few minutes later, as promised, with the completed lyrics scribbled on a notepad.

One person who didn't need George's Midas touch with lyrics was Bon Scott. 'High Voltage', the song that George had challenged his brothers to write using the chord progression A-C-D-C, was brought to vivid life with some typically sharp lyrics from Scott. (The song actually had an A-C-D-A progression, but it was close enough.) It reached the Top 10 in September, just as JPY's 'The Love Game' began its assault on the charts and the airwaves.

The band celebrated with their biggest gig yet, a free show at Sydney's Victoria Park, sponsored by 2SM. A ladder was set up next to the PA stack and Angus scampered up its rungs, *Go-Set* photographer Philip Morris scurrying behind him, snapping frantically. Angus may have been barely five foot tall but he looked enormous as he stood on top of the speakers and wailed away on his guitar. He then waded into the surging crowd, playing all the while, with manager Michael Browning and a roadie following him, hoping to prevent Angus from being swallowed alive by the mob.

Bon Scott was annoyed by the sedate nature of the crowd at the afterparty. The band was on a high; why was everyone so damned quiet? Scott took it upon himself to inform the guests: 'You people are all stuffy, and you're all fucked.'

George and Harry, who'd attended the show with their partners and children—who wore schoolboy caps, just like Angus—looked on, bemused. Bon Scott sure knew how to break the ice.

11

Saving St Peter

In 1966, George and Harry had been the only Easybeats to fully embrace the prospect of travelling to London and taking on the world. The others were torn between the band's future and personal concerns—family, going to hell—or, in the case of Stevie Wright, possibly losing the love of his life (which he did, eventually). Ten years later, Malcolm Young made it very clear to the rest of his band that their future, too, lay outside of Australia, but without meeting the same resistance. As Mark Evans noted in *Dirty Deeds*, 'It's likely that George, AC/DC's mentor, who'd come so close to breaking in the UK with The Easybeats, was dreaming of another shot. And the band was just as hungry as George.'

Author Clinton Walker once wrote that 'AC/DC was George Young's revenge'. Taking on the world was all part of the plan, George's way of correcting everything that had gone wrong with The Easybeats.

Manager Michael Browning had set in place an international deal for AC/DC with Atlantic Records in the UK, and a departure date was set for April 1976. But it would hardly signal the end of George's association with the band; the exact opposite, in fact. Before their departure, between January and March 1976, in what was fast becoming an annual ritual, the band convened in the Alberts studio with George and Harry to cut a new record, which would be called *Dirty Deeds Done Dirt Cheap*.

During these sessions, in one of the stranger moments of the band's career, Angus riffed on the traditional Scottish song 'The Bonnie Banks o' Loch Lomond' while Bon Scott sang along off-key, and 'Fling Thing' was born. George described it as a Scottish 'Amazing Grace', which was quite a stretch; it was neither amazing nor graceful. Interestingly, in 1967 George had goofed around with the same song with The Easybeats; the footage was captured by Peter Clifton and released more than 40 years later in the documentary *Easy Come, Easy Go*. George had even worn a tartan kilt for the occasion.

'Fling Thing' might have been buried away on the B-side of their single 'Jailbreak' in late June, but it did prove that the band—and their mentor—had a sense of humour. It also gave them something special to play when they finally got to perform in Glasgow.

During recording downtime, George headed out to the suburbs with the band for a gig at the Hurstville Civic Centre. Afterwards, *RAM* journalist Anthony O'Grady was backstage, taking it all in, when George spoke about an idea he had for his 'wee brother'.

'How about you dive off a 40-foot tower,' George said to Angus, 'into a glass of strawberry milk, without missing a note? Couldn't fail.'

Off stage, Angus was withdrawn, a teetotaller, but in concert he'd become a daredevil, jumping off stage to play among the crowd, spinning on his back while playing—a move known as The Dying Bug—and racing around the stage, and the crowd, on Bon Scott's brawny shoulders. He displayed the same kind of manic energy as 'Little' Stevie Wright had done in his prime.

Angus was up for pretty much anything, but George's suggestion may have been pushing it just a bit too far. 'Better save it up for a big gig,' said Angus. 'Yer probably couldn't do it twice a night till yer got use ta it.'

Back at Alberts, the songs were coming at a furious rate; those brotherly sessions at the studio piano were paying rich dividends. 'Ride On', a slow, hypnotic blues song, was a standout on *Dirty Deeds*, as was 'Problem Child', one of many AC/DC songs that hit American teenager William Bruce Bailey—later to style himself as Axl Rose—right between the eyes. The title track was a lark, inspired by the cartoon *Beany and Cecil*, which Angus loved. A character in the show, Dishonest John, would flash his card, which read: 'Dirty deeds done dirt cheap. Holidays, Sundays, and special rates.' Bon Scott had a field day—his skills as a pun-loving lyricist were advancing in step with the twin-guitar assault of the Young brothers.

Album completed, AC/DC left for London on 1 April 1976, by which time George was back working with John Paul Young.

★

Inspiration could strike George at the strangest times. One day at Alberts, he and Harry were in the lift, heading out after a long day struggling with one particularly tricky song.

'I hate the music,' George said to Harry, shaking his head.

George's frustration stemmed from the troublesome song's opening chords, which in the current version were played on a banjo. But the next day he had a solution, inserting a piano riff—and the song came to life. Yet another John Paul Young hit was born, using George's throwaway remark as the title: 'I Hate the Music'.

A *Countdown*-ready clip was compiled, using live footage of Young performing at a 2SM-sponsored show, held on a floating stage under the Sydney Harbour Bridge. JPY-mad fans jumped in the drink and freestyled out to the pontoon, hoping for a close encounter with the pop pin-up, who was decked out in his sailor suit. Sharks be damned. (Alberts' labelmates Ted Mulry Gang were on the same bill, as was AC/DC.)

Released on 5 April, 'I Hate the Music' was Young's biggest hit yet, hitting number 2 on the national chart and hanging about for twenty weeks, just like 'The Love Game' had done. JPY and Vanda/Young were an unstoppable pop force.

Even though Young was primarily a singles artist, the album that followed 'I Hate the Music' into the charts, simply titled *J.P.Y.*, was more than a collection of hits with a few novelties tacked on. One track in particular, 'Standing in the Rain', showcased the increasingly progressive recording style of George and Harry. It was a funky, soulful song that was destined for a second life a little further down the road. The *J.P.Y.* album was a Top 10 smash.

★

Back in 1975, George had spoken with the press in lieu of Stevie Wright strictly under duress; he'd held little interest in the media since the days of The Easybeats. It was therefore quite a coup for Australian *Rolling Stone* when he agreed to sit down with writer Glenn A. Baker for the magazine's July 1976 edition. The demand for George to be interviewed was proof, if it was needed, that he was now recognised by peers and punters alike as a significant figure in the Australian musical landscape, through his work with The Easybeats, Alberts, Stevie Wright, JPY and many others. He was a major player, a hitmaker, as was Harry Vanda.

The interview took place over several weeks, conducted in the studio while he was mixing AC/DC's *Dirty Deeds Done Dirt Cheap*, and at home in the 'burbs. George spoke in his typically direct, bullshit-free style; no subject was off limits.

He traced his life and career from Glasgow (his family, he said, 'were fairly musical in an amateur sort of way'), to Villawood—'coming from the hostel, we weren't actually violent, but we didn't take much shit'—and the roots of The Easybeats ('we all more or less bumped into each other there'). He also spoke about Easyfever ('You'd go into a small town with a No 1 record and, of course, everyone turns out to see you') and its downside: 'With a No 1 record, that's where all the bullshit started.'

George also spoke at length about the demise of the band. When it was over, he said, 'it was sort of like kids lost in the dark, trying to find out how the world operates'. There were also missed opportunities. '[Brian] Epstein wanted to manage us at one time,' he revealed.

He also shared a peculiar rumour. 'We had a strange piece of news the other day,' he said, 'that Snowy had died.'

(Fleet was alive and well, and working as a builder in Western Australia.)

George also disclosed that some of the legal problems of the band remained unresolved, which had brought about the need for him and Harry to use the 'Brian Russell' pseudonym at the time of the *Friends* album. 'It came to court in the last couple of weeks and it's probably going to cost us a lot of money.' He made it very clear how tough it had been for Harry and him when they returned to London after the demise of The Easybeats. They were 'flat broke', he said. 'We were skint.'

George dismissed his four-year binge as 'more or less just us having a laugh', but judging by his ability to list virtually all the acts that he and Harry had worked with, or were covered by—Tramp, Grapefruit, Paintbox, Phil Pickett, David Bowie (a big fan; he'd covered 'Friday on My Mind' in 1973), Rod Stewart, John Miles and so on—some strong memories remained. He and Harry took a lot more away from the binge than a hangover. They came to understand how the studio worked, and how records were made.

George also revealed that he now drew on his Easybeats experience to advise the acts that he worked with, so some good had come of it. 'We get the same thing across, that it all comes to an end, so don't take it all that seriously.'

And Vanda and Young's current purple patch? George was his typically pragmatic self. 'We probably did too much at once but it all worked . . . it just proved that we could do various things.'

As for AC/DC, George said that it didn't simply come together by accident; the MO had always been clear in his mind. 'To us, that was another exercise in how to get a good rock and roll band into the charts . . . To get them off the ground in such a short time, getting them off to England, and also getting them a good deal, was another exercise.'

And his future? George was unclear about what would happen next.

'I really don't know,' he said, admitting that he'd just gone through a period in which his enthusiasm for music making had waned. 'There are a lot of songs which just have to be put down on tape. It's just getting the energy and shaking ourselves out of the lethargy of our petty, bourgeois existence.' With that, George laughed out loud—he shouldn't be taken too literally—and the interview was over.

In his analysis, writer Baker put George and Harry's ongoing success down to a few key factors: 'their constant awareness of, and desire for, change and diversification in their craft' was one factor; 'their mastery of melody and commercial pop structure' was another. 'A healthy fear of stagnation and lack of interest is perhaps their greatest motivation,' Baker wrote.

Justifiably, he rated them as highly as great pop tunesmiths such as The Beatles' Lennon and McCartney, and legendary Brill Building duos Goffin and King, Bacharach and David, and Mann and Weil. 'It has been said that Vanda and Young are the last of the great songwriting teams of the 60s.'

★

The Angels returned to Alberts in 1976 to work on a new single, 'No Lies'. Since the release of their debut single, 'Am I Ever Gonna See Your Face Again', the band had relocated to Sydney from Adelaide. They now resided in a dump known as Cockroach Mansion—but at least it was closer to Alberts.

George and Harry took a keen interest in the band, often checking out their Sydney gigs to gauge the audience's reaction to specific songs.

George played the drums on this new recording; something about the drumming of Charlie King wasn't quite right. As John Brewster recalled, 'The song was pretty naff but the drum track was fantastic.'

A fraternity, of sorts, developed between the Youngs and The Angels. The band had met with Angus backstage at Sydney venue The Bondi Lifesaver, just prior to AC/DC's departure for the UK, and Angus mentioned that they were leaving some of their gear behind.

'Do you want to buy anything?'

As Rick Brewster told Angels biographer Bob Yates, 'We had no money, but we sold our old gear and somehow found the rest . . . funny how we always scraped together money for equipment and instruments.'

Angels' drummer King drove a Mini; he lived in fear of it being stolen.

'Why don't you park it in my garage?' George suggested.

Sometimes when King collected his car from George's place in Ryde, George would invite him in for a barbecue and a few drinks. King developed a strong relationship with the Young family's couch.

As for 'No Lies', George and Harry decided that it wouldn't work as a single. They sat down with Neeson and Rick Brewster and said they'd need to hire a session drummer for the album they planned on recording next. They also came to the conclusion that they'd need to fire King and hire a new drummer. Graeme 'Buzz' Bidstrup was hired, as was a new bassist, the son of rural South Australian publicans, who had the same name, Chris Bailey, as the singer of The Saints—and the classic Angels line-up was in place.

★

During his Australian *Rolling Stone* interview, George let it slip that he and Harry hadn't written together for 'about twelve months' but clearly they were ready to get back to work, because their next project would reintroduce them as recording artists, rather than background players. And yet George almost threw away the song that returned him and Harry to the charts.

Herm Kovac from the Ted Mulry Gang was developing an interest in recording and would sometimes linger in the control room at Alberts while George and Harry were working with AC/DC. He'd fire questions at George—how does this work? What does this do? What are you doing there? Kovac was pesky, but George admired his ambition.

''Erman,' George said one day, 'Borrow the eight-track if you like. Harry and I aren't using it. But just so you know, only six of the tracks work.'

George invited Kovac over to his house to collect the eight-track. When he arrived, George's wife, Sandra, greeted him and then headed into the kitchen to make some tea, while George showed Kovac the machine, a sizeable piece of equipment. George also handed him a red box containing some tapes.

'You can use these to record on,' George told him.

Duly chuffed, Kovac went home and set up the recorder. George was right; only six tracks worked, but that was two more than he had on the four-track he'd been messing around with. And it belonged to George Young, so Kovac had massive bragging rights. When Kovac settled in and played one of the tapes that George had given him, he was in for a huge shock.

Kovac started by pushing up the fader on track one. 'I heard the familiar George and Harry drum loop loping along,' he recalled. 'With fader two up I could hear George's unmistakable bass playing. Track three was a heavily compressed piano—and pushing up fader four I heard George's distinctive Dylan-esque rap, years ahead of when rap would become a genre. Pushing up faders five and six I heard Harry's voice come in with George's, both singing something about St Peter. It sounded amazing.'

Kovac felt like an archaeologist who'd just made a great discovery. There was no way he could record over this.

He quickly called George at the studio. 'Mate, I don't think I should wipe this tape.'

'Why?' a distracted George asked. 'It's just an old tape; wipe it.'

'But there's something really good on it,' insisted Kovac.

'Nah, use it,' George said.

Kovac's friendship with Malcolm Young had taught him a bit about the Young temperament. So instead of repeating himself, he tried a different tack.

'Okay, suit yourself,' he said, but rather than end the call, he left his last comment hanging in the ether for a moment. As he'd predicted, George suddenly grew curious.

'What's the song like?' he asked.

Kovac explained that it had a drum loop, bass and piano, as well as one of George's spoken vocals.

'Oh and it's got a great chorus about St Peter.'

The line went quiet for a moment before George spoke again.

"Erman, could you not erase it? And could you bring it into Alberts on Monday?'

Two days later, back at Alberts, George transferred the sketch of what would become 'Hey, St. Peter' over to a 24-track machine, and he and Harry began building the song. It took a couple of months, but what they created was more than a great pop song: it was truly innovative.

George had been tinkering with the song for some time before Kovac rescued it. The original demo, simply called 'St. Peter', dated back to the time of The Easybeats. Ted Albert particularly liked the song and had been asking George and Harry to record it, but they didn't think it suited any of their singers. It definitely wasn't a song for John Paul Young (although he did sing it 40 years later, when he took the Vanda and Young songbook on the road). It didn't fit his style, or his range, and there was a lengthy instrumental passage, some-thing rarely heard on a pop single. George also knew that pop singers didn't enjoy standing about on stage with little to do while the band indulged themselves for a few minutes.

George, with some prompting from Ted Albert, decided that he and Harry should have a shot at recording it them-selves, using his own vocal. But his attempt to sing the lyrics didn't work out so well; nor did Harry's. George described the results as 'toe curling'.

'We either had to bin the song,' said George, 'or try some-thing radical.'

George opted to try speaking the lyric, almost in a talking-blues style, hence the 'Dylan-esque rap' Kovac had heard on the tape. (Harry sang the chorus.)

'As he was singing, I slammed on the compressors and his voice went like a telephone voice,' Harry Vanda told John Tait. 'It sounded far more interesting.'

This was a genuine breakthrough—not just for the song but, as it would prove, for mainstream pop. Blondie's crossover smash 'Rapture', which featured a rap from Debbie Harry, was a good four years away. The Beastie Boys, who fused rap to rock, didn't make their first record until 1983. 'Walk this Way', the trailblazing collaboration between rappers Run DMC and rockers Aerosmith, didn't surface until 1986. Yet George Young latched onto the genre-bending idea in 1976. He was way ahead of the game.

George had been tinkering with this idea for several years. At least one song written with Harry during his UK binge, 'Can't Wait for September', a hit for the Australian band Pyramid in late 1970, featured a spoken-word passage from nineteen-year-old vocalist Erl Dalby (who later became a world-renowned martial arts instructor).

Not everyone was a fan of George's voice. *Village Voice* critic Robert Christgau wrote of the album that George's singing 'makes [actor] Rex Harrison sound like Mario Lanza'. Still, it was perfect for the track.

Another new twist was George and Harry's use of keyboards on 'Hey, St. Peter', particularly the Omni synthesizer, rather than the guitars for which they were renowned. 'It gave us a hell of a lot more scope to be spooky,' Harry told John Tait. He said the Omni created 'curtains of sound', which suited 'Hey St. Peter' perfectly.

The lyric was inspired by a conversation that George had with an African-American doorman at a New York hotel back in the time of the 1967 Easybeats/Gene Pitney tour.

'Oh well, man,' the doorman had casually said, when their conversation turned to the big issues of life and death, 'when my time comes, I am going to say to St Peter, "You can't send me to hell, because I've done my time in hell in New York."'

It was simply too good not to use, so George incorporated it into the song.

The pair agreed to cut a film clip for the song, scraping together a budget of $900. It captured the whimsical nature of the project, which George summed up as 'all a bit of fun, really. We don't want it to appear that we're chasing hits for ourselves.'

George unleashed his inner comic during the clip. At one point, he pulled off a fair impression of younger brother Angus; he even wore his little brother's cap. And despite the frequent mention of New York in the lyrics, he and Harry hammed it up against a backdrop of Sydney streets, wandering the lower end of Macquarie Street, and the Circular Quay east walkway around the Sydney Harbour Bridge. In other parts of the clip, Harry shook maracas (until one turned to dust) and sawed away on a violin and then a cello, while George chain-smoked as he banged on the keys of a piano. He then joined Harry on the mic, working his way through the chorus while wearing an Aussie cork hat. Harry opted for military garb. It seemed as though they'd raided a costume store.

It was silly, a goof, and it provided a humorous counterpoint to a lyric that had a dark heart, espousing the evil of the Big Apple, George stating: 'I've done my time in hell.' 'Hey, St. Peter' would have been perfect for MTV, but the concept of a station playing music clips 24/7 was still a few years away. *Countdown*, however, would give the clip generous exposure.

Simply by appearing in the clip, even in various costumes, George and Harry were dropping their mask of anonymity and going public. There'd be no more Eddie Avanas for the pair. The Flash and the Pan name came courtesy of Harry. When he and George decided to take a crack at 'St. Peter', he said: 'Why not? It'll only be a flash in the pan, anyway.'

Harry couldn't have been more wrong. Released in November 1976, 'Hey, St. Peter' reached number 5 in the Australian charts and charted for a remarkable 34 weeks. 'St. Peter' went on to chart highly in Belgium, the Netherlands and various other European countries. It also reached number 76 in the US when it was released there in 1977, despite an unnecessary edit of the lengthy middle section, the heart of the song.

George and Harry may have created a pop hit of their own, but George was adamant that Flash and the Pan wouldn't get in the way of his main priority: the studio. 'Even if it goes number one,' he said, 'it doesn't mean there will be necessarily more.' There was no talk of forming a proper band and touring, or any promotion beyond the film clip—and if they decided to make an album, they agreed it would be called *First and Last*. But it wasn't the end of Flash and the Pan, not by a long way.

★

This surprise hit didn't distract George from his many roles with AC/DC. He flew to the UK in August 1976 to be with the band when they were slated to play the hugely influential Reading Festival. There were many parallels between AC/DC's early months in the UK and those of George and

The Easybeats ten years earlier. The band was sardined together in a share house (in AC/DC's case, in suburban Bayswater), and had found it hard to gain a footing in the UK market—a planned tour with the band Back Street Crawler was cancelled when that band's guitarist, Paul Kossoff, died from an overdose. ('That cunt Kossoff fucked up our first tour,' a clearly devastated Bon Scott told the press.)

But AC/DC gained a foothold thanks to a weekly residency at taste-making London venue the Marquee, where they broke attendance records. The Who, David Bowie, Yes and Pink Floyd had all served residencies at the Marquee, so AC/DC was in great company. AC/DC had been personally invited to play at Reading by Jack Barrie, who ran both the event and the Marquee.

George wasn't the only 'insider' to make the trip. Manager Michael Browning was there, with his well-connected sister, Coral, who worked in the UK music industry and had helped link the band with Atlantic Records. Also in the entourage was their London booking agent, Richard Griffiths, a proper middle-class Brit whose family lived on an estate that the band visited en route for sandwiches and a game of croquet. (Griffiths would find his pot of gold managing boy band One Direction.) Harry, too, flew out for the gig.

It was a large-scale 'coming out', of sorts, for AC/DC, who needed a big push for their underperforming UK album *High Voltage*, which combined songs from their first two Vanda/Young–produced albums.

But the Reading gig was a disaster.

Playing mid-afternoon didn't suit a band best seen at the business end of the night, ideally after many drinks. The big crowd appeared more interested in getting high or getting some sun (or both) than checking out the Aussie upstarts on stage. AC/DC thrived on energy, but there was none in the air at Reading. There was also an unfortunate hassle before their set when one of their biggest UK supporters, DJ John Peel, was denied access to the stage, which further tarnished what should have been AC/DC's big day out.

When the band and entourage returned to their base in London, it was George who spoke first, and loudest. Arses needed to be kicked.

'You,' he snapped at bassist Evans. 'Why were you looking so surly on stage? What the fuck was that all about?'

Evans replied that he was frustrated by the crowd.

'You were pissed off?' roared George. 'Well, it fookin' showed, too. Who do you think you are, anyway?'

When Angus left to hide away in his room, George followed in his wake, shouting all the way. It wasn't over yet. Malcolm headed upstairs, with the intention of calming things down, but instead a full-on brawl broke out, the three Youngs rolling around on the floor, throwing punches, screaming blue murder. When Evans attempted to break up the fight by pulling George away, he, too, was dragged into the melee.

'There's a lesson to be learned here,' Evans wrote. 'Never try to break up a fight between brothers, especially when there's three of them.'

Finally, some sort of order was restored, but George had made it very clear to everyone in the band: fucking up wasn't part of the AC/DC master plan.

12

'It's the Stop That Rocks'

'Keep going! Keep going!'

George was in the control room at Alberts, screaming through the glass at his brother, Angus, who was in the midst of another blistering guitar solo.

But there was a problem. It seemed that the studio was on fire. Or at least Angus's amplifier was about to burst into flames, because it was belching smoke and sparks. Yet George insisted that Angus keep playing; who cared about a fire when he was in the middle of a great take?

Angus did as instructed and powered on to the end of the song, which was called, fittingly, 'Let There Be Rock'. Just as he wrung the last screaming note out of his guitar, his amplifier duly packed it in.

As George explained, 'There was no way we were going to stop a shit-hot performance for a technical reason like amps blowing up.'

Gear was expendable; not so great guitar solos.

AC/DC had returned to Australia in late 1976 to cut this new record, their fourth with George and Harry, and to tour.

The band's coffers had been depleted significantly during their eight months overseas; they needed a big cash injection. The album would be recorded in and around a tour.

When asked what they'd like to call their Oz tour, the band cheekily agreed on 'The Little Cunts Have Done It'. The promoter went with 'A Giant Dose of Rock and Roll' instead.

George, who along with Harry had recently been crowned the year's Best Australian Songwriter at the Australian Music Awards, spoke with his brothers before the album sessions began in earnest in January 1977. Whereas in the past it had been George who called the shots in the studio, he now had more respect for Malcolm and Angus as musicians (even if he still thought of them as kids) and wanted to sound them out.

'What kind of record do you want to make?' George asked.

'It would be great if we could just make a lot of guitar riffs,' Angus replied, 'because we're fired up after doing all this touring.'

To make the atmosphere in Studio 1 more like that of one of their live shows, George ensured that the studio was well stocked with beer and Jack Daniels at all times—and chocolate milk for the teetotalling Angus. Ashtrays, as always, overflowed: the Youngs smoked like chimneys.

'We used to come in from the gigs,' Malcolm said some years later, looking back on the making of the *Let There Be Rock* album, 'and we'd all get in and have a party and rip it up, get the fast tracks—stuff like "Whole Lotta Rosie" and "Let There Be Rock"—done right so it was the same loose feeling like we were on stage still. The studio was just like an extension of the gig.'

George did share one key bit of wisdom with Malcolm during the recording, which stuck with him for years afterwards. They were discussing Malcolm's rhythm guitar playing when George told him, 'It's the stop that rocks.' It was all about the gaps between the notes; that's where the rock-and-roll voodoo lurked.

★

Typically, George and Harry juggled hard-rock business with AC/DC with more commercial concerns. Coming off three Top 10 hits ('Yesterday's Hero', 'The Love Game' and 'I Hate the Music'), they needed to keep the John Paul Young juggernaut rolling.

Young hosted *Countdown* on 23 January 1977, sharing the set with tartan-clad Scottish popsters the Bay City Rollers, big balladeers Air Supply and *Happy Days* clones the Silver Studs. There was a cross to London to catch up with Sherbet, who'd broken into the UK Top 10 with their song 'Howzat' a few months before. (Their success riled AC/DC; how dare another Aussie act steal their thunder?) The Ted Mulry Gang also appeared, in their film clip for 'Jamaican Rum', their last single for Alberts.

During a sit-down at the end of the episode with regular host Molly Meldrum, Young defended the songs that he chose to record, something Meldrum had questioned in the press.

Meldrum was actually annoyed at George and Harry. They hadn't appeared live on *Countdown* to promote 'Hey St. Peter'; instead, they let the film clip do the work for them. Their attitude, understandably, was simple: why bother?

They had no intention of becoming a live act. Their invisibility bothered Meldrum.

In conversation with Young, Meldrum referred to George and Harry in a way that made them seem more like dictators than hitmakers. The conversation turned to 'Hey, St. Peter'. 'Vanda and Young . . . are your record producers,' said Meldrum, 'who write your songs, but who really won't go out and promote that single ['Hey, St. Peter']. So why didn't they give it to you?'

Young admitted that he'd heard 'St. Peter'—'an excellent song', he said—some eighteen months before, but that 'it didn't suit me, I don't think'.

'Will Vanda and Young write your next single?' asked Meldrum.

Young explained that he'd co-written six songs with Warren 'Pig' Morgan, his keyboardist—and Alberts studio regular—and that George and Harry had a few of their own to consider. 'We'll pick the best three, and then [release] the best one.'

Not surprisingly, it was a Vanda/Young song that made the cut. 'I Wanna Do It With You' was a less-than-subtle come-on for JPY's female fans and was released in February 1977. It was yet another of those madly catchy, mid-tempo pop/rock songs that George and Harry seemed able to dash off in their sleep, and Young sang it with his now trademark blend of energy and affability. It peaked at number 7 on the national chart. In mid-March, it briefly shared the Top 10 with 'Hey, St. Peter'—not a bad double act for George and Harry.

Young and Morgan did contribute more songs to his next album, called *Green*, which was released in May. Five of their co-writes made it onto the record; George and Harry co-wrote four. The album, however, barely scraped into the Top 20. It seemed that JPY was a singles act, after all.

★

Back at Alberts, the new AC/DC album was coming together at a steady clip. Live shows may have been the band's cash cow, but their next long player was critical. They hadn't yet cracked the UK market, and their label Atlantic was unsure whether to even release their music in the US—the *Dirty Deeds* album had been rejected. There'd been whispers of dropping them from the label. There'd also been criticism from the record company about the production of their records; they thought the band should try working with new producers, something that irked George in particular. He was as much a part of AC/DC as any of its members. How dare the Yanks suggest that he be replaced?

'I'm sure that George and Harry were less than pleased at having their production criticised', bassist Mark Evans wrote in his book, *Dirty Deeds*. 'When we returned to the studio [to make *Let There Be Rock*], the prevailing attitude was simple: "Fuck 'em. Let's see them knock this one back."'

Malcolm and Angus had accumulated a handy stockpile of riffs, crafted in various backstage areas and hotel rooms in the UK and Australia, which provided George with a rich bounty of material to work with. George and Harry's approach to recording was organic: once the central riff started to come together, Evans and drummer Rudd would join in, and if it felt right, George would direct his engineer, 24-year-old Mark Opitz, a Brisbane native who'd once jammed with legendary guitarist J.J. Cale *and* worked on the ABC kids' show *Mr Squiggle*, to start rolling the tape. Simple.

'The studio drill,' wrote Evans, 'was really an extension of the band live: cut the crap and get on with it.'

The results were there on the finished album: the title track and 'Whole Lotta Rosie'—Bon Scott's lusty ode to an oversized fan—would become AC/DC staples, songs they'd never stop playing. Other standouts, such as 'Dog Eat Dog' and 'Hell Ain't a Bad Place to Be' ('a real teeth-rattler', said Evans) became fan favourites.

With the album in the can, and George and Harry knee-deep in its mixing, the band returned to the road, ending the Giant Dose roadshow in mid-February 1977 in Perth. Frustrated by a tour that had been dogged by controversy, the band trashed their gear at the end of their set as they tore into 'Dog Eat Dog'. It would be the final Australian show that Bon Scott ever played with AC/DC.

★

George, meanwhile, was about to experience a flashback. Glenn A. Baker, who'd written the comprehensive *Rolling Stone* article on George in 1976, knew there was a bounty of unreleased Easybeats material, and asked for access to the Alberts archives. The year before, he'd pieced together a collection entitled *The Vanda & Young Story Volume 1*, which featured the various acts who'd recorded George and Harry's songs: John Paul Young, William Shakespeare, John Farnham (who'd covered their 'One Minute Every Hour' and 'Things To Do'), Stevie Wright and Ted Mulry were included. But it received a low-key release on the budget label Drum.

Baker had plans to do something else that would serve as a reminder of the key role that The Easybeats had played in the growth of Australian music. With George and Harry's recent success and acclaim, it wasn't a bad time to revisit their musical past.

The finished work, *The Shame Just Drained* (subtitled *The Vanda & Young Collection Vol 1*), was an impressive collection. The sweep of its fifteen tracks was broad, from the band's initial sessions with Ted Albert in early 1965, to their first stab at recording in the UK some eighteen months later ('Baby I'm A Comin'') and beyond. Six of the tracks were sung by George. Much of it was from the band's aborted second UK LP, the so-called lost album.

In his various post-mortems on The Easybeats, George frequently disputed some of the group's stylistic shifts, but the collection made it clear how comprehensively The Easybeats had evolved in a short time. The gulf between the raw rock of 'Little Queenie' and the expansive sprawl of 'The Shame Just Drained' was immense. The album was released by Alberts in October 1977. (A 25-track version was released in 1992.)

In his sleeve notes, Baker claimed, with some justification, 'Had all the material been released in the sequence (and quantity) it was created, then The Easybeats' impact might have been far more notable and we might today be comparing their albums alongside [The Beatles'] *Rubber Soul*, [The Rolling Stones'] *Aftermath* and other rock milestones.'

George and Harry agreed to speak with Lee Simon, the host of TV's *Nightmoves*, to discuss the record and the band's legacy, although George's thoughts seemed more focused on an upcoming holiday, a much-needed break from the studio (where they were filmed, of course). George, wearing an AC/DC T-shirt and chain-smoking, admitted that he had some good memories of the band. 'It was quite exciting, being young kids, as we were.'

So why, Simon asked, hadn't many of these songs been released before?

'We didn't think a lot of it was good enough. There were contractual problems,' George replied a tad dismissively. As to why the group ended, well, that was simple. 'The band had run its course,' George said.

While not a chart hit, *The Shame Just Drained* got people talking again about The Easybeats, and George even accepted, while talking with Simon, that he had no objection to a one-off concert: 'Who knows?' But it would be another nine years before George would seriously consider a reunion.

★

Acting on another tip from his brothers, George decided to check out a new band named Rose Tattoo. In his wildest dreams, George couldn't have imagined an act that was further removed from the *Countdown*-ready artists he'd helped become stars.

The band's lead singer, Greg Anderson, was a pint-sized, chrome-domed, heavily inked ball of fury. He'd wanted to become a singer ever since seeing Johnny O'Keefe in action. His nickname, Angry Ant—soon shortened to Angry—came about from a bar fight in Melbourne, his hometown.

The others in the band, among them bassist Ian Rilen and guitarist Pete Wells, looked as though they were on parole, or moonlighting from a biker gang. (Rilen had actually taught himself to play while in prison, so it was more than some tough-guy pose.) They were mean hombres, covered in tattoos and hard as nails, who peddled a style of raw, rocking boogie that was perfect for Aussie beer barns.

But given their mad, bad and dangerous look, they were a tough sell to record companies and the broader public. If looks could kill, Rose Tattoo were mass murderers.

As Jane Albert wrote in her history of the Alberts' empire, *House of Hits*, Ted Albert's decision to sign the band in 1977 'was a bold move—no other label would touch this gang of angry, tattooed mates'.

George, too, sensed that there was more to the band than inked skin and aggro, as Anderson recalled. 'George and Harry . . . could see past all the other stuff and see that we were a talented band.'

The first song they previewed for George was 'Bad Boy for Love'.

'You should hear the original,' Anderson laughed. 'They heard the song within the song. They were able to polish the turd.' George and Harry stripped the original down and rebuilt it into a furious rock-and-roll anthem.

As unlikely as it seemed, there was a link between Rose Tattoo and the other acts that George produced: the need for melody, for hooks. George and Harry would sit with Anderson at the studio piano—while the rest of the band 'were sleeping it off in the corner', according to Anderson— and work on his vocals. He needed to do more than shout and snarl.

It wasn't an easy adjustment, as Anderson admitted. 'Dear, sweet Harry and George, sitting there so patiently teaching me how to sing in a nice voice and sound melodic.'

Unlike The Angels, Rose Tattoo had found their target from the get-go: 'Bad Boy for Love' was a Top 20 hit upon its release in November 1977. George and Harry would go on to produce the band's first five albums.

★

George had already shortened The Angels' name; he now had a style tip for them when they reconvened at Alberts.

'Have you guys ever thought about getting your hair cut?' he asked.

George explained that it would give them an edge; every other rock band in the country had hair down to their backsides, so why not try a different look?

Angel John Brewster told George they'd do it—nobody in the band said no to George—but only when they had some cash. Their self-titled debut album, released in September and produced by George and Harry, had stalled.

'I'll sort that out for you,' said George, who soon returned with $25 and directions to a nearby barber.

Months later, when the band received their first royalty cheque, they noticed that the $25 had been deducted. It hadn't been a loan but an advance—the only time that would happen in their time with Alberts.

Around the same time, various members of the band approached George and Harry, asking if it was possible to get a more substantial advance than $25. George spoke with Ted Albert, who heard him out but made it clear that advances weren't company policy. Even the boys in AC/DC, who were making some waves on the charts and working at a furious pace, were each surviving on a modest weekly wage.

'Look,' George explained, as he broke the bad news, 'we've all been through the hard times—one day you'll thank him.'

The situation must have reminded him of his hard financial slog with The Easybeats.

A month after the release of The Angels' debut album, the band's manager, John Woodruff, delivered more bad news: the band was $10,000 in debt. There were serious discussions about chucking it in, perhaps returning to Adelaide. While in transit to their next gig, a tyre blew on their van. What else could go wrong? The Brewster brothers and Doc Neeson went to the nearest bank and, remarkably, were issued bankcards over the counter, each with a $250 credit limit. The Angels would survive a little longer.

*

George's working relationship with John Paul Young hit a rare flat spot with the song 'Where the Action Is', released in October 1977, which fizzled out at the very un-JPY chart position of number 33, despite the usual flogging on *Countdown*. But at the same time, word had been trickling back from Germany that the Young track 'Standing in the Rain', which had been released in Europe in February, had become a club hit—it had also broke into the Top 10 in Austria, Germany and the Netherlands. The continent was a whole new market for Young, one that George and Alberts were keen to exploit. But they needed to release the right song over there, something danceable, with a solid groove and a great melody—a natural extension of 'Standing in the Rain'.

'I'd been to Germany and heard the music,' said JPY. 'It was all electronic mania, all clicks and buzzes. So George and Harry gave it the treatment.'

The song given 'the treatment' didn't yet have a name. George again experimented with tape loops to get the perfect rhythm track, using the same loop that had worked so well for 'Standing in the Rain'. It was a task he clearly enjoyed—Alberts' staff would sometimes come into the studio and find George and Harry buried under strips of magnetic recording tape, meticulously piecing together a new loop, lost in their work.

While the track was coming together—it took all of a day—George turned to Harry.

'Get the book out,' he said, 'and read me out some names.' (George kept a notebook in which he wrote song title ideas.)

'What about "Love is in the Air"?' asked Harry.

'We'll work with that,' George replied.

Young was brought in to cut his vocal with the song pretty much done.

'No, no, no,' George told him when he first tried the vocal. Young was over-singing. 'What we want is a very casual attitude. Just imagine you're walking down the street and you see a friend and you say, "Love is in the air".'

'[George] schooled me in how to sing it,' Young told ABC Radio in 2017. 'It's actually a very casual delivery of the vocal.'

George and Harry worked overtime on 'Love is in the Air'; they knew it was an important song. The mixing took three weeks. They ended up with something like 50 different takes and were so immersed in the song that they couldn't tell which version was best. George did what he always did when he was unsure about something—he took the box of tapes to Ted Albert and asked for his opinion.

Within an hour Albert returned.

'This is the one,' he indicated, and it became the finished version of the song.

Alberts' Fifa Riccobono and her assistant, O'linda—who would go on to marry Malcolm Young—pitched the song to Sydney radio station 2SM along with the gift of 100 helium balloons, each emblazoned with the song's title. The DJ on air at the time took a quick slug of helium and announced, in a voice that gave a whole new meaning to JPY's nickname, Squeak: 'This is John Paul Young with his new single "Love is in the Air".'

When it was released in Australia in mid-May 1978, there was some life left in the disco movement—the Bee Gees' 'Stayin' Alive' and 'Night Fever' were still embedded in the Oz charts. 'Love is in the Air' proved to be the perfect song for the time. As JPY admitted, 'It's probably the only song I heard and instantly thought, "This has got legs, this might make it," which is testament to George and Harry.'

Though more groove-pop than out-and-out disco, 'Love is in the Air' had pure middle-of-the-road, main-stream appeal. It was also very similar in style and sound to 'Standing in the Rain', which was still in the national Top 5 when 'Love is in the Air' began its ascendancy, ending up at number 3. George and Harry might have stood accused of recycling, but they knew a good rhythm track when they created one.

But that was just the beginning of the song's extraordinary run. It would prove to be the biggest single that George ever co-wrote, outstripping even 'Friday on My Mind'. Over the next few months, 'Love is in the Air' breached the Top 10 in Austria, Belgium, the Netherlands, Germany, Ireland, Switzerland, Sweden, New Zealand and Norway. In South Africa, where JPY was already a star, it reached number 2; 'Love' was his fifth Top 10 single in the country. When he and his band The All Stars toured South Africa in 1978, they played more than 30 shows. Young took to the fishing in Cape Town like the natural-born angler that he was.

In the UK, 'Love' peaked at number 5, and JPY put in an appearance on *Top of the Pops* on 4 May, his long hair permed to perfection, appearing alongside unlikely musical bedfellows such as The Stranglers, Donna Summer and The Boomtown Rats. In the US, the song reached number 7 during October 1978, charting for more than three months. It was a red-hot time for Australians, the peak of the so-called 'Gumnut Mafia' invasion of the US. Young's Aussie peers Little River Band were just two spots ahead of 'Love is in the Air' when it peaked on the *Billboard* chart, with their sugary-sweet 'Reminiscing', while Olivia Newton-John was at number 10 with 'Hopelessly Devoted to You', a song written by Aussie expat John Farrar, formerly of Moonee Ponds, Victoria. Farrar had also penned Newton-John's Grammy-nominated 'Have You Never Been Mellow', released back in 1975.

The US success of 'Love is in the Air' was sweet revenge for George, who'd tried and failed to crack the States with The Easybeats back in his card-playing days with Gene Pitney. 'Love is in the Air' proved to be the Vanda/Young song that kept on giving—numerous foreign-language versions of the song would be cut, along with something like 300 cover versions in English.

But before its second life began in earnest, George and Harry decided that it was time to raise the *Titanic*—in song, at least.

13

George Raises the *Titanic*

George, in conversation with a *Billboard* reporter, explained the key differences between Flash and the Pan and the other acts with which he and Harry worked. 'We can take pretty much any approach we like. Anything goes,' he said. '[With] all the artists we've always produced, we've tried to stick to the plot . . . but Flash and the Pan was a completely different situation . . . We could piss around as much as we liked.'

In short, the pressure was off with Flash and the Pan. If the song didn't work, so be it—they could always get back to working with one of the many Alberts acts that they were nurturing. The simple fact that eighteen months passed between their first and second singles made it clear that this wasn't a typical commercial project—John Paul Young had released something like eight singles in that same stretch of time.

The notion of pissing around as much as they liked was all over their belated second release in 1978. As he'd proved with 'Love is in the Air' and 'Standing in the Rain', George was a smart recycler. This time, for inspiration, he simply reached for an Easybeats song, in this case the late-sixties obscurity 'The Shame Just Drained'. The riff was perfect for the new song that they were building in the studio, which they called 'Down Among the Dead Men'. Its lyrics and foreboding musical mood were a nod to the story of the *Titanic*.

Their video budget was upped to a massive $1200—a full $300 more than they'd had for 'Hey, St. Peter'. Again, simply having fun was the overriding theme of the video: George's various roles included that of a cigar-puffing card player, a pirate (complete with eye patch) and jobbing musician—he blew a trumpet as a member of the doomed cruise ship's house band. Alongside him was Harry, wrestling with a double bass, its price tag still attached. All this was intercut with archival footage of the *Titanic* on its maiden, and final, voyage.

The song was released in July 1978 and even outdid 'Hey, St. Peter', hitting a chart peak of number 4 at a time when not a lot of local acts were cracking the Top 10, despite no shortage of quality songs from acts such as The Sports ('When You Walk in the Room'), Jon English ('Words are Not Enough') and Ted Mulry Gang ('Heart of Stone'). JPY's ubiquitous 'Love is in the Air', meanwhile, was by then thirteen weeks into its lengthy run on the charts. International acts such as Gerry Rafferty ('Baker Street'), Kate Bush ('Wuthering Heights') and Patti Smith ('Because the Night') might have been riding high at the time, but it was fair to say that 'Dead Men' was the most eccentric and original cut in the Top 40. Warren Zevon may have been singing about the 'werewolves of London', and The Rolling Stones might have gone disco with 'Miss You', but who would have ever thought of writing a pop song about death ship the *Titanic*—and making it palatable for the masses?

Retitled as 'And the Band Played On', the song was a moderate hit in the UK, peaking just outside the Top 50 in late September.

Ted Albert remained George (and Harry's) biggest cheerleader, and with the success of 'Dead Men' he encouraged the pair to record an LP under the Flash and the Pan tag (the album that George and Harry had threatened to title *First and Last*). It would be the first album that George had written and recorded since the Marcus Hook Roll Band.

He and Harry duly pulled together a set of originals, with one exception—a song titled 'California', whose composer was simply credited as 'M. James', a mysterious figure who George tried to pass off as a 'lesser known German songwriter'. A little digging revealed that 'California' was the handiwork of George's brother, Alex, a man fond of a good pseudonym. It was the first time that the siblings had worked together since George's 'four-year binge' in London. The studio band included Alberts' regulars Ray Arnott on drums, piano player Warren Morgan and Lez Karski on bass.

The self-titled *Flash and the Pan* album, released in the last weeks of 1978, was all over the shop in the best possible way, swinging from the jungle rhythms of opener 'The African Shuffle' to the familiar hits ('St. Peter' and 'Dead Men') and the mellow 'Walking in the Rain', another Vanda/Young gem that would later benefit from a second life.

George was displaying a real flair for delivering sinister, world-weary narratives, from the 'silicone man with a lump on his face' of 'Man in the Middle' to brother Alex's 'California', a sombre few moments of pop noir with an apocalyptic theme: 'He pushed the wrong button,' George declared, 'and soon there'll be no place called California.'

George narrated, rather than sang, much of the record, casting a jaundiced eye over the modern world and coming up with some worrying conclusions. He was, as he admitted in 'Walking in the Rain,' 'whistling in the darkness'.

The soundscapes were deep with waves of synthesisers and loops, and unexpected twists and turns. It was hard to believe that Flash and the Pan's protagonists were former Easybeats, a band that had helped write the 1960s guitar pop/rock songbook. Yet the liner notes of the US edition made a point of citing their past, stating: '[The album] retains the fun of The Easybeats while maintaining its future musical vision.' But guitar hooks were rare; George and Harry were more interested in slinky grooves, subtle beats and generally 'pissing around'.

The album wasn't a big hit, reaching number 80 on the US charts, but it was generally well received. It went platinum in Canada; Canadian daily *The Globe and Mail* anointed it 'one of the strangest but ultimately finest records to surface in the seventies . . . the closest thing to a masterpiece we're likely to get this year'. Elsewhere, it became a cult classic. Writing in US magazine *Creem*, Jon Pareles said that the album was 'incorrigibly catchy', which, while confusing, *felt* like a compliment. US *Rolling Stone*'s David Fricke gave George and Harry credit for never underestimating 'the simple joy of a good hummable tune'. *Stereo Review* in the US rated the record 'a minor pop masterpiece'. In his coverage of the record, Australian writer Glenn A. Baker spotted George and Harry's latest musical influences, citing 'Chinese orchestras and ethnic Arabic, Turkish and Russian music [as well as] science fiction and classic cinema'.

Comparisons were many and varied, from Godley & Creme (former 10cc members with a similar flair for wit and melody) to bohemian poet Tom Waits, the eccentric electro-pop of Brian Eno and *Low*-era David Bowie. All were equally valid. Don Walker, then a budding songwriter with Cold Chisel, was a huge fan of Flash and the Pan. 'I always thought George Young, together with Harry Vanda,' Walker told *The New Daily* in 2017, 'was the finest songwriter that ever came out of Australia.'

Most reviewers had some reservations about the record, but New York's Robert Christgau, writing in *The Village Voice*, was the only critic who dismissed the album completely. As usual, he had trouble locating his funny bone, giving the album a lowly C+ rating. He wrote off 'V&Y's ruminations on socio-political realities' as 'worthy of a second-rate caper movie'.

★

Typically, George was multitasking; his focus wasn't strictly on Flash and the Pan. He and Harry had produced the debut self-titled album from Rose Tattoo, which reached a respectable number 40 in the local charts after its November 1978 release. Angry Anderson was blown away by the 'big fat Australian guitar sound' that George and Harry had been able to produce. That sound would have its admirers, too, well beyond the local pub-rock circuit. Among them was AC/DC convert Axl Rose, who, with his band Guns N' Roses, would cover Rose Tattoo's 'Nice Boys' and openly declare his allegiance to 'the Tatts'. (Rose was also a big fan of The Angels.)

Jeff Apter

Writing in *The Encyclopedia of Australian Rock and Pop*, Ian McFarlane declared *Rose Tattoo* to be 'one of *the* classic Australian rock albums'. The tracks 'Bad Boy for Love' and 'Rock 'n' Roll Outlaw' established a new blueprint for Oz rock—'heavy on the aggression, heavy on the atmosphere', in McFarlane's words.

In early 1978, George and Harry had produced AC/DC's first great album, titled *Powerage*—George had played bass during rehearsals for the record, while waiting for new bassist Cliff Williams to get his Australian working papers. The album was explosive in a number of ways; during its recording, a bomb went off at the nearby Hilton Hotel, killing three people. The explosion was so loud that staffers at Alberts raced out into the street, wondering what the hell had happened.

Malcolm Young believed that *Powerage* was the best representation of the band yet captured on tape, while Rolling Stone Keith Richards was among its many admirers. 'You can hear it,' said the one Stone who truly recognised the right rocking stuff. 'It has the spirit.'

The single 'Rock 'n' Roll Damnation', which echoed The Easybeats at their rockiest, had become the band's first chart hit in the UK, reaching number 24 in the northern winter of 1978–79. But the band's parent label, Atlantic, wasn't satisfied. AC/DC still hadn't cracked the elusive US market, despite heavy touring there in 1977 and 1978.

It was time for a sit-down to discuss the band's future beyond George and Harry.

Atlantic's rep was American Michael Klenfner, a man with an impressive moustache and a genuine love of AC/DC, who flew to Sydney in December 1978 to meet with George,

214

Harry, Ted Albert and manager Michael Browning. Klenfner made his intentions clear—the band needed to work with a new producer, ideally someone who could give their music the added sheen required to gain US radio airplay.

The only person on Klenfner's list was Eddie Kramer. Born in South Africa to parents who were active apartheid opponents, Kramer ended up in London, where he began working at Pye Studios. His résumé included studio time with Jimi Hendrix, Led Zeppelin and Easybeats buddies the Small Faces. He'd recently engineered the double LP *Frampton Comes Alive!*, the highest-selling album globally of 1976, which shifted over fourteen million copies. The man had serious form.

George remained impressively stoic throughout the conversation. He and Harry were willing to place the band's progress ahead of their own careers, even if they didn't share Atlantic's vision. As manager Michael Browning wrote in his memoir, *Dog Eat Dog*, 'George and Harry, to their absolute credit, put the band's future first . . . The band, of course, would have preferred me to tell Atlantic to back off, and then get back to work with George and Harry.'

Malcolm Young was gutted when it was agreed to move on to a new producer—George was family, for one thing; he and Harry were as much a part of the band as its members. Beyond producing their records, George often sat in with the band—he'd play bass with them at a secret Sydney gig soon after, in February 1979—and stood up for them when required, such as the time he'd shirtfronted Lou Reed's sound guys back in 1974. In an interview with Sydney radio station 2JJ, Malcolm made it pretty clear that he felt the band's hand had been forced and that George had been disrespected by Atlantic. And respect mattered a great deal to the Youngs.

George didn't dispute the decision, at least publicly. After all, it wasn't the first time a band had sacked him as producer—the Ted Mulry Gang had that dubious distinction—and the situation echoed the flashpoint in 1966 when United Artists insisted that The Easybeats move on from Ted Albert and produce records with Shel Talmy, a shift that had led to the classic 'Friday on My Mind'. He'd been here before; he understood the commercial needs of a big record label.

George left his brothers with a key piece of advice: 'Go ahead. Don't let them mess with what you are. Always remember you're a rock-and-roll band.'

The drama didn't end with George and Harry's firing. After preliminary sessions with Eddie Kramer in Miami in February, Malcolm called Browning with a demand that would prove hugely beneficial for AC/DC: 'Get us the fuck out of this situation, Browning. It just isn't working.'

At the same time, George, while he was no longer AC/DC's producer, was hardly out of the loop. Malcolm had been discreetly sending him demos of the new songs being recorded with Kramer, seeking his input.

Browning duly connected the band with hot-shot producer on the rise Robert 'Mutt' Lange, which led to their breakthrough album *Highway to Hell*. But Browning would suffer fallout from George's sacking—Malcolm fired him in May 1979. Browning believed that this may have been payback for the events that led to George's dismissal.

'I was on the AC/DC shitlist,' he wrote. 'No doubt about it.'

★

Not long after, George was tangled up in another drama involving an Alberts band that he'd produced and mentored. The Angels' LP *Face to Face*, released in mid-August 1978, was a big hit, parking itself in the Oz charts for a remarkable 79 weeks and selling 70,000 copies. 'Take a Long Line', the first song to truly capture their raw rocking ethos, was on high rotation at 2SM and would chart for more than six months. The album was co-produced by the band and engineer Mark Opitz, a protégé of George's at Alberts.

Opitz swore blind that George's focus in the studio was so intense that he 'could look at an ashtray and make it move'. Opitz also had George to thank for his $100-a-week salary; he'd insisted that Ted Albert pay Opitz properly. As he settled into life at Alberts, Opitz would sometimes wind George up. George hated bands like Steely Dan and The Doobie Brothers, which he dismissed as 'bullshit'. One day, Opitz snuck into the car park and cheekily slapped a Doobie Brothers sticker onto the bumper of George's new Lancia, which escaped his notice for months.

Opitz also grew to understand the relationship between George and Harry. 'George was the heart of the operation, Harry was the soul. George was machine-like; Harry added the icing on top.'

When The Angels raised concerns about no longer working with Vanda and Young as producers, George told them, simply: 'We're just down the hall.' He was still their mentor; that wasn't in doubt. He provided the band with a drum loop that would form the basis of their song 'No Exit', the title track of their next album, released in June 1979, which was equally successful.

The Angels toured Australia with Easybeats admirer David Bowie in late 1978. The Thin White Duke watched them during the tour's first soundcheck and announced: 'I really like your music.' Then he invited the band to dinner. Bowie even checked out the band when they played the Bondi Lifesaver during a night off from the tour, mingling with the sweaty punters at the front of the stage.

On the back of such admiration, manager John Woodruff was itching to get The Angels an overseas deal, and felt that Alberts' focus was more on establishing AC/DC offshore. He flew to the US to sniff out a deal by himself. Buoyed by news of their rabid Australian following, Epic in the US offered them a contract, but The Angels still had one album to make for Alberts.

Woodruff, armed with American attorney Owen Sloane, a music business veteran, met with Ted Albert back in Sydney and told him that The Angels were breaking their contract. A shocked Albert—he'd funded Woodruff's trip to the US—called George and Harry into the meeting. Woodruff later admitted that he didn't handle the situation very well.

'I went in on the attack,' he remembered. '[George and Harry] were offended and felt snubbed, as I probably would have been.'

Ted Albert rescinded the band's contract and never spoke with Woodruff again. George, meanwhile, phoned John Brewster, who was in Melbourne.

'I hear you're leaving us,' George said. He was genuinely upset by their decision; he'd given wise counsel to the band in much the same way he'd advised AC/DC. George let Brewster know Ted Albert's feelings: he felt that Woodruff was directly responsible for the schism. Brewster had tears in his eyes when he hung up the phone. He knew that George had been the band's mentor and felt his loss deeply.

As Angels' biographer Bob Yates wrote, 'The mentoring by George Young couldn't be underestimated. His quality control and high standards. The suggestions he made'— Neeson ditching the bass, taking over as lead singer and developing the 'Doc' persona, toughening the group's sound and sharpening their image—'fundamentally changed the band . . . George and Harry were high-quality advisers.'

First he'd been shelved as AC/DC's producer, and now he was estranged from The Angels. It had been a rough stretch for George.

★

George wasn't the only one doing it tough. Since the release of 1975's *Black Eyed Bruiser*, Stevie Wright had been in freefall. He'd been through deep-sleep therapy at Chelmsford; he'd also endured methadone treatment to try to wean himself off heroin. He'd overdosed in 1976 and nearly died, resulting in a stint in rehab centre Odyssey House. At one point, he took a job in the warehouse at Alberts, a humiliating comedown for the former Easybeat and voice behind the classic 'Evie'.

Stevie Wright, however, still had one great performance left in him. Appropriately enough, it was during 2SM's Concert of the Decade, staged on the Sydney Opera House steps on 4 November 1979. With something like 100,000 people looking on from the forecourt, and plenty more watching from boats on the harbour, Wright took the stage in the afternoon, hell-bent on reminding the huge audience that he could still out-sing and out-perform newer stars such as Skyhooks, Jon English and Sherbet.

Backed by some of the musicians whom George and Harry utilised at Alberts, among them pianist Warren Morgan, Wright threw himself, physically and emotionally, into all three phases of 'Evie'.

The years, and his travails, had taken their toll: Little Stevie's eyes had lost their sparkle, and there were deep lines etched into his face, which was hidden by a full beard. But as Wright showed from the moment he began singing, he still had the moves, throwing karate shapes and big kicks in the direction of guitarist Kevin Borich as he hurled himself about the cramped stage. When the band segued into the solemn second phase of 'Evie', the crowd grew noticeably quiet. Wright, his eyes closed tightly, had them under his spell. Even the stage crew and hangers-on stopped to watch and listen.

Wright shed his sports coat for the big finale, prowling the stage like a dog off the leash, roaring the song's harrowing coda as if he was reading from his diary. As the song gained more and more momentum and then thundered to a close, Wright channelled his Easybeats days, pulling off a knee drop that was worthy of James Brown, totally in sync with the band. It was spellbinding—a legendary Australian song being performed by one of its most legendary vocalists.

Tellingly, when the song was resurrected by supergroup The Wrights at the fundraising WaveAid concert in 2005, it took three vocalists—Bernard Fanning, Phil Jamieson and Nic Cester—to replicate Wright's feat.

*

AC/DC, meanwhile, had actually prospered from their very reluctant shift from George and Harry to South African–born producer Mutt Lange. Within weeks of Wright's triumphant return at the Opera House, their new album, *Highway to Hell*, reached a US chart high of number 17. Finally, the band was poised to take over the world, which had always been George and Malcolm's game plan. They'd even gotten themselves into the black for the first time, after five years of living hand to mouth.

But with the band in London and about to start work on a new album that was bound to make them superstars, tragedy struck. On the morning of 19 February 1980, Bon Scott's lifeless body was found in the back of a car in the suburb of East Dulwich. After a big night out, he'd fallen asleep, choked on his own vomit and died. Scott was 33.

The Alberts and AC/DC inner circle was stunned, as was the broader music community. Scott had lived fast— as Billy Thorpe put it, he loved 'a smoke, a drink and a stink'—but he had seemed bulletproof, indestructible. He'd become a big brother figure to Malcolm and Angus, and both were shocked beyond belief when the news broke.

Back in Oz, George and Harry paid their respects to the man who'd helped transform AC/DC into a 'real band', as George had said at the time of Scott's hiring, in the form of a simply worded tribute that ran in the pages of *RAM*. It read: 'A great singer, a great lyricist, a great friend, one of a kind. We'll miss you.'

Few knew how close George and Bon had grown. George would frequently host Scott and the other band members—'AC/DC's inner sanctum'—for barbecues when they were in town. 'There was a real bond,' said Scott's son, Benjamin.

★

George had spread his creative wings far and wide, from the mainstream pop of John Paul Young and William Shakespeare to the boozy rock of AC/DC and The Angels, and the genre-jumping Flash and the Pan, but he and Harry had worked with few female acts in Australia. That was now about to change.

Sharing the stage with Stevie Wright at the Sydney Opera House in 1979 were Wright's two backing vocalists, known collectively as Cheetah, who would soon become George and Harry's latest protégés.

A sister act, Cheetah comprised the London-born, Melbourne-raised Hammond sisters, both beautiful women—raven-haired Chrissie and blonde Lyndsay. Chrissie, just like Stevie Wright and John Paul Young, had paid her dues in *Jesus Christ Superstar*, playing the role of Mary Magdalene. Chrissie then joined the original line-up of Air Supply with Graham Russell and Russell Hitchcock, fellow *Superstar* alumni. The striking sisters had undertaken a variety of studio work, backing up Jon English and Mark Holden; they'd also sung on George and Harry's pet project, Flash and the Pan.

By the time of the Concert of the Decade, they were in transition from EMI, where they'd released two singles, to Alberts, with whom they signed in April 1980. George and Harry pushed them in a harder rock direction than their earlier releases, resulting in 'Spend the Night', a heavy-breathing, innuendo-laden power ballad that wouldn't have been wasted on Meatloaf and Jim Steinman. Released in September 1980, it reached the Top 30.

'They were tough rockers but decent guys,' Chrissie said of George and Harry. 'They saw us as strong women, rather than being the tits, the teeth and the glam; they produced us as rockers, which was very innate. Our lyrics, our stage performance was very much in the male vernacular.'

With 'Spend the Night' entrenched in the local charts, and with overseas interest in the duo building, the Hammond/Vanda/Young team set to work on a full-length album, which was released in 1981.

*

George may have kept his profile low, divvying up his time between the family home in Ryde and the Alberts studio, but he did find time to wander out into the spotlight, if he deemed a cause worthy enough.

In the latter part of the seventies, George and Harry, along with other local identities such as Sydney DJ Bob Rogers, became part of a group lobbying the Australian Broadcasting Tribunal to grant an FM radio licence for Sydney. According to a report in *The Sydney Morning Herald* on 10 June 1979, a consortium that included George, Harry, Rogers and savvy businessman and former DJ Rod Muir had been 'lobbying for FM to be opened up for two and a half years'. Who could be a better spokesman for FM radio than the man currently supplying radio with hit after hit?

The week before the article ran, the federal government announced that they were going to grant two FM licences for stations to operate in Sydney.

'This is a major breakthrough,' said Muir—and in more ways than one, as it turned out.

With Muir at the helm, and with Chris Gilbey, formerly the A&R man at Alberts, among the shareholders, 2MMM began broadcasting on 2 August 1980. (Muir's father-in-law, Sir Ian Turbott, was the chairman of the board.) 'Because your ears have brains' was the station's tagline. Their playlist specialised in meat-and-potatoes rock, which worked brilliantly for George, Harry and Alberts; bands such as AC/DC, The Angels and Rose Tattoo quickly became 2MMM staples. By the mid-1980s, it had become one of the city's highest-rating stations, with George and Harry providing a good chunk of their playlist.

14

Walking in the Rain Redux

George had initially agreed with Harry that Flash and the Pan would live up to its moniker, but it now seemed too good a creative outlet to cast aside. He and Harry got to work on their second long-player, which surfaced in 1980, in and around working with Cheetah and Rose Tattoo. It was titled *Lights in the Night*, a less-than-subtle nod to an interest that George had developed in all things extraterrestrial.

The past decade had been a lively time for UFO sightings all over the world, which may well have sparked George's curiosity. In 1974, the Yugoslavian Air Force claimed to have chased UFOs during training flights, while the occupants of space station Skylab 3 snapped blurry images of a mysterious unknown object. In Victoria, a pilot named Frederick Valentich informed air traffic control that he had just seen a UFO; seconds later, he disappeared from the radar, and the planet, forever. Hollywood was all over the phenomenon, too, with blockbusters such as Steven Spielberg's *Close Encounters of the Third Kind*, released in 1977, cashing in to the tune of US$300 million worldwide. No wonder George was seeing lights in the night.

The LP's cover, designed by American Janet Perr, who'd go on to work with everyone from rapper Vanilla Ice to jazz great Miles Davis, was a comic book–style illustration of a boy watching a dice fly through the air. On the three visible sides of the dice were the American Sign Language signs for the letters 'U', 'F' and 'O'. On the back cover of the album, visible through some scratches, was the artwork for Flash and the Pan's first album.

George loved a visual pun as much as he enjoyed messing around with musical styles. He also paid some dues, dedicating the album to the recently deceased Bon Scott.

The first single and video was 'Media Man', another of George's less-than-subtle slams. This time his target was ego-ridden journalists ('Easy on the eyesight/. . . Mass appealing tonsils'), this being the era of outspoken US identities such as Phil Donahue and Larry King, and, closer to home, the bronzed and hirsute talking heads on shows such as *60 Minutes*. The people asking the questions were now the stars; somehow, the tables had been turned. The witty, rapid-fire video clip would have been great fodder for MTV, but George and Harry were still just ahead of the curve, because the music network wouldn't begin broadcasting until August 1981.

The title track, 'Lights in the Night', was a standout of the duo's career, not just the album. While an orchestra-sized wave of keyboards and synthesizers lingered in the background, George was in the most sombre of mindsets. He was alone, 'Talking to the ceiling/Feeling kinda ill', casting glances into the night sky, wondering exactly what is out there, hoping it's better than life on Earth. 'If the bottle doesn't get me,' George pondered, 'the thinking will.' It was a hypnotic mood piece. In the words of one long-time fan, commenting on YouTube, 'I still feel the existential nausea.'

The album, while not a big hit, gained widespread release throughout 1980, in the US and Canada, the UK and much of Europe, and Japan, too. In Australia, it performed moderately on its June release, peaking at a lowly number 78 and charting for only seven weeks. But it was another influential record, a precursor of albums such as *Boomtown* by Americans David & David, a commercial and critical hit in 1986. The two Davids, like George, had a jaundiced view of modern life and the Me Generation.

*

George may not have been setting the charts on fire, but his brothers had hit a hot streak. Released just months after *Lights in the Night*, AC/DC's 'comeback' record, *Back in Black*, featured new vocalist Brian Johnson, and was also dedicated to the memory of Bon Scott, whose spirit lived on in many of its tracks (so much so that fans speculated that he'd either written some lyrics before he died or was somehow raised from the dead during the recordings). The album's stark black cover, meanwhile, would later be memorialised in the razor-sharp satire *This is Spinal Tap*.

The band had taken George's 'Keep it Simple, Stupid' ethos to its zenith with second-time producer Mutt Lange, resulting in a series of concise, powerful and anthemic window-rattlers, best heard in 'Rock and Roll Ain't Noise Pollution', 'Hells Bells', the hit single 'You Shook Me All Night Long' and the title track. There was hardly a superfluous note in the entire record. Three months after its US release, the album had sold more than a million copies in America alone and would go on to sell a staggering 30-million-plus copies, making it the most successful hard-rock LP of all time.

They may have long been ousted as producers by the time of *Back in Black*, but for George and Harry there was an upside: the big spike in sales of AC/DC's back catalogue, the records they'd produced. (Producers claim 'points' on albums they produce, which generate royalties.) By the time *Back in Black* hit platinum status, *Let There Be Rock* had sold 500,000 copies.

When AC/DC returned to Australia in mid-February 1981, for their first tour since 1977, Atlantic had a change of heart about releasing *Dirty Deeds Done Dirt Cheap*, the 1976 LP George and Harry had produced that until now the label had deemed unfit for release. The band agreed to its belated release, but they insisted that a sticker was to be displayed on the record specifying that 'Young/Young/Scott/Evans/Rudd' had cut the record, so it wouldn't be confused with the current line-up. They also demanded that it be discounted by 10 per cent.

George wasn't surprised by the news. He knew how the industry operated, especially when there was a dollar to be made. 'It was business, pure and simple,' George said of the label's move to finally release the LP. 'Suddenly the album interested them.' By the end of 1981, *Dirty Deeds* had sold two million copies globally, another handy windfall for George.

After AC/DC's rapturously received Sydney Showground show on 23 February 1981, George, Harry, their partners and children were among a small crowd that gathered in a marquee set aside for VIPs. Ted Albert marked the occasion by handing out various gold and platinum records to the band—for the records produced by George and Harry. George had mentored his brothers well, all the way to the bank.

What George didn't realise, though, was that his days as AC/DC's producer weren't quite over yet.

★

In much the same way that George and Harry were adept at writing songs in many styles, covers of their songs also came in many shapes and forms. Probably the oddest, and at the same time one of the most highly regarded, emerged in October 1981. Androgynous 33-year-old Jamaican-American supermodel Grace Jones, a woman with legs like goalposts, razor-sharp cheekbones and a monotone voice that made talking clocks sound expressive—as well as a thing for undressing on stage—covered 'Walking in the Rain', from the first Flash and the Pan album.

Jones had a flair for bending familiar songs into odd new shapes. Her 1980 LP, *Warm Leatherette*, featured versions of Tom Petty's 'Breakdown', Roxy Music's 'Love is the Drug' and the Pretenders' 'Private Life'. Her follow-up, *Nightclubbing*, reimagined not only 'Walking in the Rain' but also Bill Withers' 'Use Me' and the title track, a David Bowie/Iggy Pop collaboration. Jones made her presence felt when she went on the promotional circuit, slapping smarmy British TV presenter Russell Harty when she felt she was being ignored. Jones was not a woman to mess with. She was fierce.

Jeff Apter

'Walking in the Rain' was one of an impressive six singles lifted from the album, which fused jazz, pop, groove and New Wave with Jones's not-really-singing vocal style, which echoed George's method on the Flash and the Pan records (only chillier). The album was a hit, charting highly in the UK, US, Australia (where it went platinum) and parts of Europe—especially Germany, a country always receptive to George's music, where it sold 250,000 copies. British weekly *NME* crowned it their album of the year, while the magazine's rival, *Melody Maker*, ranked it among their top 10 of 1981. 'Walking in the Rain', which opened the album and was lifted as a single, charted in Australia, Germany and New Zealand.

When Harry Vanda heard Jones's version, he was impressed. 'It almost sounds as if the song could have been written for her,' he said.

There was no avoiding the irony: George and Harry had spent four tough years in London, striving to write hits for anyone and everyone—and now high-profile acts like Jones were seeking out their songs. All George and Harry had to do was count the royalties.

*

When he wasn't saving Flash and the Pan songs from being erased, Ted Mulry Gang drummer Herm Kovac tried to give other bands a leg-up. One of them was named Girls Talk, whose singer, an eager Northern Beaches local named Mark Kitchen, would ride his motorbike to Kovac's house to play him his band's demos. The band had formed in 1976; its core members were singer Kitchen, bassist Ian Hulme, guitarist Brad Carr and Lindsay Tebbutt on drums.

In 1982, Kovac handed George a demo of the band—it was given 'cheekily', in Kovac's words, because it wasn't the 'done' thing to simply hand George a demo.

Nonetheless, George called Kitchen after hearing the demo.

'I really like what you're getting together,' he said. 'Come into the office and we'll have a talk about it.'

'I couldn't believe it when he did,' admitted Kovac.

George convinced Ted Albert to offer the band a deal. Kitchen was a huge Easybeats fan; he was overawed by the experience of simply stepping inside the Alberts studio when he and the band set to work.

'The ethos of the place, the history of it all. It was incredible to be part of that, just amazing,' he said on radio in 2018.

George suggested a change of name to the Choirboys; Kitchen changed his name to Mark Gable; and production duties were given to Jim Manzie, of the band Ol' 55. George and Harry sat in as executive producers, an overseeing role. The Choirboys' self-titled debut album dropped in July 1983; three singles were released, and the band snagged support spots with the likes of The Angels and Rose Tattoo.

The album wasn't a big hit, but the band's star seemed to be on the rise when they were asked to join Cold Chisel's Last Stand tour towards the end of 1983. But Gable ruptured his vocal cords, rendering him unable to sing, and the band entered a tough two-year hiatus waiting for him to recover.

Although he couldn't sing, Gable still managed to say all the wrong things at Alberts, alienating the label and George in the process. Gable later said, 'I tried my damnedest to destroy it by upsetting the hierarchy', and the band shifted to Mushroom Records for what would be significant success a few years further down the line, with the song 'Run to Paradise'. It became an Oz rock standard—one of the few that George didn't produce.

★

The Alberts studio in King Street in Sydney, George and Harry's sonic playground, now truly deserved its reputation as 'the house of hits'. Terrific songs had come to life in the room courtesy of AC/DC, John Paul Young, The Angels, Rose Tattoo, Cheetah and many others. Its walls were adorned with the scrawls of the many acts that had come to think of it as their recording home, their base. George and Harry had now spent several years filling the studio's ashtrays and emptying out the fridge while crafting an amazing array of songs destined for the Great Australian Songbook. It had been the hottest streak of their creative life, and complete validation of Ted Albert's belief in them.

The Alberts studio, while grimy, possessed an indefinable magic, which George and Harry tapped into deeply. 'There's a certain kind of school of sound that comes out of there,' said Doc Neeson. 'Those guys just have a real feel for rock and roll and when you work with them it rubs off.'

But progress, especially in an ever-expanding city like Sydney, had little time for history or magic. In the early 1980s, Sydney City Council had begun enforcing new fire ordinances on buildings in the city. Boomerang House, due to its vintage, would require extensive updates to continue operating. Radio station 2UW, which Alberts owned, had already been forced to shift base from the city to Neutral Bay, on the northern side of the harbour, because of these ordinances. At the same time, developers had been snapping up CBD properties in advance of what was to become the Centrepoint shopping complex. When Alberts were offered $12 million for the building, they accepted and set to work relocating some of the staff, and the studio, to new digs. Their new address was also in Neutral Bay, at 9 Rangers Road.

George and Harry, along with long-term Alberts staffers such as Fifa Riccobono, drank a last toast to the studio on the day of its closure in 1984, but some in the party were so deeply connected to the site that they were reluctant to leave. George had to talk Riccobono into stepping inside the lift and leaving King Street for good.

'I couldn't look back,' she told Jane Albert. 'It was tragic.'

It was the end of an amazing era in Australian music.

There were also changes afoot with the Alberts' roster of artists. John Paul Young's deal with Alberts lapsed in the early 1980s. His final record with George and Harry was a 1979 album named *Heaven Sent*, which lacked a big single and barely made the Top 100.

'I could never really put my finger on what the hell I wanted to do next,' Young admitted. 'And George and Harry couldn't help me—because if I didn't know then they didn't know.'

Young had two children to care for and, lacking the ambition of George and Harry—by his own admission— he would soon shift careers, from international pop star to Newcastle radio DJ.

AC/DC were now global superstars who rarely spent time in Australia. While George still offered his counsel, the band was now represented by powerful managers and business teams in the US. The Angels, meanwhile, had left for Epic, having alienated Alberts in much the same way as the Choirboys. Cheetah had relocated to the UK in 1982 soon after the release of their one album, *Rock & Roll Women*, recorded with George and Harry. (Mark Evans, the former AC/DC bassist, sometimes played in their backing band.) Ironically, Cheetah were a big hit at the 1982 Reading Festival, the event where AC/DC had bombed in 1976; they played before a crowd of 120,000, shrugging off repeated cries of 'Get your tits out' and slaying the crowd with their powerhouse voices. But the duo disbanded in 1984, preferring life as session musicians.

It truly was a time of flux for many of the artists that George had helped nurture, so perhaps it wasn't such a bad time to start again in a new studio. Multiple studios, in fact: Ted Albert had commissioned three new ones at the Neutral Bay site, one specifically for recording jingles and ads, which had become a handy money-spinner for the company.

★

When the Neutral Bay site opened for business, George and Harry settled into an upstairs studio, which they used for writing and production. But, as Harry would tell Jane Albert, the heady period that he and George had enjoyed throughout much of the 1970s was over. 'It almost became semi-retirement,' he admitted. That was fair enough, too, given that he and George hadn't stopped moving since The Easybeats had exploded back in 1965. Harry had a family to tend to; George's daughter, Yvette, was growing up. Things were changing.

George was also struggling to find motivation. Since returning from London in 1973, he and Harry had produced huge albums and even bigger hits, building numerous careers in the process and establishing themselves as among the world's finest production teams. What more did the pair have to prove?

George wasn't seen as frequently in Neutral Bay as he had been back in the city. One Alberts staffer who'd been with the company for several years admitted to never having met George at all. George typically entered the building, checked in with Harry and his nephew, Sam Horsburgh Jr, who worked at the studio, and went about his business. He became less of a presence at Alberts.

Yet George still held hopes of resurrecting Stevie Wright's career. When he and Harry had decided to craft another Flash and the Pan album in 1982, which was titled *Headlines*, they came up with an intriguing idea: make Wright the focal point of a group that would tour in support of the album. (The Hammond sisters contributed to the record, as did Sherbet drummer Alan Sandow.)

A press release that accompanied the album drove the point home. It declared: '*Headlines* brings into focus the always-present contribution of vocalist Stevie Wright who now assumes a more prominent position in the group.'

This served a couple of purposes—not only would it help set Wright's career back in motion, but it would also relieve George of any need to promote the LP, which was hardly his favourite pursuit. Wright and the band could do all the promo. Wright didn't actually contribute to the album but he did ham it up, hidden behind a face mask, in a video for the song 'Where Were You'. Released in August 1982, *Headlines* became a hit in parts of Europe, especially Scandinavia, and the song 'Waiting for a Train' made the Top 10 in the UK. It was George's first hit in the UK as a performer since 'Friday on My Mind'. The album was well reviewed by Australian *Rolling Stone*, which said that the record 'paint[ed] a rather schizoid picture of contemporary society'.

But the plan to get Wright involved came to nothing; he had shot himself in the foot so often that he probably didn't have any toes left, and again his drug habit took precedence over his music. He was arrested in early 1984 and charged with breaking and entering; this came only days after he had checked out of the West Mount drug rehab centre west of Sydney. Then he was arrested for heroin possession. Addiction, clearly, still had its claws deep in Wright.

George probably had the sense that his long, complicated relationship with the brilliant yet troubled Wright, which dated all the way back to the Villawood hostel, was over.

Yet in 1986, remarkably, that turned out not to be the case.

15

An Uneasy Return

Ever since their split in 1969, there'd been repeated whispers of an Easybeats reunion, ranging from that bizarre press release of 1972 announcing that 'the Easy Beats [*sic*]' had signed to an American label, to the three Sydney shows where George and Harry had helped out Stevie Wright in 1974. There had also been rumours of a re-formation in 1979, but those went nowhere, and again in 1983, when Stevie Wright told a writer from *Juke* magazine that it was only a change of venue that scuppered a possible re-formation.

'We had our lawyers working out the deal,' he said, 'but at the last minute they tried to change the venue and we just said, "Forget it."' (There's no record of the others agreeing, in principle, to this reunion.)

The Easybeats were never much of a gang. When they split, with the exception of Harry and George, they went their own ways: Wright into a personal minefield, dotted with occasional creative bursts; bassist Diamonde to the New South Wales north coast, psychiatric care and God; drummer Fleet to a solid family life in Perth and a building business. They weren't the types to swap Christmas cards or stay in touch, although George tried his best to help Wright, either as a musician or regular working stiff: in fact, it was George who recommended that Stevie take the job at Alberts.

Whenever there was a suggestion that they get the band back together, George would insist that he and Harry were too busy in the studio, which wasn't far from the truth. But by the mid-1980s, after one more Flash and the Pan album, titled *Early Morning Wake Up Call*, they drifted into a sort of semi-retirement, so George's standard excuse no longer rang true.

Interest in the band had never completely faded. There were Glenn A. Baker's reissues—*The Shame Just Drained* had sold several thousand copies locally and in the US—along with a steady stream of cover versions, mostly by high-profile Oz bands. Melbourne rockers The Sports pulled off a typically high-energy cover of 'Wedding Ring' in September 1979, making it to the fringes of the national Top 40. Singer Stephen Cummings admitted to being 'obsessed' by The Easybeats. The Divinyls, fronted by Chrissy Amphlett, who was so dynamic that she could have been mistaken for a female Stevie Wright, cut the Young/Wright track 'I'll Make You Happy' as the B-side of their 1983 hit single 'Science Fiction' (on the insistence of their producer, former Vanda/Young protégé Mark Opitz). Amphlett's cousin was Little Pattie, 1960s Oz pop starlet, a contemporary of The Easybeats. The Three O'Clock, an LA band of the 'Paisley Underground' scene, covered 'Sorry' in 1983. There'd also been re-releases of the first two Easybeats albums on vinyl, in 1982.

Other covers would be hits by the end of the decade, including The Saints' take on 'The Music Goes Round My Head', which George and Harry helped to produce. Mark Opitz produced 'Good Times' for INXS and Jimmy Barnes, which impressed George so much that he burst drunkenly into a recording session to tell Opitz that it was 'the best cover version of any of our songs . . . it's fucking great'. And every time Stevie Wright was mentioned in the press—usually in the court reports—he was billed as 'the former Easybeat'. David Bowie and Meatloaf had name-checked either the band or Harry and George during recent interviews. Clearly, The Easybeats still had a high recognition factor.

In September 1986, David Fricke, a writer for US *Rolling Stone*, tracked down Stevie Wright. Fricke was a major Easybeats fan. 'The Easybeats combined the songwriting depth of The Beatles with the raw surge of The Rolling Stones,' he wrote in the article titled 'The Easybeats: Where are they now?'

During the interview, Wright opened up about his post-Easybeats life and his fall from grace. 'The effect was devastating,' Wright admitted, 'going from the stardom of The Easybeats to sweeping floors. But I had to survive.'

Wright said that he'd finally kicked heroin in late 1985, after a long period in which 'my career was going up at the same rate as my addiction. One blew out the other in the end.' Wright had recently played a solo show at the pub where he now lived. The show was well received, and he felt the time was right for The Easybeats to return to the spotlight.

'A lot of groups are doing our material in their stage acts,' he told Fricke. 'So why not do it with the original sound and the original singer?'

Wright also spoke about the possibility in a conversation with his friend, George Crotty, back in 1981, snippets of which were later published in *Australian Record Collector* magazine. 'Nobody's said no,' Wright admitted, when asked whether the band might re-form. 'To actually put it together would take quite a lot of finance. You have to find a promoter who can back up the enthusiasm with the money.'

In 1986, the money did appear, in a most peculiar way.

Terry Hunter was the publican at the hotel where Wright lived and had taken on the challenging role of managing the career of his famous resident. This basically meant supplying Wright with all the Southern Comfort he could drink. Hunter was bold enough to propose a meeting with George and Harry, on Stevie's behalf, to see if they'd consider re-forming the band for a tour. Wright was broke, his career was in the gutter; an Easybeats reunion could provide one more shot at glory—and some real money.

The pair met with Hunter, and seemed reasonably receptive to the idea, but made two demands: they wanted a guarantee of $250,000 to finance the tour, and they needed to know that the others—not only Wright, but Dick Diamonde and Snowy Fleet—were up to the task. In no way did George want to commit himself to a humiliating exercise in nostalgia. And he did have his doubts, as did Harry, who told a reporter that 'the only thing Snowy has banged in 17 years' was a hammer and nail. He shared George's concern about how the re-formed band might look. There was a legacy to maintain. 'We [have] no intention of making asses of ourselves.'

There were also concerns about Wright's addiction. As he'd admitted to his friend, George Crotty, 'I found stopping [heroin] wasn't too difficult, but it was staying clean that was hard.' Falling off the wagon mid-tour would be a disaster and a very public humiliation.

Hunter immediately set about sourcing funds, and found there were plenty of backers willing to invest—most simply wanted, with good reason, to see Australia's greatest rock-and-roll band in action one more time. The tour, if it happened, would be promoted by Michael Chugg, who'd attempted to manage Stevie Wright a few years before. An associate of Chugg's, a major Easybeats acolyte named Mark Longobardi, who was also a promoter, agreed to help.

With the money in place, and Diamonde and Fleet willing to get involved, George and Harry agreed to a secret rehearsal in Sydney during June 1986. Fleet arrived with the snare drum he'd used on 'Friday on My Mind', quite the talisman. Diamonde turned up sporting an earring and goatee. He looked vastly different to the 1960s version of Dick Diamonde. They'd all aged in different ways—Snowy was getting a bit thin on top, Stevie's weathered face reflected his tough recent times, while George and Harry looked like what they were: successful men shifting gears into a comfortable middle age. Harry now lived in posh Rose Bay, by the harbour.

Sam Horsburgh Jr, George's nephew, was the only non-band member permitted inside the rehearsal room at Damien Gerrard studios. He was there to record the rehearsal, which George and Harry could later listen to and determine if the band still had something to offer. Their decision to get involved hinged on it.

George and Harry arrived at about 1 p.m., and the mood was friendly; the five exchanged greetings and war stories for an hour, before plugging in. The first song they attempted was 'She's So Fine', and as soon as a note was struck, it was as though the past seventeen years just faded away. 'We just rolled into it as if nothing had happened. The chemistry was still there,' Harry reported afterwards. When the six men emerged from the rehearsal room at around 4 p.m., George typically kept a poker face.

But on listening to the rehearsal tape, his doubts receded.

The news of The Easybeats reunion broke in late August, and a press conference was held on 1 September 1986 at the Sebel Townhouse in Kings Cross. In front of a backdrop of black-and-white footage of the band in the 1960s, and a soundtrack of their hits, the five Easybeats took their seats. At least one reporter noted that George and Harry didn't seem that comfortable; they looked 'as if they'd been talked into something they already regretted'.

When they posed for photographer Bob King, George, wearing a cream-coloured sports coat, was to the far right, set slightly apart from the others, nursing a cigarette. George's inscrutable expression made it impossible to determine exactly how he felt about the reunion. Perhaps he wasn't quite sure.

The overriding message from the press conference was that this was a one-off; it wasn't the start of The Easybeats Mk II. There'd been a flurry of bands re-forming of late, among them *Countdown* stars Dragon and Skyhooks, but this wasn't going to be the case with The Easybeats. There'd be shows in all the capital cities in late October and November, maybe a live album or a TV special taken from one of the gigs, but then they would be done for good. It was strictly a five-night stand.

Stevie was enthusiastic ('This will be five guys getting together for a couple of weeks of fun'), while Harry waxed not-quite nostalgic: 'I see the old photos now and I can't relate to me being there.'

George spoke guardedly. 'There's always reservations. You get the feeling some things should be left as memories.' He went on to say that the tour was a reaction to public demand, nothing more. 'There's people out there who want to see it and this is the last chance to do it. I've got a little bit of doubt but now that it's on I'll give it my best shot.'

It was typical George Young: zero spin, no bullshit.

There was also the question of what they would play. Given the vast sweep of their back catalogue, would they play songs from the many phases of the band, or maybe write some new material? Definitely not. In fact, if anything, this was their chance to get back to being the band George wished they had been in the first place: a tight rocking combo.

Harry spoke on behalf of everyone. 'We're not out to prove any musical points,' he said. 'We're just playing what we used to play then.'

Afterwards, the band posed in an attempt to replicate a press conference shot from 1967, although they decided to forgo wearing the matching suits (with ruffles) that they'd worn nineteen years before. Street clothes would do just fine.

Press coverage was enthusiastic, to a point. Sydney music writer Stuart Coupe wrote that 'Friday on My Mind' 'was one of the first records I ever owned' but wondered what the point of the tour could be. As far as George and Harry were concerned, 'They obviously don't need the money so one can only assume it's being done for the benefit of the other three members.' He was right on the money; Wright's future financial wellbeing, in particular, was one reason that George agreed to get involved. (In a separate interview,

Wright said that they were doing it for the money, because they didn't make any the first time around.)

Coupe spoke with band archivist Glenn A. Baker, who was in the tour entourage. He admitted that George was the wariest regarding the reunion. 'Up to two or three weeks ago . . . George was sincerely telling his close friends that he didn't think it would happen,' Baker said.

'Vanda and Young have been very protective about The Easybeats' legacy over the years,' he continued, 'and I don't think they're going to do anything to put it at risk.'

*

Over the next eight weeks, during rehearsals at a 'secret location', the band fine-tuned their set. There were no surprises. They would play all the hits—'She's So Fine', 'Wedding Ring', 'Sorry', 'Friday on My Mind'; throw in a few favourites, such as 'St. Louis'; and include a couple of songs from Stevie's work with George and Harry, namely 'Evie (Part 2)' and 'Hard Road'. They'd even tackle the old weepy 'In My Book', though it was unlikely that Stevie would reach for the onion skin this time around. The idea of tackling something more experimental—say, 'The Music Goes Round My Head' or 'Heaven and Hell'—was quickly dismissed. It probably wasn't even considered. A few keys were adjusted to suit Wright's 1986 voice but, apart from that, the music remained unchanged. They'd play the songs that five guys on stage could comfortably handle; there'd be no extra players, no strings, no keyboards. This was all about nostalgia—do the favourites, give the crowds a thrill, and then, certainly in George's case, put The Easybeats to bed forever.

With no new Easybeats product to flog, Alberts, who would be closely involved in the tour, pieced together an 'Easybeats medley', a three-and-a-half-minute salute to their hits. It was packaged as a single and released to coincide with the tour, but didn't chart.

The first gig of the tour was on 30 October at Festival Hall in Melbourne, the scene of much madness during the height of Easyfever. The response was no less enthusiastic as the band took the stage in 1986; they received a standing ovation. The group responded accordingly, tearing into 'I'll Make You Happy', Wright throwing himself around the stage as he'd done in the mid-1960s, while George and the others comfortably locked into a solid groove. After an hour-plus set and a barnstorming 'Friday on My Mind', they were called back for a second encore. Lacking another song to play, they simply repeated 'She's So Fine'. The response was euphoric; their former fans, who'd aged along with the band, danced in the aisles of Festival Hall as if it was 1965 all over again. There was even a surge of female fans towards the stage at the end of the show.

Harry Vanda, for one, was chuffed, stating afterwards: 'It felt as if we'd never been off the road.'

In a classic case of conflict of interest, Glenn A. Baker, who would introduce the band each night, reviewed the show for *The Age*, although there's no question his reaction was heartfelt.

'The band delivered a white hot 90-minute performance of such passion and energy that it was possible to believe a time machine had taken the audience back to 1965,' he wrote. Tellingly, a mention of George, who in Baker's words 'anchored the proceedings,' came with a mention of his now famous brothers. As teenagers, Malcolm and Angus had proudly boasted of being George's brother; now George was billed as 'the elder sibling of AC/DC's Angus and Malcolm Young', which showed how far their star had risen. Times had changed.

Riding high from their Melbourne triumph, the band, now briefly back in Sydney, agreed to be interviewed on video. They were shot in an empty rehearsal room, working their way through 'St. Louis'.

'How do you feel about being back on the stage with all the old guys?' an unseen narrator asked Stevie after the rehearsal.

'Ah, it's a magic vibe,' the singer responded.

Snowy was equally enthusiastic. 'Fantastic!' he replied. 'I've been a rock-and-roll star for about three weeks now.'

Harry spoke on both his own and George's behalf, and brought a touch of levity to the conversation. 'George and myself,' he said, 'we view it very much like a reunion thing. Like an old school class.'

George, typically, kept his feet firmly on the ground. When asked about his strongest memories of the 'glory days', he replied: 'Ahh, the hysteria, obviously.' Then, after a pause: 'The lack of money.'

Harry Vanda spoke with Stuart Coupe a few shows into the tour. He was surprised by the make-up of the audience. He expected the crowd to be roughly 75 per cent old fans and the rest curious onlookers, 'younger kids coming along to see what the fuss was about. But it's the other way around.'

★

Despite its auspicious start, as the tour rolled on, George and Harry's concerns gradually turned into reality. Stevie Wright was drinking too much, and the reaction in Perth to their re-formation was so underwhelming that a proposed show at the city's Entertainment Centre was cancelled. It was a major disappointment for Snowy Fleet; there'd be no hometown gig for him. But a Canberra show was added to the itinerary, for 15 November.

There was a flare-up at Adelaide airport, en route to the show at the Apollo Entertainment Centre. Stevie Wright demanded, loudly, to be given some booze, and airport security hovered nearby, sensing a problem. Harry, the most Zen-like of men, shirtfronted Stevie, demanding that he tone it down before he did something hasty. George sat nearby, clearly fuming, pretending to read a newspaper. One of George's biggest fears—that Wright was unstable and unreliable—was coming to life right in front of him.

George celebrated his 40th birthday on 6 November, the day before their gig at the Sydney Entertainment Centre. It's highly unlikely that he would have imagined spending his birthday on stage with The Easybeats. *Again.* After all, it was George, way back in 1967, who had told a British reporter, 'I can't see us stretching it out until people call us old men.'

The Sydney show was recorded for a possible live album, which never eventuated. Stevie Wright was especially chatty throughout the gig, insisting at one point that the crowd sing 'Happy Birthday' to George. His garrulousness could have been because of the booze or the nerves; it was probably both.

'I bought [George] half a dozen roses and a card,' Wright said, as his gift was laid at George's feet by a roadie. 'There ya go!'

Wright's voice by now was shot, and he was missing a lot of notes. It seemed as though he was overplaying the genial host to compensate for his shortcomings as a singer. As they were about to begin 'Come and See Her', Wright told the full house, 'None of the boys are out to sing the nasty words because me granny's here and me aunty's here'— meaning the 'Gonorrhoea, gonorrhoea' chant that had surfaced during The Easybeats' first go-round. Then, as they launched into 'Evie (Part 2)', he instructed the crowd to 'boo us if you don't like this one'. Wright also exhorted the crowd to 'put your arms around each other and give yourselves a cuddle because you've survived this long'. It wasn't clear if he was referring to surviving the show itself or the fact that the band and much of their audience had made their way to middle age.

At the end of the night, Wright turned to George and asked: 'What song is there still to be played, mate?' Then they rocked 'Friday on My Mind', and the house lights came up. Show over.

In his review of the show for *The Sydney Morning Herald*, Bruce Elder summed up the conflict at the heart of The Easybeats reunion: was it strictly an exercise in nostalgia, and, if so, why did George and Harry, men with active creative careers, bother to get involved? What was left to prove?

'The fans came,' wrote Elder, 'hoping for nothing more than a moment, a chord, a vocal nuance which would wipe away 17 years . . . In this, they were not disappointed.

'But finally the result was little more than good journeymen hit playing . . . The Easybeats were loved as a memory. Why did they feel the need to tamper with the illusion of their own greatness?'

Friday on My Mind

Writing in *The Canberra Times*, Stuart Coupe was more succinct and even less impressed, admitting that he left after three songs. He wrote: 'As Johnny Thunders sang, "You can't put your arms around a memory—don't try".'

Shows followed in Brisbane and Canberra, and again Wright's drinking caused problems for the others. Just hours before their concert at the Brisbane Entertainment Centre, Harry grabbed Wright, who was stumbling drunk, and with the help of his wife, Robyn, rushed the singer to a doctor for vitamin shots, which enabled him to get through the show.

Not surprisingly, there was no lavish afterparty in Canberra, the final date of the tour. The band members simply shook hands and disappeared into the darkness. Stevie Wright later admitted that he went home after that last show and cried: 'I was very sad when it was over.' Harry Vanda insisted that he had no regrets, even though he acknowledged that 'it's always been a bit hard to come to grips with what the group means to a lot of people. In fact it was a bit threatening meeting those expectations.'

As for George, the end of the tour probably stirred up unpleasant memories of the last hurrah of the band in 1969, when they had each walked away with a paltry $800 for several years' hard slog (and in hefty debt to Alberts). Because of the Perth cancellation and various other mishaps, the band didn't receive the promised $250,000. George and Harry waived their share of the money that was eventually forthcoming, ensuring that Wright and Diamonde were taken care of.

And that was it; The Easybeats were finally done and dusted. George couldn't have been more relieved.

249

16

London Calling, One More Time

If George needed a change of scenery after the dramas of The Easybeats reunion, he couldn't have dreamed up a better offer than the one that came his and Harry's way in 1987: how would they like to spend a two-month working holiday in the south of France? And how did they feel about working once again with AC/DC? George and Harry had helped the band with the 1986 album *Who Made Who*, the soundtrack to Stephen King's film *Maximum Overdrive*, primarily on the insistence of Angus. AC/DC's 1985 album *Fly On the Wall* was poorly reviewed, and it dawned on Angus that some of the band's best work had been done with George and Harry. This would be the first full-length album recorded with George and Harry since 1978's *Powerage*.

'I always think we did great rock tunes when we worked with my brother,' he told *Classic Rock* magazine.

Angus went as far as to state that he preferred George and

Harry's work to that of Mutt Lange, despite what the sales sheets revealed.

'I like what we did with [George] better.'

AC/DC's fortunes had fluctuated, relatively speaking, since the breakout success of *Back in Black*. *For Those About to Rock We Salute You*, released in late 1981, had sold four million copies in the US alone—great numbers for most bands. But given that *Back in Black* had sold more than twenty million copies in the US, it was seen as a failure. Subsequent albums—1983's *Flick of the Switch* and 1985's *Fly on the Wall*, both self-produced—barely made platinum status in the US. The band's sales were in steep decline. Acts such as Bon Jovi and Guns N' Roses had stolen the band's thunder, and a good chunk of their audience.

Maybe George and Harry could recapture the spark that had made their earlier Bon Scott–era albums so vital. Malcolm admitted that the band needed inspiration. He felt that they had lost their footing: 'We needed to get the old feeling back again.' As Angus said of their decision, 'We just ignored the influence of the record company and any [outside] producers.' It was time to bring everything back in-house.

On paper, the site for the recording, which began in August 1987, couldn't have been more ideal. Miraval Studio was built inside a twelfth-century chateau in the picture-postcard-perfect Provence region, not too far from the French Riviera. Pink Floyd had recorded parts of their album *The Wall* there, while the sheer dimensions of the studio—it was 300 square metres, with a 10-metre-high ceiling—made Alberts look like a dogbox. The Miraval control room alone was larger than the entire Alberts studio.

But the reality proved to be something else altogether: the on-site residence had no air conditioning, and beds were nothing more than mattresses on the floor. Everyone's sleep was disturbed by the sounds of insects and scorpions scurrying across the floor. It was quickly decided that the troupe should stay elsewhere.

George had to confront a larger problem when he and the band got to work. His brother, Malcolm, had a serious drinking problem. Malcolm was no wowser—he loved a spliff and a drink—and until recently he had been able to guide the good ship AC/DC with the steady hand he'd maintained since 1974. But there'd been uncharacteristic dramas, including a flare-up with often wayward drummer Phil Rudd, which had led to Rudd's exile from the band. Malcolm had also clashed backstage with Mötley Crüe's Nikki Sixx and had had to be dragged away from the poodle-permed bassist, Malcolm screaming, 'I'll bite your fucking nose off.' He was no longer in control—and control had always been crucial to Malcolm, as it was to George.

George, in his usual manner, addressed the problem head on.

'If you don't get your act together,' he told Malcolm, 'I'm out of here.'

Malcolm pulled himself together sufficiently to get through the sessions, but his problems were far from over.

One upside of working again with George and Harry was that they gave Angus free rein to rock the joint. 'I'm just gonna play a bit of rock music here,' Angus declared, and proceeded to do just that—tracks such as 'Heatseeker' and 'Ruff Stuff' were the stark evidence.

Blow Up Your Video, released in January 1988, wasn't the blazing return to commercial glory that the band had intended it to be; it simply matched the returns of their previous two albums. Yet in a very positive review for US *Rolling Stone*, writer Jim Farber rated it the band's best work since *Back in Black*. 'Maybe *Blow Up Your Video* will finally convince those who have doubted the truth about AC/DC: it's the metal band that plays solid-gold rock & roll.' It did, however, kickstart a return to top form for AC/DC the live act—during the 167-date tour, they sold out London's Wembley Arena four times and consistently filled stadiums of 10,000 to 20,000 people across North America, Europe and Australia. Those venues would grow considerably larger over the next decade as demand for the band increased.

George gave a rare interview to US *Rolling Stone* on the release of the record, where the matter of Malcolm's boozing arose. George spoke about confronting Malcolm in the studio and how the Young clan handled such dramas. 'In our family, if we have a problem, we deal with it ourselves. There's no point in people telling us we gotta stop this or that.' In the end, George wasn't so sure that his strong words had changed anything: 'I don't recall it having any effect.' Yet as the band readied itself for the lengthy North American leg of the album tour, Malcolm withdrew from the band, and the world, and checked himself into rehab. Proving how clannish the Young family was, his nephew, Stevie Young, stepped in on rhythm guitar. He was the son of Stephen, the eldest brother of the Young clan, and a dead ringer for Malcolm.

★

George, meanwhile, accepted a new post with Alberts soon after finishing work with Malcolm, Angus and the band. He agreed to become the company's rep, based in London. It had been some fifteen years since he and Harry had returned from the UK, and it had been a remarkably successful run. Now it was time for a change.

His brother, Angus, had a flat in St John's Wood, and George and his family moved in. George's goal was pretty straightforward: check out what opportunities there were for Alberts to expand into the UK. He'd see if there were artists worth signing and also sniff out studios that were for sale. George had a long list of contacts from the time of his four-year binge, which he could readily tap into now.

Ted Albert employed Peter Dawkins as general manager of J. Albert & Son UK. Dawkins, an expat Kiwi, had been a drummer, even jamming with Jimi Hendrix at London club The Speakeasy. He'd also worked as both a record producer and label man with Australian Crawl, Matt Finish, Billy Thorpe, Mi-Sex and Dragon—he had a stellar CV. In London he would work directly with George, scouting both talent and studio space.

George wrote to Ted Albert in early 1989, reporting back from London. He made it clear that he thought the UK remained the centre of the rock-and-roll universe—'I still have the feeling that this place is ripe for some action,' he noted—while he still firmly believed that distance remained the biggest problem for Australian acts (an opinion that had copped some criticism back in the 1960s). 'Altho [sic] successful acts will break out from Australia,' George wrote, 'I feel it will always be too remote from the trends, fashions, etc.'

AC/DC had proved that to be true. Although Malcolm and Angus retained property in Australia, they were rarely sighted in Australia. Malcolm's neighbours in the genteel Sydney suburb of Balmain would hear the sound of an electric guitar coming from his home studio and know that Malcolm was home, but his Gretsch was rarely heard outside of Christmas time. When not on the road, their business was based in the UK and the US, the two centres of the rock-and-roll business. They recorded in the south of France or in the Bahamas.

George signed off his letter to Ted by saying that a decision to move into the UK market would depend upon two things: money and desire. 'I feel this is the crux of the matter,' George wrote in closing.

It was a much-needed change for George. He was still making music—another Flash and the Pan album, titled *Nights in France*, had been a moderate hit for him and Harry, generating a pair of Flash and the Pan favourites: 'Ayla' and 'Money Don't Lie'. Both became club anthems and Top 10 hits in Europe. George's nephew, James Young, sat in on the drums. But it was George's only other project for 1987. (In the spirit of keeping it in the family, George's nephew, Sam Horsburgh Jr, engineered Flash and the Pan's final album, 1992's *Burning Up the Night*.)

George and Harry had also recorded Mark Williams, who'd been a double threat back in his native New Zealand—a pop star and a TV personality. Williams possessed impressive dreadlocks and even more impressive dance moves. After twelve indifferent years in Australia, Williams had signed to Alberts, and his single 'Show No Mercy', produced by Vanda and Young, was a platinum-plated hit, reaching the Top 10 in Australia and New Zealand. Williams got to perform the song at the 1990 NRL grand final, before a massive live and

TV audience. Its success came as a huge relief for Williams; at the age of 36, he was at risk of disappearing into the pop wilderness. An album written and produced by George and Harry, *Mark Williams ZNZ*, was released in August 1990.

George and Harry were also dipping their toes into new territory: film. In 1988, Ted Albert and producer Tristram Miall had established the M&A Productions film company. After seeing the stage version of *Strictly Ballroom*, Albert commissioned up-and-coming Sydney filmmaker Baz Luhrmann to write and direct a film adaptation. This would be Albert's entree into the world of film. George and Harry would help, naturally, with the music.

Albert had bought a large space in Rosebery, in the southern suburbs of Sydney, with a plan to convert it into what he called a 'one-stop film, television and music complex', à la Sydney's Fox Studios. His development application was knocked back, yet his interest in film remained.

But there'd been changes behind the scenes with Ted Albert and the company.

In 1988, Albert had been approached by major label Polygram: would he consider selling up? They were interested in acquiring Alberts' publishing and/or record catalogue, which, of course, included AC/DC's music, a highly valuable commodity. Though the offer was unsolicited, it was tempting; Polygram, a Dutch company that had been in the record business since 1962, had deep pockets, and at the time was valued at more than US$5 billion. Albert also knew that because of AC/DC's runaway success, Alberts' stocks had never been higher, quite literally. He also knew that none of his siblings were interested in running the family business, so the decision was entirely his.

Albert was cautious; he made it known to Polygram, via a letter to his US lawyer, that the business wasn't for sale, 'unless they made an offer that we could not refuse'.

Still, Albert floated the idea at the next board meeting, and the board was supportive. Yet while the board's okay was crucial, he placed just as much importance on George and Harry's opinion. They were as vital to the company as board members, maybe even more so. After all, they jointly owned a large chunk of the company's catalogue, and the record-label side of the company probably wouldn't exist if they'd not returned to Sydney in 1973. When they met with Ted, both agreed that it could be the right time to sell, even though it might mean, for George, an end to his UK sojourn.

Albert also consulted with Malcolm, who had as much to lose as George—perhaps more, due to the value of AC/DC's music and publishing. Malcolm was fine with the prospect of selling, but his okay came with a caveat: he needed assurance that AC/DC would end up with the right publisher and with even better terms.

Albert wrote to George in early 1990, updating him on the possible sale. He said that the 'word is certainly out' about the offer, because other companies had expressed interest in buying Alberts. But then Albert pulled out, most likely because a Polygram executive had been boasting of the sale as if it was a done deal, and word made its way back to Ted. He was offended by the notion that an executive had been spreading the message around the local industry that he was selling up. He'd made it clear from the get-go that the idea of selling wasn't his; he'd only do it if he was made an irresistible offer.

George, for the time being at least, would stay in the UK as an Alberts employee.

★

In September 1990, upon the release of the latest AC/DC album, *The Razors Edge*, Ted Albert had a hefty pair of subwoofers installed in his car. He particularly loved the opening track, 'Thunderstruck', a latter-day AC/DC classic, which he'd crank to maximum volume as he powered along in his Mercedes—it was quite a shock to his upscale Eastern Suburbs neighbours. In a letter to Malcolm Young, Albert said he was 'blown away' by the record and promised that he'd increase the band's royalty rate, 'as a way of saying thanks for our long association and for the success that you have brought to my company'.

Soon after, Albert was given a Lifetime Achievement Award at the annual ARIAs, a richly deserved accolade.

On 10 November, Ted Albert was at a family gathering when he suffered a heart attack. The efforts of family and friends to revive him could not save his life. He was 53. Albert had rarely discussed his heart condition with anyone.

George was quickly notified and, despite his shock, managed to call Malcolm, who was in New York. George was gobsmacked; his mentor and friend of the past 25 years was gone, and much too soon. Malcolm was equally devastated.

'I don't think we've ever met anyone so genuine and that you can trust as a person,' Malcolm said of Albert. 'We owe Ted a lot.'

Calls started coming in from all around the world, from people who knew and respected Albert. The feeling among them was the same: they were stunned. Albert's US attorney, John Clark, fielded many of the calls. 'I never knew anybody in the industry in the past 30 years who did not like and respect Ted Albert,' he said.

A service was held for Albert on 20 November. George sat with Harry Vanda and Fifa Riccobono, who'd left the company in 1987 but was still very much part of the Alberts family. Harry, who'd grown particularly tight with Ted over the past few years, spoke on behalf of himself and George, directing his words to Albert as if he were still alive.

'You were our guide through many difficult times,' said Harry, 'yet because of your vision you made the many dreams we shared come true.'

George had suffered three heavy blows in a relatively short time. Five years earlier, George had lost his father, 'Pop', who had died at the age of 74. His eldest brother, Stephen, died in 1989, aged 56. Now Ted Albert was gone.

George and Harry soon sat down with Ted's brothers, Robert and Tony, and lawyer John Clark, to discuss the future. Could they keep going without Ted, the glue that had held everything together at Alberts? Ted was their friend, the man who'd been their advocate when they were The Easybeats, a lifeline during their years in London and their sounding board during their heyday. They were partners.

'Look, what has happened is a terrible, miserable thing,' Robert Albert told them, 'but we hope you'll continue with Alberts because we have every intention that the business must carry on.'

And so it was agreed. Fifa Riccobono returned to run the label, while George headed back to London to continue his work there. The company took out a five-year lease on a property in Islington, while Rose Tattoo's former manager, Robbie Williams, was hired to work with George, replacing Peter Dawkins, who'd returned to Australia.

In Ted Albert's honour, the Australasian Performing Rights Association (APRA) established the Ted Albert Award for Outstanding Services to Australian Music, which quickly became one of the most coveted gongs in the local industry. George and Harry would claim the award in 1995. They'd been inducted into the ARIA Hall of Fame in 1988, but the Ted Albert Award resonated more powerfully with them. Ted was family.

Tragically, Ted Albert didn't live long enough to savour the runaway success of *Strictly Ballroom*. With Ted's wife, Antoinette—known as Popsy—taking over as co-producer, the movie was a critical and commercial smash, the highest-grossing Australian film of 1992. It took in a whopping $80 million globally—all on a modest $3 million budget. It scooped the pool at the annual Australian Film Institute Awards; among its eight wins were awards for best film, best director and best screenplay. It also won awards at Cannes and the BAFTAs, and was nominated in the Best Motion Picture—Musical or Comedy category at the Golden Globe Awards (only to lose to the Robin Williams cross-dressing vehicle *Mrs. Doubtfire*).

In his four-star review, influential American film critic Roger Ebert captured *Strictly Ballroom*'s nature precisely, describing it as a movie that 'crosses Astaire and Rogers with Mickey and Judy and adds a dash of "Spinal Tap".'

Three Vanda/Young songs were included on the sound-track: 'Yesterday's Hero', 'Standing in the Rain' and 'Love is in the Air'. Thanks to its pivotal role at the climax of the movie, 'Love is in the Air' became a hit all over again, reaching number 3 on the Australian charts and hitting the Top 10 in Denmark and New Zealand. It also kickstarted the second phase of the pop career of John Paul Young, while the film launched the flamboyant directorial career of Baz Luhrmann.

George must have been relieved that something positive had come out of the terrible loss of Ted Albert. But the hole that Ted's absence left was undeniable.

17

In Rock We Trust

Apart from the fact that he was no longer working to survive, there was a strong whiff of deja vu to George's endeavours in London—once again, he was seeking out new acts to record, just as he and Harry had done during their four-year stretch. But this time Harry was back in Sydney, still at Alberts, still writing songs, which, in his own words, 'gave me something to do'. Their partnership, but not their friendship, was gradually unravelling.

One of the bands that George worked with in the UK was named Huge Baby. In keeping with their enigmatic status, the band used only first names—Sal was the singer, Kay played guitar, Az was on bass and Matt played the drums. They'd built a heady buzz in the fickle UK music scene well before Alberts got involved with them.

Writing in *NME*, journalist Johnny Cigarettes piled on the hype with a trowel when he crowned one of their records Single of the Week. 'This is an evil, malevolent and unspeakably scary record which you should only play in the hours of daylight, if accompanied by a priest.'

There was chaos at their gigs; guitarist Kay believed that getting hurt at a Huge Baby show was a stamp of credibility in the indie-rock world. 'People are actually queuing up to tell us they were injured at our last gig,' he told *NME*.

There was also a fair bit of chaos off stage: the band ran through managers and labels before signing with Alberts. Allegedly, they were turfed out of EMI's London offices on the brink of being signed and whimsically rejected another major label's 'massive' offer.

But despite all the hype, nothing much came of their relationship with George and Alberts UK, likewise that of another of the label's signings, a band called Silverstone.

By 1998, George was working with a new partner, an Irishman named James Cassidy. There were more signings, including acts such as Happylife, The Answer and Violent Delight, covering the spectrum from punk to pop. After seeing The Answer play live, George insisted that the Northern Ireland rockers were the best band Alberts had signed since AC/DC. A band named Breed 77, who played what was described as 'Gibraltarian flamenco metal' and who packaged their debut album in a fold-out crucifix, also signed to Alberts.

But none generated a hit record. The weak Aussie dollar also created an unwelcome challenge for George and Alberts' UK plans. In 1998, the exchange rates were dire, at their worst down to AU$3 per British pound. Given that Alberts UK financing came out of Australia, it was proving untenable.

The well was running very dry, as was George's desire to keep going. He'd lost another sibling; Alex, the so-called 'black sheep' of the family, with whom George had worked on so many projects, died in 1997 aged 59. George had now moved with his family to Lisbon, Portugal. He told Harry that he had decided to move there because the country had lax smoking laws.

'People don't know me there,' George told a nosy reporter during a brief return to Australia, 'and better still, they don't care.'

George spent his time dabbling with software and gadgets—and keeping up with the soccer scores. And smoking, of course. Portugal was good in that regard.

He even filed a patent for a training apparatus, a device for 'improving and assessing the skill and reactions of soccer players'. It was a complex invention, containing some nineteen specific components. George had always been an inventor; it was just that now gadgets took the place of songs.

*

Unlike George's foray into the UK market, AC/DC's recent fortunes had experienced an upswing. In the wake of the 1988 album that George and Harry co-produced, *Blow Up Your Video*, their album sales had picked up—1990's *The Razors Edge* shifted five million copies in the US alone, their biggest seller since 1980's *Back in Black*.

The band's shows were now big-budget events, with pyrotechnics, massive video screens and audiences teeming with Angus clones ('Angis') and glowing devil horns. They played more than 150 concerts promoting 1995's *Ballbreaker* album, filling stadiums from Chile to the Czech Republic, Darwin to Dublin. Each show opened with a video featuring MTV brats Beavis and Butthead attempting to sneak into the band's dressing room, only to be chased off by a female security guard, under orders from Angus. Box office takings for most shows ranged from US$500,000 all the way to US$1 million and beyond. AC/DC was big business.

Interestingly, their set was still dominated by songs from the Alberts era, including 'Let There Be Rock', 'T.N.T.', 'Whole Lotta Rosie' and 'Dirty Deeds Done Dirt Cheap'. Perhaps, then, it didn't come as a huge surprise when the band enticed George out of his bucolic exile to produce their new album. There was also a more unfortunate reason for their choosing George: Canadian producer Bruce Fairbairn, who'd produced *The Razors Edge* and the 1992 *AC/DC Live* album, as well as huge hits from Bon Jovi and Aerosmith, was scheduled to work with them again but died suddenly from a heart attack in May 1999, aged just 49.

George began recording with the band in September 1999 at the Warehouse Studio in Vancouver. In the absence of Harry Vanda, Mike Fraser, who had worked on *Ballbreaker*, helped George. (Fraser had mixed 'Thunderstruck', the song with which Ted Albert loved to test the integrity of his Merc's subwoofers.) Warehouse Studio, the site of Vancouver's former City Hall, was owned by Canadian star Bryan Adams, who had taken the 1980s power ballad all the way to the bank. What the clean-living, vegan Adams made of three chain-smoking, trash-talking Young brothers has never been revealed, although Malcolm Young joked with singer Brian Johnson about the experience of working with three Youngs. 'It's like a shit sandwich, isn't it, Brian?' he said. 'And you're trapped in the middle.'

George maintained a solid work schedule over the next two months—his workday started at 11 a.m. and would sometimes run as late as midnight. Sundays were his only day off. It was

George's trademark no-bullshit/get-the-job-done approach in action. Most of the album's twelve songs were nailed in a few takes; George even encouraged Malcolm to play a rare guitar solo, a feature of the song 'Can't Stand Still'.

Singer Johnson, a guy fond of cloth caps whose voice was equal parts gravel and whisky, joked that George was so organised that if his penis broke in half, George would be able to find him the perfect replacement—and in record time.

'We were working pretty hard,' Johnson told *Guitar World* in a more serious moment. 'It was good, though. George always had a game plan. I hate it when you're hanging around waiting for the next decision. George always had it all worked out.'

Upon its release in February 2000, *Stiff Upper Lip* continued the uptick in the band's fortunes. It was certified platinum in North America, where it climbed as high as number 7 on the *Billboard* album chart. It sold another million copies in Europe, peaking at number 12 in the UK; it also reached the top chart position in Austria, Finland, Germany and Sweden.

In a favourable US *Rolling Stone* review, David Wild welcomed George's return. 'The album has two factors in its favor: It's even louder than normal, and it was produced by George Young . . . which means *Lip* is old-school all the way,' Wild wrote.

'Let it be said: These guys still know how to crank it to eleven.'

The 143-date world tour to promote the album culminated in several dates with the one band that the Youngs had always respected: The Rolling Stones. It was a fitting finale to the last record that George would ever produce for his brothers. If AC/DC really was George's 'revenge' for The Easybeats—and there's no reason to think it wasn't—he'd accomplished more with them, and for them, than he could ever have imagined.

★

A year after the completion of *Stiff Upper Lip*, it was time to reassess the AHR agreement between George, Harry and the late Ted Albert. They agreed that there was no point in continuing with it, now that Ted was gone, Harry was in Sydney and George was based in Europe. The work was done—and they'd all become wealthy men. (In 2013, the combined wealth of George, Malcolm and Angus was estimated at US$233 million by *Business Review Weekly*, who listed the Youngs as the 48th wealthiest Australian family.)

'There comes a time when things run a natural course,' Harry told Jane Albert, 'and there's no point pretending they haven't.'

The agreement, which had been in place for 27 years, was terminated. George and Harry's shares in the company were bought out by Alberts, and they both settled into a comfortable retirement. The Alberts UK studio would close its doors in 2007.

Yet if George was intending to fade quietly, then the Australian music industry had other ideas. In late May 2001, APRA published a list of the Top 30 Australian Songs of the previous 75 years, which had been adjudicated by 100 industry influencers. 'Friday on My Mind', George and Harry's working-class anthem that was inspired by life at the hostel *and* The Swingle Singers, came in at number 1.

AC/DC's 'It's a Long Way to the Top (If You Wanna Rock 'n' Roll)', brought to life by George and Harry in the Alberts studio, ranked number 9 on the list.

As was typical, it was Harry who turned up to receive the gong when the top 10 from the list were announced at the 2001 APRA Awards ceremony. He guested on guitar with Sydney indie rockers You Am I on a version of 'Friday', and at the end of the night he joined many others whose songs were in the top 10—Daddy Cool's Ross Wilson, Midnight Oil's Peter Garrett, and Vanda and Young acolyte Don Walker from Cold Chisel—to receive their awards. George was notable by his absence.

A year earlier, a cover of 'Friday' by an unlikely pair— pop belter Vanessa Amorosi and behatted country king Lee Kernaghan—had been the official NRL Friday Night Football theme, heard weekly on Channel 9 at 8.30 p.m. 'Love is in the Air', meanwhile, was judged to be the Most Played Australian Song Overseas at the APRA Awards of 2004, thanks to its *Strictly Ballroom* rebirth and continued airplay throughout Europe. The song was unstoppable, almost 30 years after its original release.

In 2003, while speaking with writer Debbie Kruger, George admitted that 'I haven't written a song for 12 years or so'. Yet even when he was in retirement, his work was being heard everywhere.

*

Melbourne band Dallas Crane were a rare new signing with Alberts, joining the label in 2003. They were rock purists, whose bloodline could be traced back to the bands that George and Harry had produced at Alberts: AC/DC, The Angels, Rose Tattoo. They'd taken their name from a Port Melbourne company named Dallas Crane Transport, whose base they'd used to rehearse material for their debut album (rehearsals paid for in beer). Their first release after signing with Alberts was a three-track EP named *Ladybird*, in November 2003.

One winter's night in 2006, while playing a pub gig in Melbourne to launch a new single called 'Curiosity', the band made an extraordinary sighting in the crowd. Standing at the back of the room, quietly taking it in, was none other than George, who was in Australia visiting family. He was soon to turn 60, and what remained of his hair was now ash-grey, though the gap between his front teeth gave him away. George was tanned and looked healthy; life in Lisbon clearly suited him.

He liked the band enough to join them backstage, and they fell into a comfortable groove, George cracking racy dad jokes and shouting drinks. He even posed for a selfie.

While in Oz, George checked in on Harry, who was recording a new album called *In Too Deep* with John Paul Young. It would be Young's first studio record in ten years.

'How's the family?' George asked Young, a question that he'd ask the singer whenever they met. Family meant the world to George.

Then George strapped on a bass and played on a track called 'Isn't it Sunshine'. It was his final recording credit.

'George was like a ghost,' said Young. 'He'd just suddenly appear.'

★

When he returned to Europe, George became unwillingly entangled in one of the stranger situations of his life, which dated back to 2002, in a trendy Notting Hill pub called the Churchill Arms. A man had taken to introducing himself to budding musicians as 'George Young from Alberts'. He'd hand his targets copies of AC/DC product as some kind of proof, while ingratiating himself with his intended victims.

The 'faux George' told his marks that he could get them jobs in the music industry, but first they'd have to enrol in an event management course. This would, of course, require a cash deposit, which he promised would be fully refunded when the course started. He also offered cheap concert tickets, among various other sweeteners.

Half a dozen hopefuls, aged between 30 and 45, fell for the scam. It came to the attention of the law when Alberts in Sydney began receiving emails from those who'd been defrauded. They hadn't only lost money; some had handed over credit card details and others their passports. One victim, a man who identified himself simply as Fernando, coughed up almost AU$1700 over time, as did several others who fell for the man at the Churchill Arms.

'He works by imposing pressure,' Fernando told *The Sydney Morning Herald* in May 2006, 'saying that it's a once in a lifetime opportunity.'

This, he added, was usually accompanied by lots of yelling and aggressive behaviour. At one point, after pressuring Fernando for more cash, the impostor insisted that he sell his jacket.

Perhaps his boldest ruse was convincing the promoter of a Finnish jazz concert that AC/DC would perform there.

There was also the promise of a 'farewell tour' of Australia, including a show at Uluru, with all proceeds going to charity. A keen promoter lost some $50,000 in planning costs.

Victims posted warnings on an AC/DC fan site, alerting others to the fraud.

The real George, when contacted, expressed sympathy for the victims, saying, 'I hope the cops catch him quick.'

In July 2006, a man named George Karounis appeared in Sydney's Downing Centre Local Court, facing 121 charges of fraud, which allegedly involved him posing variously as a stockbroker and as a director of a travel agency firm. Though the 'fake George' scams weren't among his charges, two of the people caught up in those scams said he bore a strong resemblance to the man who had ripped them off. Karounis denied any involvement and no one was ever charged with impersonating George.

★

Despite George's very low profile, the accolades and recognition continued. A selection of Australian acts, including The Living End, The Cruel Sea and The Veronicas, recorded the Vanda and Young songbook for a 2008 album named *Easy Fever: A Tribute to The Easybeats and Stevie Wright*, which was packaged with a separate disc of the originals. The cover of George and Harry's 'Evie', recorded by 'supergroup' The Wrights, whose line-up featured a member each of Powderfinger, Grinspoon, Spiderbait, Jet, The Living End, Dallas Crane and You Am I, returned the classic song to the Oz charts, reaching number 2 in March 2007. Harry Vanda produced the track, for the second time.

The same year, *Australian Musician* magazine selected George and Harry's meeting at Villawood in 1964 as 'the most significant event in Australian pop and rock music history'. In 2009, APRA launched the inaugural Vanda & Young Global Songwriting Competition. (Its winners have included Megan Washington, Kimbra and Amy Shark, all highly rated writers.)

Director Peter Clifton's footage of The Easybeats in the UK in 1967, long thought lost, was restored and screened at the Sydney Film Festival in 2012, then released on DVD in 2015.

In 2013, The Angels' Doc Neeson—the man who once took George literally when he suggested that he throw fish at his audience—recorded his take on George and Harry's 'Walking in the Rain' in the current Alberts studio. Neeson, who had recently been diagnosed with a brain tumour, felt a strong connection to the song, as he'd tell a writer from *The Age*. 'It really made me think about George and Harry's songwriting because lyrically, it's like a stream of consciousness; almost an existential thing,' he said.

When talk turned to performing the song, Neeson said it typified one of George's favourite maxims. 'It requires quite a lot of restraint,' he said. 'In that respect it's a good example of . . . what George used to say a lot: "Keep it simple, stupid".'

In December 2013, soon after Neeson recorded 'Walking in the Rain', he performed the song during a live show of SBS's *RocKwiz*, shot at Sydney's Enmore Theatre, which was devoted to the music of Vanda and Young. (It was one show of a three-show run.) A bowler hat perched low over his brow, his face puffy, singing in a low growl, Neeson delivered the last great performance of his life. He died on 4 June 2014, aged 67.

Alongside Neeson on the *RocKwiz* bill was Wally De Backer (aka Gotye) and his band The Basics, who, decked out in pirate hats, provided the backing vocals for 'Down Among the Dead Men', played 'I'll Make You Happy' and rocked the bejesus out of the third part of 'Evie'. Singer Gossling—who sang 'Falling in Love Again' and 'Love is in the Air'—and Isabella Manfredi from The Preatures, who nailed the challenging second part of 'Evie', also featured, as did The Church's Steve Kilbey, who led the ensemble into the big finale, 'Friday on My Mind'. The *RocKwiz* house band, meanwhile, dusted off 'My Old Man's a Groovy Old Man', the song that linked Bon Scott and George Young all those years ago.

As tributes go, the *RocKwiz* special was the rarest of things: both musically accomplished and presented in the best possible manner. The crowd went absolutely nuts.

★

The health of George's brother, Malcolm, had been in decline for several years. It was Angus who first noticed the changes, in 2008, when they were working on the belated follow-up to *Stiff Upper Lip* at the Warehouse. Malcolm had always been the most organised member of the band, yet he was forgetting the simplest of things: guitar basics, as well as day-to-day matters. Malcolm consulted a US specialist and was diagnosed with 'shrinkage of the brain'; he was prescribed medication and was given, in Angus's words, 'good care'.

Before beginning the gruelling world tour for the new album, *Black Ice*—168 shows spread over 20 months—Angus sat down with Malcolm.

'Are you sure you're up for it?' he asked.

'Shit, yeah,' Malcolm replied. 'I'll keep going until I can't.'

Malcolm proved true to his word, but the tour was, at times, a struggle. There were nights when Angus glanced across to Malcolm and sensed that he wasn't connecting with the music. He seemed elsewhere, adrift. Before every show, Malcolm sat backstage, working through the songs—some that he'd been playing for more than 30 years. He'd never needed to do that before.

Malcolm, much like George, was a stubborn type of fellow, so his bandmates didn't question his ability to make it through the tour. He'd committed to it, and he'd make sure he finished the job, as hard as it was some nights. But when the tour finally wound up, with a massive stadium show in Bilbao, Spain, on 28 June 2010, in front of 37,000 raucous fans, everyone in camp AC/DC sensed that it was the end of the road for Malcolm. He was drained, physically and emotionally. He was only 57 years old.

His health took a nosedive soon after the end of the tour (which grossed a handy US$446 million). Malcolm was diagnosed with a lung problem, then with heart trouble. He underwent extensive surgery. He also had a pacemaker installed.

Then, in early 2014, when the band assembled to discuss a new album, Malcolm spoke with the others. 'I just can't do it anymore,' he said.

It was a massive admission for such a determined man.

Malcolm was admitted to Lulworth House, an upscale care facility in Sydney's Eastern Suburbs. Images emerged of Malcolm being led by the hand around the grounds by a carer—it was almost impossible to reconcile the man in the photo with the tough little bantam who'd wielded his Gretsch guitar like a weapon for so many years. There was an emptiness in Malcolm's eyes; he seemed bewildered, lost. It was heartbreaking. In early 2015, his family released a short statement: 'Malcolm is suffering from dementia and the family thanks you for respecting their privacy.' It wasn't a great time for the Alberts musical family: Stevie Wright, after his many battles, died from pneumonia on 27 December 2015, aged 68. In a statement, David Albert said this of Wright: 'Stevie will be sadly missed by all who knew him and countless more who did not know him but loved his music. We have lost one of Australia's greatest frontmen who has left an indelible mark on our musical landscape. He has always been a much-loved part of the Alberts family.'

The new AC/DC album, *Rock or Bust*, had appeared in November 2014. Malcolm didn't play on the record—nephew Stevie stepped in again—but his stamp was all over it, just as Bon Scott had made his presence felt powerfully on *Back in Black*. Among the liner notes was a dedication: 'And most important of all, thanks to Mal, who made it all possible.' There was a photo of Malcolm and Angus's guitars, leaning against a Marshall amp. The simple caption said it all: 'In Rock We Trust'.

*

With so much focus on Malcolm's struggles, the next piece of news out of the Alberts' camp, on 22 October 2017, was an equally staggering blow: George had died at the age of 70. He had yet again slipped under the radar; no one outside of his family had known of his ill health. The last time John Paul

Young saw George was in July 2015, when George turned up unannounced at the Channel 7 studios in Melbourne, where JPY was competing in *Dancing with the Stars*. JPY had to assure production staff that George was a friend, because no one on the set recognised him.

'George was very secretive,' remembered his friend from the Villawood hostel, Brian Lee. 'He once told me, "When people ask what I do, I tell them I like to fool around. If they're going to find out what I do, they'll find out without me telling them."'

Even more typically, the cause of George's death was not made public. All that was made known was that he and his family had moved to Singapore after several years in Portugal. He lived there quietly, although he *had* been speaking with Harry Vanda about one more Flash and the Pan record at the time of his death. And it was in Singapore that he died.

'It is with pain in our heart that we have to announce the passing of our beloved brother and mentor George Young,' AC/DC said in a group statement. 'Without his help and guidance there would not have been an AC/DC.'

To this, Angus, speaking on his and Malcolm's behalf, added a more personal tribute. 'You could not ask for a finer brother. For all he did and gave to us throughout his life, we will always remember him with gratitude and hold him close to our hearts.'

Accolades for George filled newspapers, websites and blogs. 'George Young should be recognised as the sonic architect of Australian rock music,' stated *The Guardian*, and rightly so. 'The Easybeats guitarist and AC/DC producer wasn't just a star in his own right, but a behind-the-scenes industry giant.'

'Genius doesn't even seem like a strong enough word when describing George Young,' stated the ABC. 'Music would not be the same without George Young.' He was 'Australia's early pop music champion', an 'architect of heavy metal', a 'love song mastermind' and a 'reluctant pop star'.

The Sydney Morning Herald declared George to be 'AC/DC's Svengali'. Jimmy Barnes added this tribute: 'What a huge loss for music. A great songwriter, producer and a great human being.'

Dallas Crane posted a heartfelt message on Facebook: 'Dallas Crane want to say thanks for putting the lines on the map for us all, and for giving us a few solid chuckles on your way through. Rest well George Young.'

On the day of his death, the National Film and Sound Archive inducted 'Love is in the Air' as one of its 'Sounds of Australia'. It was one of many fitting tributes to the man.

On 28 October, ABC's *Rage* devoted an entire program to George's music, from The Easybeats through to AC/DC and Flash and the Pan, from Stevie Wright to John Paul Young and beyond. His back catalogue easily filled the four-hour program. A few weeks after his death, ABC screened the mini-series *Friday on My Mind*, a colourful and convincing portrait of The Easybeats' rise and demise. British actor Will Rush capably filled George's shoes, portraying him as a tough and determined lad straight out of the hostel, and the driving force of the band.

Rush admitted that he was 'gutted' that George didn't get to see the show. 'It's not so much of a portrayal as it is a tribute and a homage to George . . . how he took his family from nothing and created quite a dynasty.' Critical reaction to the show was positive.

Then, barely a month after George's death, Malcolm Young passed away. He was 64. The huge wave of emotion that poured out from Malcolm's many fans, peers and pundits relegated George's death, at least on a public level, to the shadows. And it's quite likely that's exactly what George would have preferred. He was an intensely private person, right to the end.

Epilogue

The years have been kind to 69-year-old John Paul Young. His once flowing locks may have turned grey and been trimmed back to a more conservative length, but the gleam in his eye hasn't dimmed a bit. His voice remains strong, as do his natural charm and charisma. Young could sing the phone book and his rusted-on fans would still swoon. The old sailor suit is gathering dust somewhere in the back of his closet; he now wears a well-cut suit worthy of Tony Bennett. As for his audience, the *Countdown*-era boob tubes and mullets have been replaced by modest haircuts, sensible shoes and, in some cases, mobility walkers. But that doesn't mean their love of the music has faded. The opposite is true, judging by the reaction of tonight's full house: everyone in the crowd has braved a bone-chillingly cold winter's night to check in with the man they simply call JPY.

Almost two years after George's death, JPY is undergoing a late-career renaissance. Four years ago, he took a show called *The Vanda and Young Songbook* on the road, and demand remains strong. Tonight's show, at the stately

1000-seat Anita's Theatre on the New South Wales South Coast, is a sell-out. Among his touring band is 77-year-old Warren 'Pig' Morgan, who played keyboards on many of Young's original recordings. On bass is Rockwell T. James, who, like Morgan, is a long-time veteran of Young's backing band, The Allstars.

John Paul Young is one of the last men standing from the golden era of George Young and Alberts. Ted Mulry is gone—he died in 2001, on the eve of his 54th birthday, from a brain tumour—as are Ted Albert and Stevie Wright (Young provided a haunting, soulful rendition of 'Evie (Part 2)' at Wright's service). John Cave—aka William Shakespeare—died, penniless, in 2010, aged 61. Bon Scott and Malcolm Young are dead, and so, of course, is George. None of them lived what you'd call a long life. George barely made it to three score and ten. The songs have outlived so many of their makers. Harry Vanda, despite some health concerns, is almost the last man standing.

JPY's set list tonight is the definitive Great Australian Songbook, Vanda and Young creations that time has not diminished in any way, shape or form. Young plays the lot, from The Easybeats' 'St. Louis' and 'Friday on My Mind' to AC/DC's 'Long Way to the Top' and Flash and the Pan's 'Hey, St. Peter', 'Down Among the Dead Men' and a killer version of 'Walking in the Rain'. He also throws in Ted Mulry's 'Falling in Love Again'—insisting that the song was once destined for Engelbert Humperdinck—and, boldly, all three parts of 'Evie', a challenge for anyone, let alone a singer just a year shy of 70. Yet he delivers it brilliantly, channelling the wild spirit of Stevie Wright. The audience laps it up.

Of course, he also plays the songs that George and Harry

crafted for him, the tunes that made him famous: 'Standing in the Rain', 'Yesterday's Hero', 'Pasadena', 'I Hate the Music', 'Love is in the Air'—which gets the crowd up on their feet—and many more. The response is euphoric; the show has all the devotion of a Hillsong gathering but with none of the proselytising.

Everything is set up perfectly by Young's funny and chatty narrative, mostly drawn from conversations with George in the Alberts studio—sometimes his backstories run longer than the songs themselves. He reveals that George and Harry wrote 'Where the Action Is' as a sort of sequel to 'Friday on My Mind'. 'It's my own working-class anthem,' says Young, who tonight reworks the lyrics and adds a little local flavour to the song: 'He was a boy from Port Kembla/She was an uptown girl from the northern suburbs of Thirroul . . .' Then there's the backstory to 'Keep on Smiling', as revealed to Young by George—it's the story of a man who got caught with his pants down—and 'Silver Shoes and Strawberry Wine', from the Marcus Hook Roll Band album, which documents a case of 'accidental' incest.

'It can happen,' Young says, with a shrug.

He jokes about Molly Meldrum and crotch-grabbing, as well as revealing the high jinks among the cast of *Jesus Christ Superstar* and leading the audience through an impromptu version of 'Dinah' (as in 'Show us your legs . . .'), a favourite song of Ted Mulry. He also speaks, with more than a little pride, about how 'Love is in the Air' was declared one of the iconic Sounds of Australia in 2017. Its fellow inductees included the theme to Play School and 'Louie the Fly'.

It's a great night, incredibly well received. For much of the crowd, JPY and The Allstars are playing the soundtrack to

Jeff Apter

their youth. *To their lives*. And it wasn't that hard to imagine that somewhere, somehow, George Young was looking on, taking it all in, grinning his gap-toothed smile and thinking to himself, 'Not bad, son. Job well done.'

Acknowledgements

Nothing beats a good team, and my last few books have enabled me to work with the same terrific people, namely Jane Palfreyman, Samantha Kent, Emma Driver, Dannielle Viera and Luke Causby. Thanks to one and all. Let's try and keep the band together, okay?

This project required some heavy lifting research-wise, and some people deserve special thanks: Bill Small (RIP) for his extensive knowledge of everything Easybeats, and for his guidance and advice; Mike Griffiths for his remarkably detailed work on George Young's 'four-year binge'; and Luke Winterton and Michael de Looper for their assistance.

I'd also like to thank the following authors for their support. Bob Yates (author of *The Angels*) and John Tait (*Vanda and Young: Inside Australia's hit factory*)—both went above and beyond in helping me separate fact from 'faction'. Murray Engleheart and Arnaud Durieux's *AC/DC Maximum Rock & Roll*, meanwhile, remains an invaluable resource, as does the remarkable Steve Hoffman Music Forums (https://forums.stevehoffman.tv/threads/the-easybeats-album-by-album-thread-pt3.388716/)

The following folks also deserve a hearty shout-out: John Paul Young, Herm Kovac, Glenn Goldsmith, Michael Dwyer, Philip Morris, Bob King, Tony Mott, Stephen Fleay, Michael Browning, Phil Manning, Mark Evans, Gered

Mankowitz, Chris Gilbey, Colin Beard, Glenn A. Baker, Janet Perr and Stuart Coupe.

Special thanks to Brian Lee, George's friend from the days of the Villawood Migrant Hostel, who helped reveal the real George, the man behind the music. Thanks also to Tam Lee.

As ever, the resources of the State Library of New South Wales, which connected me with the incredibly helpful Jill Molan, and the National Film and Sound Archive, were invaluable.

I've recently taken to mentioning the books I was reading while writing—to wit, Susan Orlean's *The Library Book*, Bob Mehr's hugely readable *Trouble Boys: The true story of The Replacements* and Mitchell Zuckoff's remarkable *Fall and Rise: The story of 9/11*, all of which inspired me in their own unique way.

My wife Diana, children Christian and Elizabeth and our ever-expanding menagerie (Neela, Cat, Poe and the floating three) each deserve a supersized thank you as well.

Selected Discography for George Young

THE EASYBEATS STUDIO ALBUMS

EASY (1965)

It's So Easy/I'm a Madman/I Wonder/She Said Alright/I'm Gonna Tell Everybody/Hey Girl/She's So Fine/You Got It Off Me/Cry, Cry, Cry/A Letter/Easy Beat/You'll Come Back Again/Girl on My Mind/Ya Can't Do That

IT'S 2 EASY (1966)

Let Me Be/You are the Light/Women (Make You Feel Alright)/Come and See Her/I'll Find Somebody to Take Your Place/Someway, Somewhere/Easy as Can Be/I Can See/Sad and Lonely and Blue/Somethin' Wrong/In My Book/What About Our Love/Then I'll Tell You Goodbye/Wedding Ring

VOLUME 3 (1966)

Sorry/Funny Feelin'/Say You Want Me/You Said That/Goin' Out of My Mind/Not in Love With You/Promised Things/The Last Day of May/Today/My My My/Dance of the Lovers/What Do You Want Babe/Can't You Leave Her

GOOD FRIDAY (1967)

River Deep, Mountain High/Do You Have a Soul/Saturday Night/You Me, We Love/Pretty Girl/Friday on My Mind/

Happy is the Man/Hound Dog/Who'll Be the One/Made My Bed Gonna Lie in It/Remember Sam/See Line Woman

Released in the UK in May 1967; retitled *Friday on My Mind* for the US release in May 1967, with 'Hound Dog' exchanged for 'Make You Feel Alright (Women)' and tracks resequenced. Later released in Australia as *Friday on My Mind* in October 1970, with the track listing matching the US release.

VIGIL (1968)

Good Times/What in the World/Falling off the Edge of the World/The Music Goes Round My Head/Can't Take My Eyes Off You/Sha La La/Come In You'll Get Pneumonia/See Saw/Land of Make Believe/Fancy Seeing You Here/Hello, How Are You/Hit the Road Jack/We Can All Live Happily Together/I Can't Stand It

In the US, *Vigil* was released as *Falling off the Edge of the World*, with an altered sequence and different cover art, in October 1968.

FRIENDS (1969)

St. Louis/Friends/Watching the World (Go By)/Can't Find Love/Holding On/I Love Marie/Rock & Roll Boogie/Tell Your Mother/The Train Song/What Becomes of You My Love/Woman You're on My Mind

'FOUR-YEAR BINGE' 45 RPM SINGLES SELECTED DISCOGRAPHY

Paintbox—Get Ready For Love (Alexander)/Can I Get To Know You (Vanda/Young)
A Shock/Orange Production; Young Blood, YB 1013, 5 June 1970, UK

* George Alexander [Alex Young] sang lead vocal on A side; Harry Vanda lead vocal on B side

Moondance—Lazy River (Vanda/Young)/Anna St. Claire (Alexander)
A Shock Production, engineered by Brian Hatt; A&M, AMS 792, 19 June 1970, UK

* George Alexander [Alex Young] sang lead vocal on A side; Harry Vanda lead vocal on B side

Also issued in The Netherlands, Germany, Norway and Sweden. It made number 13 on the Swedish charts, as broadcast on the radio show *Tio i Topp*, 28 November 1970.

Tramp—Vietnam Rose (Vanda/Young)/Each Day (Alexander)
A Shock Production; Young Blood, YB 1014, July 1970, UK

* Iain Campbell sang lead vocal on A side; Harry Vanda lead vocal on B side

John Miles—Why Don't You Love Me If I Could See Through (Errington)
A Becket/Shock Production, recorded in Orange Sound Studios London; Orange, OAS 508, September 1970, UK

John Miles—Why Don't You Love Me (Vanda/Young)/Send Your Son to the War (Errington)
A Shock Production, recorded in Orange Sound Studios London/Produced by Danny Becket, recorded in Orange Sound Studios London; Pink Elephant, PE 22.535-H, 1970, Netherlands

* The Dutch B-side has a misprint with 'You're' in the title

John Miles—My World Belongs to Yesterday (Vanda/Young), 1970

* Unreleased until it was included on the double CD *Their Music Goes 'Round Our Heads*, Columbia, 4716532, in 1992

Whichwhat—Vietnam Rose (Vanda/Young)/Shame and Solution (Terry Penn)
Beacon, BEA 169, 23 October 1970, UK

Pyramid featuring Erl Dalby—Can't Wait for September (Vanda/Young)/Let Me Be Yours Until Tomorrow (Goffin/ King)
A 'Banner' production for 'World Of Sound'; Du Monde, DM 325, October 1970, Australia

* *Go-Set* chart: peaked at #24. Brisbane charts: peaked at #18. Sydney charts: peaked at #15

Eddie Avana—Children (Hemmings/Vanda/Young)/Sarah (A. Eland)
Children arranged by Nicky Walsh, produced by Miki Dallon/ Sarah arranged by Tom Parker, produced by Miki Dallon; Young Blood, YB 1020, 27 November 1970, UK

* Harry Vanda sang lead vocal on A side; George Alexander [Alex Young] possible lead vocal on B side; 'A. Eland' possibly a pseudonym

Ted Mulry—Falling in Love Again (Vanda/Young)/Louisa (Mulry)
An Albert Production; Albert Productions, AP-9338, December 1970, Australia

* *Go-Set* chart: peaked at #16

Buster—Pasadena (Hemmings/Vanda/Young)/Priscilla (Pickett)
Produced by Phil Pickett & Tony Cox for Zonk Productions; Parlophone, R 5881, 29 January 1971, UK

* Phil Pickett sang lead vocal on A side

Heavy Feather—Beautiful and Black (Maynard/Vanda/ Young)/Ceilings (Ray Cane)
Friday Music, produced by Nigel Hutchinson and Ray Cane/ White Dove Music, produced by Nigel Hutchinson and Ray Cane; Penny Farthing, PEN 756, 26 March 1971, UK

* Phil Pickett sang lead vocal on A side

Tony Williams—Lazy River (Vanda/Young)/Man Made World (Wilkins/Frechter)
Produced by David Mackay; Columbia, DB 8790, 21 May 1971, UK

* A side has a misprint crediting it to 'Vander—Young'

Shortcakes—I Can Try (Vanda/Young)/Save Me (J. & S. Bell)
Friday Music, Shock Productions for Marsam Music, arranged by Zack Laurence; Decca, F 13185, 4 June 1971, UK

Grapefruit—Sha-Sha (James)/Universal Party (Alexander)
Friday Music/Apple Music; A Friday Production, musical director: George Alexander; Deram, DM 343, 24 September 1971, UK

* George Alexander [Alex Young] sang lead vocal on both sides; 'James' was a George Alexander pseudonym

Haffy's Whiskey Sour—Shot in the Head (Vanda/Young)/ Bye Bye Bluebird (Vanda/Young)
Friday Music, A Friday Production; Deram, DM 345, 5 November 1971, UK

* Iain Campbell sang lead vocal on both sides

Jeff Apter

Vanda and Young—Lazy River (Vanda/Young)/Free and Easy (Vanda/Young)
Albert Productions, AP-9710, 11 November 1971, Australia

* George Young sang lead vocal on both sides

John Miles—Pasadena (Hemmings/Vanda/Young)
Rumoured to have been recorded in 1971; still unreleased

Mosaic—Bye Bye Bluebird (Vanda/Young)/Bird of Time (Titley)
Friday Music, arranged by Tony Cox, produced by Phil Pickett; Parlophone, R 5928, 12 November 1971, UK

* Phil Pickett sang lead vocal on A side

Steve Ryder—Ain't It Nice (Vanda/Young)/Remember Me (Mulry)
Produced by Ted Albert and Tony Geary; An Albert Prod. Rec.; Blue Mountain, BM 1003, 10 December 1971, UK

* Steve Ryder was a pseudonym for Ted Mulry

John Young—Pasadena (Hemmings/Vanda/Young)/Better Go Back to Bed (Napier-Bell/Vanda/Young)
Produced by Simon Napier-Bell; Albert Productions, AP-9765, 16 December 1971, Australia

* *Go-Set* chart: peaked at #16; the backing track may be a Vanda and Young demo, with John Paul Young singing over the top of George Young's lead vocal

Alison McCallum—Superman (Vanda/Young)/Take Me Back (Mulry)
Produced by Simon Napier-Bell, recorded in Australia/ Recorded in Australia—Australian composition; RCA, 102019, 20 January 1972, Australia

* Real name Alison MacCallum, but spelled 'McCallum' on the single; a Vanda and Young demo was sent to Ted Albert. *Go-Set* chart: peaked at #12

Worth—Don't Say You Don't (Vanda/Young)
Produced by Martin Clarke, engineer: Mike Ross; A U.K. Production, Friday Music Ltd; CBS, CBS 7728, 28 January 1972, UK

* Misprint credits it to 'Vander/Young'

Bobbi Marchini—You're the Hand that Feeds My Love and I Won't Bite You (Napier-Bell)/ London Town (Vanda/Young)
Produced by Simon Napier-Bell; Albert Productions, AP-9815, 3 February 1972, Australia

The Hendrys—Life is Getting Better (Vanda/Young)/United We Stand** (Simons/Hiller)
Friday Music, produced by Michael Jacobsen/Belwin-Mills Music, produced by Peter Jacobsen; Pye, 7N 45119, 4 February 1972, UK

* Misprint credits A side to 'Vander-Young'

Fluff—Dance Dance Dance (Young)/Don't Say You Don't (Young/Vandenberg)
Producer: Peter Swettenham; Kinney Music/Friday Music; Decca, F 13273, 11 February 1972, UK

Jeff Apter

Band of Hope—Working Class People (Vanda/Young)/Stay
on My Side (Vanda/Young)
Decca, F 13274, February 1972, UK

* Projected single, withdrawn. 'Working Class People' was recorded and
released by Peter D. Kelly in 1973.

Erl Dalby—Candy (Vanda/Young)/Pasadena (Vanda/Young)
Produced by Ted Albert; Banner, BK-4574, 1972, Australia

John Miles—Yesterday (Was Just the Beginning) (Vanda/
Young)/Road to Freedom (Paul Morrison)
Recorded in Orange Sound Studios London; A Shock
Production, Friday Music/ Recorded in Orange Sound
Studios London, produced by John Miles, Orange Pub.;
Orange, OAS 208, 24 March 1972, UK

Jeremy Paul—What Becomes of You, My Love (Vanda/
Young)/What I Want To Know (Napier-Bell)
Produced by Simon Napier-Bell; Albert Productions, AP-9877,
27 April 1972, Australia

Tina Harvey—Working My Way Back to You (Vanda/
Young)/Tina's Song (King)
Arranger: Johnny Arthey, producer: Jonathan King; UK
Records, U.K.2, 2 June 1972, UK

Colin Areety—Poco Joe (James)/To Give All of Your Love
  Away (Havens)
Produced by Friday Productions, Friday Music/Produced by
  Friday Productions, Carlin Music; Deram, DM 360, 4 August
  1972, UK

* 'James' was a George Alexander pseudonym

Marcus Hook Roll Band—Natural Man (Vanda/Young)/
  Boogalooing is for Wooing (Waller)
Friday Music Ltd, produced by Wally Allen/Carlin Music
  Corp., produced by Wally Allen; Regal Zonophone, RZ
  3061, 18 August 1972, UK

* George Young sang lead vocal on A side; misprint credits it to 'Vander-Young'/Wally Allen: lead vocal on B side

Toblerone advert—Triangular Bees (Vanda/Young/Allen)
September–October 1972

* Co-writer Roderick Howard Allen was a British advertising executive

Paintbox—Come On Round (Vanda/Young)/Take It From
  Here (P. Bonner/M. Eastman)
Produced by Paul Bonner, Friday Music/Produced by Paul
  Bonner, Ed. Kassner Music; President, PT 384, 13 October
  1972, UK

Marcus Hook Roll Band—Natural Man (Vanda/Young)/
  Boogalooing is for Wooing (Waller)
Produced by Wally Allen; Capitol, 3505, December 1972, US

* Misprint credits it to 'Vander-Young'. KOL Seattle chart for 28 February
1973: #36; included in 'Best discoveries', WCCC Hartford, Connecticut,
16 March 1973, and 'Looking ahead at the best', WKXY Sarasota, Florida,
23 March 1973 / 'Waller' is Wally Allen

Marcus Hook Roll Band—Louisiana Lady (Vanda/Young)/ Hoochie Coochie Har Kau (Lee Ho's Blues)
Produced by Wally Allen, Friday Music Ltd/Produced by Wally Allen, Ardmore & Beechwood Ltd; Regal Zonophone, RZ 3072, 5 January 1973, UK
* Harry Vanda sang lead vocal on A side; Wally Allen lead vocal on B side

Peter D. Kelly—Hard Road (Vanda/Young)/100% Rock and Roll Medley (Kelly/Morris)
Produced by George Alexander for Very Good Music Co.; Feldman/Very Good Music/Sunbury; RCA Victor, RCA 2317, 9 February 1973, UK

John Miles—Hard Road (Vanda/Young) You're Telling Me Lies (J. Miles)
Produced by John Miles & Dave Humphries, recorded in Orange Sound Studios; Feldman/Orange Music; Orange, OAS 209, 16 February 1973, UK

Peter D. Kelly—Working Class People (Vanda/Young)/ Change Your Mind (Kelly/Morris)
Produced by George Alexander for Very Good M., Friday Music Ltd/Produced by Peter D. Kelly for Very Good M., Very Good M./Sunbury; RCA Victor, RCA 2363, 4 May 1973, UK

John Miles—One Minute Every Hour (Vanda/Young)/ Hollywood Queen (J. Miles)
Produced by John Miles & Dave Humphries, recorded in Orange Sound Studios London; Feldman/Orange Music; Orange, OAS 213, 29 June 1973, UK

MARCUS HOOK ROLL BAND

TALES OF OLD GRAND-DADDY (1973)
Can't Stand the Heat/Goodbye Jane/Quick Reaction/Silver Shoes/Watch Her Do It Now/People and the Power/Red Revolution/Shot in the Head/Ape Man/Cry for Me

FLASH AND THE PAN

FLASH AND THE PAN (1978)
The African Shuffle/California/Man in the Middle/Walking in the Rain/Hey, St. Peter/Lady Killer/The Man Who Knew the Answer/Hole in the Middle/Down Among the Dead Men/ First and Last

LIGHTS IN THE NIGHT (1980)
Media Man/Headhunter/Restless/Welcome to the Universe/ Make Your Own Cross/Lights in the Night/Captain Beware/ Atlantis Calling

HEADLINES (1982)
Jetsetters Ball/Don't Vote/Waiting for a Train/War Games/ Where Were You/Love is a Gun/Up Against the Wall/Psychos on the Street/Hey Jimmy/Phil the Creole

EARLY MORNING WAKE UP CALL (1984)
Early Morning Wake Up Call/Communication Breakdown/ Barking at the Moon/Downtown Too Long/Opera Singers/ Midnight Man/On the Road/Look at That Woman Go/Fat Night/Believe in Yourself

NIGHTS IN FRANCE (1987)

Money Don't Lie/Nights in France/Ayla/Yesterday's Gone/
Drawn by the Light/Hard Livin'/Saviour Man/Bones

BURNING UP THE NIGHT (1992)

Living on Dreams/Vacuum of Emotion/Ivy Love/Searching
for a Headline/Bad Love/Do It/On the Level With You/On
My Way/Burning up the Night/Only the Bad Survive/Secret
Eyes/3 Into 2

JOHN PAUL YOUNG STUDIO ALBUMS

HERO (1975)

St. Louis/Pasadena/Friends/Silver Shoes and Strawberry Wine/
The Love Game/Yesterday's Hero/Bad Trip/Things to Do/
The Next Time/Birmingham

J.P.Y. (1976)

Keep on Smilin'/Won't Let this Feeling Go By/The Painting/
Take the Money/Good, Good, Good/I Hate the Music/
Standing in the Rain/If I Could Live My Life Again/Give It
Time/I Still Got You

GREEN (1977)

Gay Time Rock 'n' Roll City/Just Can't Go/Down on My
Knees/Shake That Thing/I Wanna Do It With You/I Know
You/The Same Old Thing/Here We Go/Bring that Bottle of
Wine Over Here/One of These Times

LOVE IS IN THE AIR (1978)

The Day That My Heart Caught Fire/Fool in Love/Open Doors/Lost in Your Love/Red Hot Ragtime Band/12° Celsius/Lazy Days/Love is in the Air/It's all Over/Lovin' in Your Soul

HEAVEN SENT (1979)

Heaven Sent/Don't You Walk That Way/I Don't Wanna Lose You/Love You So Bad It Hurts/Hot for You Baby/Can't Get You Out of My System/I Ain't Ready for Love/Bad Side of the City

NOW (1996)

Happy the Man/Groovin'/Just One Look/I'm Walkin'/I'm Left, You're Right, She's Gone/Ain't That a Shame/Medley: Blue Moon, Stormy Weather/Love is in the Air/Silver Shoes and Strawberry Wine/I Hear You Knockin'/St. Louis/Hard Road

WILLIAM SHAKESPEARE

CAN'T STOP MYSELF FROM LOVING YOU (1974)

Can't Stop Myself from Loving You/Can't Wait for September/ Woman/My Little Angel/Can't Live Without You/On Saturday Night/Love is Like a Cloudy Day/Goodbye Tomorrow, Hello Today/Lean a Little Bit on Me/Just the Way You Are/Time/ Feelin' Alright

CHEETAH

ROCK & ROLL WOMEN (1981)

Bang, Bang/Suffering Love/Spend the Night/Rock 'n' Roll Woman/Scars of Love/My Man/N.I.T.E./Come and Get It/ Let the Love Begin/I'm Yours

STEVIE WRIGHT

HARD ROAD (1974)

Hard Road/Life Gets Better/The Other Side/I Got You Good/ Dancing in the Limelight/Didn't I Take You Higher/Evie (Parts 1, 2, 3)/Movin' On Up/Commando Line

BLACK EYED BRUISER (1975)

Black Eyed Bruiser/The Loser/You/My Kind of Music/Guitar Band/The People and the Power/Help, Help/Twenty Dollar Bill/I've Got the Power

THE ANGELS

THE ANGELS (1977)

Take Me Home/You're a Lady Now/Goin' Down/Shelter from the Rain/Can't Get Lucky/Am I Ever Gonna See Your Face Again/You Got Me Runnin'/High on You/Hot Lucy/ Dreambuilder

ROSE TATTOO

ROSE TATTOO (1978)

Rock 'n' Roll Outlaw/Nice Boys/Butcher and Fast Eddy/One

of the Boys/Remedy/Bad Boy for Love/T.V./Stuck on You/
Tramp/Astra Wally

ASSAULT & BATTERY (1981)

Out of This Place/All the Lessons/Let it Go/Assault & Battery/
Magnum Maid/Rock 'n' Roll is King/Manzil Madness/
Chinese Dunkirk/Sidewalk Sally/Suicide City

SCARRED FOR LIFE (1982)

Scarred for Life/We Can't Be Beaten/Juice on the Loose/
Who's Got the Cash/Branded/Texas/It's Gonna Work Itself
Out/Sydney Girls/Dead Set/Revenge

SOUTHERN STARS (1984)

Southern Stars/Let us Live/Freedom's Flame/I Wish/Saturday's
Rage/Death or Glory/The Pirate Song/You've Been Told/No
Secrets/The Radio Said Rock 'n' Roll is Dead

MARK WILLIAMS

MARK WILLIAMS ZNZ (1990)

Show No Mercy/Fix of Love/Spell is Broken/Heavy Woman/
Good Thing/Love Electric/Shanghai Lily/You're So Cool/Feel
for the Night/Fool No More

Albums listed are only those written and/or produced by
George Young and Harry Vanda. For additional informa-
tion on George Young's various credits as producer, musician
and songwriter, see AllMusic: www.allmusic.com/artist/
george-young-mn0002328580/credits

Selected Bibliography

Albert, Jane: *House of Hits: How the Albert family shaped the history of music and entertainment in Australia*, Hardie Grant, 2010

Altham, Keith: 'Easybeats didn't copy The Beatles', *New Musical Express*, 3 December 1966

Anon: 'How The Easybeats got a big US contract', *The Sydney Morning Herald*, 3 April 1966

Anon: 'Beatle man sends for The Easybeats', *The Sydney Morning Herald*, 5 June 1966

Anon: 'Bomb hoax: 100 taken off plane', *The Sydney Morning Herald*, 11 July 1966

Anon: 'Easybeats in hysterical farewell', *The Canberra Times*, 11 July 1966

Anon: 'Tragedy struck The Easybeats . . .', *The Australian Women's Weekly*, 20 July 1966

Anon: '"We sat quietly eating our plum puddings while the family fought on!"', *Go-Set*, 17–24 August 1966

Anon: 'Life lines of The Easybeats', *New Musical Express*, 17 December 1966

Anon: '"We won't head a rock revival," say Easybeats', *Beat*, March 1967

Anon: 'The Unknown Blues get better known', *The Sydney Morning Herald*, 30 April 1967

Anon: 'The Easybeats are coming home—in triumph', *The Sydney Morning Herald*, 7 May 1967

Anon: 'A big welcome home for The Easybeats', *The Sydney Morning Herald*, 14 May 1967

Anon: 'Millionaires of '67', *Daily Mirror*, 22 May 1967

Anon: 'Star says wife depressed', *The Sydney Morning Herald*, 6 June 1967

Anon: 'Easybeats find a new drummer', *The Sydney Morning Herald*, 23 July 1967

Anon: 'Easybeats—Falling Off the Edge of the World' (review), *Billboard*, 9 September 1967

Anon: 'Why Dave likes Sydney', *The Sydney Morning Herald*, 20 July 1969

Anon: 'Sedate welcome for The Easybeats', *The Sydney Morning Herald*, 24 September 1969

Anon: 'George and Stevie talk to Mitch', *Go-Set*, 18 October 1969

Anon: 'George Young interview', *Let There Be Light*, numbers 5 & 6, 4 September 1992

Anon: 'The vastly different sides to George Young's genius', Double J, 23 October 2017, <www.abc.net.au/doublej/music-reads/features/>

Apter, Jeff: *High Voltage: The life of Angus Young*, Nero Books, 2017

Apter, Jeff: *Malcolm Young: The man who made AC/DC*, Allen & Unwin, 2019

Baker, Glenn A.: '13 years of rock and roll: George Young remembers The Easybeats', *Rolling Stone*, 11 July 1976

Baker, Glenn A.: 'The Vanda Young Story', *Bomp*, no. 18, March 1978

Betrock, Alan: 'Stevie Wright: *Hard Road*', *Phonograph Record*, March 1975

Blake, Marcus: 'The Wizard of Oz (Pt. 1): Australian producer Mark Opitz', *Blurt Magazine*, 17 October 2011, <www.blurtonline.com>

Browning, Michael: *Dog Eat Dog*, Allen & Unwin, 2014

Cashmere, Paul: 'Easybeats Stevie Wright to get a public funeral in Sydney with fans welcome,' *The Sydney Morning Herald*, 30 December 2015

Chugg, Michael: *Hey, You in the Black T-Shirt*, Pan Macmillan, 2010

Clifton, Peter (director): *Easy Come, Easy Go* (film), 2012

Costantino, Romola: 'Easybeats galore', *The Sydney Morning Herald*, 16 May 1967

Coupe, Stuart: 'Legendary band back in action', *The Canberra Times*, 9 November 1986

Crotty, George: 'Interview with Stevie Wright 1981', unpublished

De Looper, Michael: *The Easybeats*, Australian Artists (series), Big Three Publications, October 2014

Dwyer, Michael: 'Legends pay tribute to Vanda and Young', *The Sydney Morning Herald*, 7 December 2013

Dwyer, Michael: 'A message from George Young: "Avoid over-hype"', *The Sydney Morning Herald*, 23 October 2017

Engleheart, Murray & Durieux, Arnaud: *AC/DC Maximum Rock & Roll*, HarperCollins, 2006

Evans, Mark: *Dirty Deeds: My life inside and outside of AC/DC*, Allen & Unwin, 2011

Farrelly, Midget: 'How the surfer can learn from the sailor', *The Sydney Morning Herald*, 25 June 1967

Fricke, David: 'The Easybeats: Where are they now?', *Rolling Stone*, 11 September 1986

Hardy, Phil & Laing, Dave: 'The Easybeats', *The Faber*

Companion to 20th-Century Popular Music, Faber & Faber, 2001

Harry, Bill: 'The Easybeats: Two in a row?', *Record Mirror*, 11 February 1967

The J Files: 'George and Malcolm Young' (radio program), Double J, 23 November 2017, <www.abc.net.au/doublej/programs/the-j-files/george-and-malcolm-young/10274408>

Kent, David: *Australian Chart Book 1970–1992*, Ambassador Press, 1993

Kruger, Debbie: *Songwriters Speak*, Limelight Press, 2005

Kusko, Julie: 'A family reunion for The Easybeats', *The Australian Women's Weekly*, 15 October 1969

Makeig, Maggie: 'Shock Pop Riots', *Everybody's*, 15 December 1965

McCabe, Kathy: 'George Young helped craft the Australian sound but preferred the music to do the talking', 27 October 2017 <www.news.com.au>

McCulley, Jerry: 'Meet Vanda & Young: The unlikely pop duo behind AC/DC, The Easybeats, and Flash & the Pan', Gibson, 14 July 2008, <www.es.gibson.com/News-Lifestyle/Features/en-us/meet-vanda-and-young-the.aspx>

McFarlane, Ian: *The Encyclopedia of Australian Rock and Pop*, Allen & Unwin, 1999

McKenna, Kevin: 'In the poor heart of Glasgow, political loyalties melt away', *The Guardian*, 8 February 2015

Mordue, Mark: 'Prehistoric sounds: In search of an Australian rock 'n' roll', *The Sydney Morning Herald*, 28 December 2004

Morris, Philip: *It's a Long Way: From Acca-Dacca to Zappa*, Echo, 2015

Murphy, Damien: 'Back in Black: George Young, AC/DC's Svengali dies', *The Sydney Morning Herald*, 23 October 2017

O'Grady, Anthony: 'Australia Has Punk Rock Bands Too, You Know', *RAM*, 19 April 1975

O'Grady, Anthony: 'Gonna Be a Rock 'n' Roll Singer, Gonna Be a Rock 'n' Roll Band', *RAM*, 23 April 1976

Opitz, Mark with Wallis, Luke & Jenkins, Jeff: *Sophisto-Punk: The story of Mark Opitz & Oz rock*, Ebury Press, 2012

Roxon, Lillian: *Lillian Roxon's Rock Encyclopedia*, Grosset & Dunlap (Tempo Books), 1974

Souter, Gavin: 'The enormous thistle', *The Sydney Morning Herald*, 8 March 1966

Tait, John: *Vanda & Young: Inside Australia's hit factory*, NewSouth Publishing, 2010

Unterberger, Richie: 'Interview transcripts from the *Urban Spacemen* archive: Shel Talmy', 2010, <www.richieunterberger.com/talmy.html>

Valentine, Penny: 'Will the Real Easybeat Step Forward?', *Disc and Music Echo*, 1968

Veitch, Allan: 'Now The Easybeats are poised for the big time . . .', *The Sydney Morning Herald*, 13 November 1966

Veitch, Jock: 'Young world', *The Sydney Morning Herald*, 18 February 1968

Walker, Clinton: *Highway to Hell: The life and death of AC/DC legend Bon Scott*, Pan Macmillan, 1994

Walker, Clinton: 'Overcoming the cringe: A potted history of Australian rock and pop', *The Sunday Mail*, 2006

Walsh, Mike: 'Dylan—one for the "in" crowd', *The Sydney Morning Herald*, 3 April 1966

Walsh, Mike: 'Rolling Stones' book a sell-out', *The Sydney Morning Herald*, 22 May 1966

Walsh, Mike: 'Cliff out at the end of the year?', *The Sydney Morning Herald*, 10 July 1966

Walsh, Mike: 'A new Columbus discovers America', *The Sydney Morning Herald*, 24 July 1966

Walsh, Mike: 'Step Back becomes a hit here—at last', *The Sydney Morning Herald*, 18 September 1966

Walsh, Mike: 'Take a "trip" in a disco', *The Sydney Morning Herald*, 30 October 1966

Walsh, Mike: 'What's happened to the Stones?', *The Sydney Morning Herald*, 13 November 1966

Walsh, Mike: 'Why it's not a record Christmas', *The Sydney Morning Herald*, 11 December 1966

Walsh, Mike: 'A grand piano on the sand', *The Sydney Morning Herald*, 5 February 1967

Walsh, Mike: 'Underground for the new music', *The Sydney Morning Herald*, 12 March 1967

Walsh, Mike: 'A tough break for The Easybeats', *The Sydney Morning Herald*, 18 June 1967

Walsh, Mike: 'Those drugs and the stars', *The Sydney Morning Herald*, 25 June 1967

Welch, Dylan: 'AC/DC rocked by ID scam', *The Sydney Morning Herald*, 4 May 2006

Welch, Dylan: 'Dirty deeds rock music legend', *The Sydney Morning Herald*, 1 July 2006

Wigney, James: 'Easybeats drama *Friday on My Mind* is a tribute to the late, great George Young and Stevie Wright', *Herald Sun*, 21 November 2017

Yates, Bob: *The Angels*, Random House, 2017